Contents

List of Illustrations

Chapter 1

Chapter 2

Chapter 3

Chapter 4

Chapter 5

Chapter 6

Chapter 7

Chapter 8

To: Jordan Connelly

From: Dr Ahmad ...

15th March 2019.

Congrats on your various
endeavours.

Acknowledgements

In my humble view, Great Britain has been enhanced by the rich and diverse tapestry culture of its people, many of whom are the descendants of migrants from virtually all parts of the world. In completing the praiseworthy task, Dr. Chris Johnson's intensive research is unique amongst his peers, in giving a true and balanced picture of the critical contribution of South Asian communities to the current life and soul of this country - **Dipak Shelat, immediate-past Director of the Institute of Asian Businesses (now ABCC), part of the Greater Birmingham Chambers of Commerce**.

History never lies if attempts are made to portray facts objectively. Dr Johnson's brilliant effort at capturing a segment of South Asian's economic history in Britain is worthy of many commendations. *The Anatomy of South Enterprise* is a fitting tribute to the cultural, economic, education and social contribution of South Asian communities across three generations in Britain since the early 19th century - **Harminder Kaur Bhogal, Founder of Community Education Academy of Leadership (CEAL), West Midlands, England.**

The Anatomy of South Asian Enterprise tells the stories of Commonwealth citizens from South Asia who have made (and still are making) an invaluable contribution to British. society. The author of this compelling work, is himself a well-respected member of this community and has invested much time and effort to ensure that this segment of Britain's history is known – **Councillor Rupinderjit Kaur, Wolverhampton Council, West Midlands, England.**

In yet another lucid analysis on ethnic entrepreneurship, Dr. Johnson's latest book, *The Anatomy of South Asian Enterprise*, further redefines the critical importance of generational migrants' contribution to Britain from 1800s to the present. A compelling read for everyone who is interested in understanding the impact of wealth creation on human development" – **Dr. Stan. A.M. Lopes, Director of Global Enterprise Development Services (GEDS), London.**

As a third generation entrepreneur, I am so happy to have a book that contains facts and figures about our business history and other matters of interest. The author has done both the South Asian community and Britain as a whole very proud, by making this piece of work accessible to all - **Sumit Jain, Entrepreneur, England.**

i

Preface

It is widely acknowledged from current literature, that profiling ethnic firms can be problematic especially in industrialised societies where (enterprise) diversity is confused with multiculturalism or cultural pluralism. Why? Because of the complex history of ethnic groups which is further compounded by experts' lack of understanding of the dynamics of inter and co-ethnic trading patterns.

The purpose of this book, *The Anatomy of British South Asian Enterprise*, is to give recognition to this section of society whose economic contribution remains selective in academic and mass media circles. Frequent stereotyping or typecasting hasn't dampened the enterprise spirit of members of the second and third generation of British South Asians in their quest towards self-determination. Their various endeavours have helped to strengthen the economic and social fabric of the UK.

Numerous studies have also highlighted the presence of minority ethnic firms but reports have not examined in any great detail, organisation and performance strategies. Instead class, ethnicity, religion or faith and deprivation indices, have been used to evaluate the work of business owners, for the most part.

It is for this reason why the biological term '*Anatomy*' is appropriated for this book as a lever for examining the origin, development and growth of firms, based on an industry sector perspective. This model allows for a better understanding of the challenges and prospects including the degrees of diversity and heterogeneity, prevalent amongst British South Asians.

Yet whilst the complexity of each group hinges on respective cultures and faiths, through risk-taking and niche market opportunities, business owners contribute billions to the Treasury. In essence therefore, their input reflects a cumulative economic value exceeding £30 billion per annum by minority firms.

Therefore, *The Anatomy of British South Asian Enterprise* book is a fitting commendation for this particular cohort of entrepreneurs whose self-determination is exemplary to both group power and national pride. Through wealth creation activities – in the commercial, industrial (semi-industrial) and social enterprise sectors – members of this community have impacted on the regeneration of disadvantaged inner-cites areas particularly. From all indications, this trend is set to continue for the foreseeable future.

It is hoped that this book will be a welcome addition to other published material; that is, journals, research papers and literature reviews on minority ethnic firms. By examining British South Asian entrepreneurship through a gender, youth and 'ethnic sub-groupings' prism, this book raises the bar of the ethnic firm sector, a subject that mainstream has been examining since the last century.

Besides entrepreneurs, this book is ideal for government departments, learning institutions, policy makers, professionals and researchers. It can also be used as a reference text for students embarking on Enterprise Development and International Business Management programmes.

This book is dedicated to my **parents, siblings, children and grandchildren** for supporting my publishing endeavours and enterprise support activities. **Bill Kirkman** MBE, a friend and confidante whose guidance has enabled me to progress beyond the sphere of human limitations. The indefatigable **Harminder Kaur Bhogal** and her dedicated team at Community Education Academy of Leadership (CEAL), for pushing the boundaries of educational entrepreneurship to new heights. **Councillor Rupinderjit Kaur** for supporting heritage excellence amongst diverse communities, especially those of South Asians. To **Glenys Jones** and **Ruth Edgcumbe** for their quiet, but dignified interest in this ground-breaking work.

Arif Ali of Hansib Publications who gave me the opportunity to profile numerous (generational) minority ethnic communities, businesses and social enterprises during 1994 and 1997. **Lions Club of Hornsey** for the recognition and support given to my involvement in civic enterprise affairs. The **Council of Asian People** in Haringey who gave rare insights into the worthy contribution of South Asians to the London economy. Editor in Chief of *British Bangladeshis Who's*, **Mr. Mohammed Abdul Karim (Goni)** who gave unfettered access to members of his business community. Publishers of the **Sikh Directory** for making the work of Sikh business owners and their communities accessible. Publishers of **Power 100: The Future Leaders** and **Women Power 100** for making material available on Pakistanis in Britain and overseas. **Dr Chandra Laksamba**, Founder/Co-ordinator at the *Centre for Nepal Studies UK* and **Mr. Sushil Singh** of the *NepaliSamjUK* for their generous commitment and desire to publicise the unsung labours of British Nepalese. **Mr. Ruwan Warnakulasuriya**, Editor in Chief, *The Lanka Times*, for providing vital links to Sri Lankan business network-associations. To **Dipak Shelat** who gave expert guidance and support in the 'makings' of this book, by maximising his vast experience of the South Asian community in the West Midlands particularly.

Sroosh Kouyhar of Coventry Refugee and Migrant Centre and **Dr. Sarindar Singh Sahota OBE**, for offering our research team advice and guidance on the geographic dispersion of British-based Afghanis. Their tremendous concern for economic and social justice is highly commendable. **Parag Bhargava** of Suman Marriage Bureau fame, for his 'pearls of wisdom' into the diversity of minority communities in West London.

To some of our young stalwarts - **Mark Johnson**, our beloved son who showed glowing appreciation and interest in this ground-breaking work. **Shivarjun Bhogal** whose talent symbolises a new generation of enterprise pioneers. **Miriam Iqbal** who dedicated time and commitment to gather primary information for this book, particularly the Sri Lankan chapter.

This publication is a fitting momento to the millions of young people keen on starting a business as well as those who are either operating fledging enterprises and/or on the verge of expanding new frontiers of business and industry in the 21st century. They like others, have duly inspired this 'labour of love'. Blessings and happy reading to all.

Introduction

The need for *The Anatomy of British South Asian Enterprise* book illustrates the importance of this productive segment to the British economy. This publication aims to contribute to our understanding of the factors influencing the organisation and performance of these firms. It also helps to provide a clearer understanding of the strategic role South Asian entrepreneurship plays within the broader matrix of the British ethnic firm sector. This book is timely too, because it signifies the further recognition given to minority ethnic communities by policy makers and media commentators alike.

Thus the term '*South Asians*' (**www.southasianconcern.org/**) is used in this book to mean business owners who are originally from either the Indian-subcontinent or born of British South Asian parentage. The enterprise contribution of **Afghans Bangladeshis, Indians, Nepalese, Pakistanis** and **Sri Lankans** will be examined in totality since most of the literature on British South Asian firms is restricted to owners of Bangladeshi, Indian and Pakistani origin due to their numerical strength and presence.

Equally, the contribution of Afghanis, Nepalese and Sri Lankans business owners need to be featured within Britain's entrepreneurial corridors. Like the other three groups, they impact on diversity relative to culture, faith and allied persuasions. South Asians who are classified as 'Indian Africans' or 'East African-Asians' will be included in this book. Tens of thousands who lived in East Africa, emigrated to Britain in the 1960s; in the case of 'Indian Ugandans', they left to escape political persecution (**Sen 2013**).

The **2011** census reported an estimated 3.3 million South Asians residing in the UK comprising Afghans (56,000), Bangladeshis (451,529), Indians (1,451,862), Nepalese (50,881), Pakistani (1,174,983) and Sri Lankans (200,000). In total, this segment of the UK population makes up between 0.7% and 2.30% (**EHRC 2009: ONS 2011**). A more recent count showed that persons of 'country of birth' of South Asian origin in the UK, were estimated to be 1.79 million, with Indians and Pakistanis comprising 795,000 and 503,000 respectively (**ONS 2015**).

Contrary to popular opinion, British South Asians reflect a true and broadly stratified community, rather than a [limited] homogenous group. Their history is reflected by the uniqueness in culture, business, enterprise, faith, science, technology and other disciplines.

Therefore, the term '*Asian*' is restrictive in this sense, since it encompasses multi-layers of '*Asian-ness*' namely Chinese, Japanese and other 'Oriental-type' groups which are not the real subjects of this book. However, because of the popularity of the word '*Asian*', this author will apply it interchangeably only in areas where sourced materials are cited or referenced for this book.

Much of the research on minority ethnic firms including South Asians, remain largely exploratory. (**Ram and Jones 2007**) Ethnicity, culture, faith and other socio-economic variables are commonly used to evaluate the impact of this group to British society. In light of the 'diversity agenda' however, (**Jones 2012; Klean, 1990; Ram and Smallbone 2001**) a more industry sector focus is required when examining the organisation and performance of minority firms in total.

Factors that contribute towards South Asian females' access to finance and other credit facilities are not fully understood. Why? There is a blurred distinction between understanding minorities vis-a-vs their cultural, faith, social and related practices, all of which are not fully analysed within the context of ethnic entrepreneurship (**Clark & Drinkwater 2007**). Yet the second and third generation of female business owners have started businesses with access to finance not being a problem (**Hussain and Martin 2005; Dhaliwal, 1998**).

The growth of new creative industries by South Asian women also typified the 'gender alternative' of this sector by owners who are predominantly professionals and who recognised the need to either 'give something back' to society or better still, commercialise their interests and talent (**Fielden and Dawe 2005**).

Women make up 51% of the UK population, but only 29% are self-employed. Experts suggest that with the increasing number of females opting for enterprise start-ups, an estimated 600,000 extra such firms can contribute an added £42 billion to the British economy (**BIS 2011**).

The diversity issue is further compounded by inequalities such as poor funding allocation for new and existing ethnic firms. The closure of enterprise development agencies (**RDA 2012**), along with bank bailouts, illustrates the contradiction between 'prioritising' monopoly interests versus 'a lesser demand' for minority interests.

Vertovec (2007) referred to "transformative diversification" in Britain as one that resulted from the nature of immigration. Such movement he added can be seen from the various ethnic groups and the countries of their origin present in Britain today. (**Vertovec 2007**)

However, in the midst of celebrating diversity, minorities continue experiencing institutional discrimination although this age-old practice has not necessarily dampened the spirits of British South Asians and others, in their movement towards economic independence.

In fact, migrants have used prejudice as a catalyst to intensify 'opportunity structures' in niche markets where ethnic communities are mostly affected by economic deprivation and social exclusion (**Ram and Smallbone 2003**).

A House of Commons report cited further inequalities in the patchwork quilt-type technical assistance offered to ethnic firms. (**NABA 2010**) Business owners felt that their communities have a critical role in boosting international trade. They contended that most procurement initiatives are 'London-centric' and that the authorities did not often appreciate the South Asian business contribution to other UK Regions.

As owners struggled in their attempts to trade in open markets, they have used 'self-supporting mechanisms to create opportunities for their firms' (**Ibid 2012**). Public institutions set up to offer SME support reportedly have advisers who lack cultural sensitivity, poor 'social fitness' and a questionable track record of multi-sector industry experience or expertise.

This situation is prevalent especially in cases where would-be owners have difficulty in obtaining (specific) industry guidance and support for new start-ups. Thus the 'one-fit-all' [size] model is not the most appropriate for start-ups or existing firms particularly if knew or existing companies are operating in in the services sector (**2013**).

Therefore, *The Anatomy of British South Asian Enterprise* should not be perceived as another academic exercise or ethnic project. While a range of published materials have been used to illustrate business operations from an industry sector perspective, case studies, quotes and other informal citations have also been used to give this book credibility (**Levent and Wang, 2009**).

Indeed, the use of constructive theory should not be limited to prescriptive statements and rehearsed themes, but its application should be evidenced proportionately. Implicitly, the use of theoretical principles for a book on the British South Asian firm sector, serves as an informative guide and educative function as some theorists suggest **(Volery, 2007)**.

Consequently, there is an urgent need for live examples (via case studies and citations) on the organisation and performance of British South Asian firms. Essentially, the contribution of three generations of South Asians to British society makes this book a valid addition to the enduring legacy, conjuncture of the country's ethnically diversified business sector.

The publication of the 'Spinder Files' **(http://www.sikhentrepreneur.com/dr-spinder-dhaliwal/)** gave further insights into South Asian firms' enormous contribution to the British economy. However, little is known about the value-add and/or their real impact on local and regional economies, even though they dominate much of the literature on minority/ethnic entrepreneurship.

There is a historic interconnectedness between business and South Asian diasporic communities involving the transnational movements of people, capital, commodities, technologies, information and cultural forms **(Brah 1996)**.

Principally, this book complements existing works on business development particularly in key sectors in which minorities are demonstrating their unique sterling entrepreneurial qualities via self-employment route-activities.

This author has over 30 years of combined experience in *business, enterprise and civic affairs*, underpinned by a multidisciplinary parallel in *industrial relations and sociology, the mass media, youth affairs, marketing, business administration and management,* coupled with *media (the press) business* and *civic awards* respectively.

Additionally, there has been a long standing relationship with South Asian societies –at home and abroad - with more formal relationships established through multiple business associations and trade networks. The publication of high profile individuals and their institutions in the ethnic press **(Hansib 1994-97)** also provided ample opportunity to understand and appreciate the dynamics of British South Asians enterprise performance inter alia their communities.

Later, these writings were followed by performance reviews, enterprise support and regeneration initiatives for minority ethnic firms in 'hard to engage' inner-city areas. Since then, through independent consultancies via Global Enterprise Development Services (GEDS), this author has offered services on advice and guidance, business planning, bid writing, labour market intelligence (LMI) coupled with organisational governance services for British South Asian and other firms.

In part, these services have helped owners to gain market entry with less hindrance, whilst existing businesses have reported improvements in competing with different markets. Particularly, these services have improved the confidence and self-esteem of several owners and enabled them to enjoy mutually beneficial relations with agencies and institutions.

This book represents the second in a series of publications on ethnic firms in Britain. The first was *British Caribbean Enterprises: A Century of Challenges and Opportunities (2008)* for which the author received the 'Obama Shield'. *The Anatomy of British South Asian Enterprise* is therefore another effort at validating the importance and relevance of a performance excellence model for the minority ethnic firm sector (**EU 2012; Harding 2005; Mascarehas-Keyes 2007**).

The publication, *Multicultural Britain* (**2012**) highlighted the growing presence of ethnic communities in aspects of national life –from consumption patterns to entrepreneurial practices according to various businesses and the professions. The authors suggested that the concerns and interests of this section of society should be given greater coverage in the British media, than is currently the case.

Prior to the late 19th century, trading between the Indian sub-continent also described euphemistically as the 'British Raj' (**http://en.wikipedia.org/wiki/British_Raj**) was prevalent, and during that period, Indian student-émigré, Saik Deen Mahomet, opened the first 'curry' restaurant in Britain (**1810**). At that time, the British ruled the Indian sub-continent, Africa, the Caribbean and other Commonwealth dominions. The region which was once a single, diverse civilisation, represents today, a plurality of separate cultures, languages, religions and customs.

A history of feuds involving religious and communal strife, along with external interference, resulted in the 1947 partition, with the west of India becoming

Pakistan and later in 1971, the east of Pakistan giving way to Bangladesh. It should be noted that the division created ostensibly, two 'Punjabs' – the 'Indian Punjab' on the northeast and the 'Pakistan Punjab' to the west.

Later, Bhutan, Nepal and Sri Lanka emerged as nation-states though it is perceived that India influences much of the Bhutanese and Nepalese economy in relation to finance and trade matters (**Krishen 2001**).

However, like most historic conflicts, the disintegration of the Indian sub-continent along the lines of independent nation-states has benefitted regional and global trade. On the one hand, whilst partition left residual tensions in the region, the idea of having a collective 'national-identity' has grown even stronger over the last 60 years.

Cricket tournaments involving Afghanistan, Bangladesh, India, Nepal, Pakistan and Sri Lanka, showcase the most visible evidence of identity and a remarkable sense of patriotism and loyalty to 'tribe' and country. On the other hand, self-government has boosted the creation of regional institutions such as the South Asian Regional Community (SARC) and the Association of Southeastern Nations (ASEAN).

In particular, SARC is pivotal to the region's functional and technical co-operation including trade agreements comprising Bangladesh, Bhutan, India, Nepal, Pakistan and Sri Lanka and other South Asian regional-states (**SARC 2012**).

Indeed, it was Mahomet, a Bengali-Indian traveller, surgeon and entrepreneur who was the catalyst for the first British Indian-owned curry house in the early 1800s reminiscent of Britain's historic interest in the sub-continent's goods and services. Other Indian nationals followed his example by exploiting 'curry niche markets thereby giving rise to the current 'British curry' label.

Consequently, the establishment of 'balti houses' in city centres where a high concentration of Indian/South Asian communities live and operate successful businesses, reflects the growing affinity Britons have with ethnic cuisine. When the national press remarked that 'Chinese stir fry' (**Hills 2012**), had become a popular British cuisine, diners still continued to enjoy a 'good curry' according to reviews of South Asian restaurants in Britain.

By the mid-20th century, a new wave of immigration stimulated further start-ups in food retailing, creative industries, (textiles) manufacturing and other sectors in inner-cities across much of England. By the end of that century, the trend continued with the formation of South Asian firms in Northern Ireland, Scotland and Wales.

On the domestic front, British South Asians' overall input into the minority ethnic purchasing power is around £300 billion (**2012 estimates**). There is an estimated 320,000 minority ethnic-led SMEs in the UK contributing close to £25 billion to the economy, representing 6% of the total SME Gross Value of £430 billion.

Government and independent reports on self-employment rates for minority ethnic groups vary considerably. We endeavoured to source the best possible data available to provide readers credible evidence of this labour market trend. For instance, British South Asian self-employment rates were as follows: Bangladeshis 13.8%, Indians 11.9%, Pakistanis 27.2%, Nepali 2.6% (**Urwin, 2011**) - See also Chapters 2,3,4,5,6 and 8.

However, these figures should be treated with caution since there are thousands of informal or 'shadow' business activities that go unreported within minority communities across the country (**Sepulveda, Syrett and Lyon 2008**).

In addition, the migration patterns of South Asians have also contributed to the outflow of remittances to members' countries of origin. Remittances to South Asian countries amounted to $123 billion in 2015 while outward money transfers were $16 billion in 2014 (**World Bank 2015**).

Aside of personal benefits, remittances contributed to the gross domestic product (GDP) of the region; that is roughly 6% of total domestic earnings. It is also the case that owners make a significant contribution to the export market although there has been no comprehensive research on the value-add of international trade in goods and services.

Notwithstanding restrictive practices, a main feature of South Asian firms is the level of owners inter and co-ethnic trading practices in various industries. Commentators have referred to this trend, although the interplay of trading loyalties among business owners is yet to be fully analysed (**Basu and Altinay 2002**).

Apart from the money transfer 'trade', increasing trends in female-owned firms, the evolution of youth entrepreneurship coupled with challenges and opportunities for British South Asian enterprise development, are topics for examination in this book.

As part of the evidence collection for this book, case studies are included according to an industry sector axis (embodying key business segments) as part of the overall UK Standard Industrial Classification (SIC). Music, publishing, theatre and visual arts were profiled as distinctive business segments of the *Creative Industries Sector*. This approach is aimed at aiding readers to have a better understanding of the contribution South Asian firms are making to the British economy. The structure of the book is therefore defined and explained in the chapter outlines below:

Chapter 1 [Afghan Enterprise Landscape] – examines the contribution of Afghanis to Britain's business and the professions. Their 'unknown' impact on local economies along with diverse cultures, are highlighted through live case examples.

Chapter 2 [Thriving Markets for Bangladeshi Traders] - sets the scene on the levels of entrepreneurship of British-based Bangladeshis in this book. It shows the impact members of this group have on the ethnic market as well as their influence on the business environment that will be explored.

Chapter 3 [Global Trends in Indian Entrepreneurship] - explores the strategies British Indian business owners have used to globalise the operations of their firms in the face of intense competition in the marketplace of ideas, goods and services.

Chapter 4 [Nepalese Enterprise Dynamics] - takes a broad view of the gradual evolution of British-based Nepalese firms. They have used challenges to create opportunities for market advantage.

Chapter 5 [The Durability of Pakistani Industries] - looks at the broad aspects of the dynamic and multifaceted business culture of this group. Their effects on ethnic entrepreneurship and influence on British society are also considered.

Chapter 6 [Phenomenal Rise of Sri Lankan Commerce] - is set in the context of actions taken at a national and international level by Sri Lankans to maintain their competitive spirit. Their 'back home' conflicts are used as a catalyst to infuse further, their enterprise culture, which is also examined in this book.

Chapter 7 [The Third Age Entrepreneurs] – this chapter focuses on key issues young British South Asians face in their quest towards either setting up or managing commercial firms and social enterprises. Consideration is given to their overall attitude towards business activities.

Chapter 8 [Conclusion - Strategies for Business Enterprise Growth] - analyses various challenges and other issues affecting British-based South Asian firms and recommendations for sustaining competitive advantage in the marketplace of ideas, goods and services.

Chapter 1 Afghan Enterprise Landscape

"When I came to Britain, I wanted to continue doing business to help the community" – **Owner of Aman's Jewellers**.

Introduction

The contribution of migrant communities irrespective of their circumstances, should be acknowledged, and where possible, publicised. The case of Afghanis who fled their country due to prolong civil unrest and are contributing towards economic and social development, is an important pivot in Britain's [ethnic] entrepreneurial dynamic.

This chapter therefore focuses on the significant input Afghanis are making at integration and in so doing, maximising opportunities in the commercial and social enterprise sphere. Information for this chapter was obtained from referenced studies, online directories, media features, interviews and evaluation of employability and enterprise training sessions attended by Afghan learners. On completion of this chapter readers should be able to:

- Understand the reason for Afghanis migration to Britain;
- Appreciate the issues affecting this migrant-settler community;
- Recognise the impact of their industriousness on local economies; and
- Learn about the interconnectedness between Afghanis and other South Asians.

Migration Journey

Afghanis emigrated to Britain and other parts of Europe including Germany and the Netherlands in thousands, as they fled years of civil unrest that destroyed human lives, careers and businesses. Several came as highly skilled doctors, scientists, engineers and technologists whilst others were artisans and other unskilled personnel.

Their desire was two-fold; to seek refuge and work to support their families and other loved ones. Afghan migration to the UK began in the 1980s, then the 1990s and at the beginning of 2000 (**IOM, 2007**).

The Office for National Statistics reported that there were 60,000 people born in Afghanistan and 29,000 Afghan nationals living in the UK (**ONS, 2013**). This data might be an underestimate as during 2006 and 2007, over 40,000 births of children to Afghan parents were recorded (**Jones, S 2010**).

Exact figures are also difficult to determine because of fluctuations involving Afghanis who enter Britain vis-à-vis those who leave owing to changes in residence/non-residency status.

Except for London, Afghanis live in other UK Regions, as national census figures have reported (**Home Office, 2010**). Other areas where this community is dispersed are the North East, North West, Yorkshire & Humber, Midland Counties (East and West), East of England, South East, South West, Wales, Scotland and Ireland. The male-female ratio is approximately 64:36, with an estimated 33,000 or 33% of Afghanis under the age of 35. An average 19,000 or 25% of young Afghanis are between 16 and 25 years old.

Other distinctive features lie in ethnicity, language and faith-based practices (**Fig 1**). The two foremost national languages are Pashto and Dari (Persian), with the majority of Afghanis being Muslims. Other faith practices are Sikhism, Hinduism, Christianity and Judaism. The latter faith is evidenced by the presence of a small Afghan-Jewish community in London with a synagogue (**2014**) -See also **Chapter 8**.

Figure 1.1 Main Afghan ethnic groups
(*Source: The National Centre for Language 2009*)

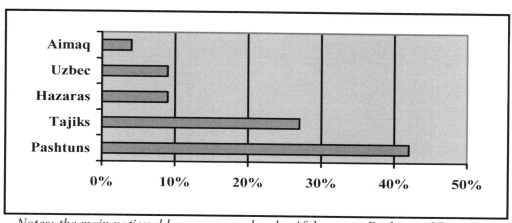

Notes: the main national languages spoken by Afghans are Pashto and Dari Persian.

Socio-economic Indicators

In the context of their official 'refugee' or 'asylum' resident status, Afghanis are categorised ethnically as either '*Other*' or '*Other Asian*' in the broader 'Asian/South Asian' definition. (**ONS 2015**) Such labelling detracts from the distinctiveness of this relatively new migrant community. For instance, their cultural, economic, faith and social identify-features are frequently ignored in the milieu of claims and counterclaims of them being part of a cohort of 'economic migrants' and thus poorly educated.

Generally, typecasting communities has negative consequences and there is evidence pointing to Afghanis who feel incapable of being successful entrepreneurs and professionals in Britain. In a 2009 study, an Afghan male observed:

"I think it's really important that Afghans be registered as a distinct minority. You asked how many Afghans are here. We would know if they were registered, as Somalis are Pakistanis are, Bangladeshis are, why not Afghans? We always get registered as
'Asians'. The related problems are lack of quotas [for ethnic minorities or Afghans specifically] in jobs, there is no real opportunity for them to get anywhere. You have to be exceptional to break out of that and get a good job" **(2009).**

Recurring studies on the presence of Afghanis in Britain, refer to key factors that are vital for their integration. The following prerequisites are also applicable to other migrants who wish to be integral of British society: -
- Secure immigration status;
- Tolerance;
- Proper housing tenure;
- English language fluency;
- Effective social networks; and
- Sustainable help and support of a professional or competent individuals. (**Rutter, Reynolds & Sheldon 2007**)

Other issues include authorities' lack of recognition and non-acknowledgment of Afghanis overseas qualifications. This has resulted in many experiencing 'a loss in professional status' and being forced to accept jobs that are incompatible with levels of academic attainment.

Men are mostly affected and it is perceived as a reason for 'undiagnosed depression' within sections of the community (**Bloch, 2002**).

Attainment Levels

There is no substantive data on the academic and vocational attainment of Afghanis in Britain. Evidence shows that upon arrival in Britain, whether skilled or unskilled, many are forced to take jobs such as mini-cabbing, pizza delivery and work in restaurants and shops due to the lack of formal [English/British) qualifications.

For men, any type of work is vital especially for the upkeep of their family. It is a source of dignity and pride since employment is seen as the 'honourable' alternative to claiming welfare benefits.

One study noted that the reason for 'certified' Afghanis not accorded professional status, was because of 'a lack of training opportunities', often linked to lack of English Language fluency (**DCLG, 2009**).

Children of Afghanis who're resident in Britain have opportunities for education. This exposure offers them essential language and other skills to improve confidence and general well-being (**Fig 1.2**). Below are excerpts of two young Afghanis-a female Londoner and a male West Midlander - who excelled at GCSE exams.

Figure 1.2 GCSE successes for young Afghanis

Two A* and nine A-levels: *"I wanted to do well and work hard. You need to dedicate your whole life to it. I didn't go out much because you need to understand this is your future. I'm not sure what I want to do when I grow up yet my ambition is to go to university"* -16 year old student, South London (*Evening Standard, 20 August 2015*).
Maths, English, Physical Education: *"I am feeling good. When I started I didn't know anyone. I've been pushed hard, to my limits, and it's helped me to get the results I need. The staff are teachers, but they're like friends too. You can talk about your problems with them"*- 16 year old student, Birmingham (*The Guardian, 20 August 2015*).

The above comments are indicative of the aspirations of younger Afghanis who attended schools with diverse student populations and adapted well whilst excelling in their educational pursuits. These examples are also a predictor of young migrants' value for a sound education to achieve satisfactory lifestyles for the future – via traditional employment or establishing start-ups in business and the professions.

Vocational Training

Local agencies provide vocational training for 'newly-arrived' migrants who are resident in the UK. Firms utilise public funding with private investment to offer programmes in '*Commercial English*' and *Enterprise Start-ups*' among other courses.

The West Midlands-based **Bright Learning Academy**, is an education institute that provides a high calibre of training for individuals of all ages. In 2014/2015 Afghanis aged 25-30 comprised over 25% of all learners enrolled for language courses. Their ambitions to succeed were noticeable from the feedback below.

"*I really want to learn new skills so that I can work.*" (**26 year-old female**)

"*I am thinking of setting up a nursery when I finish this course and do a degree programme.*" (**30-year-old female**)

"*Looking at running a food business in the future.*" (**28 year-old male**)
"*We want to know more about business in the UK.*" (**Group of Afghan students**)

The Carramea Community Resource Centre in South Harrow (London) organises various courses for migrant residents. From June to August 2015, the centre hosted a local 'Employability and Business Skills' project. A total of 100 learners primarily from the ethnic community attended this innovative course. The evaluation produced these results: -

- 12% of Afghanis attended the course (aged 25-40 years).
- Nearly all had Level 2 attainment levels.
- 90% had an existing English Language qualification.
- Afghanis completed units in interpersonal skills, customer care, communication skills, CV writing, teamwork, job interviewing techniques, money management and job search skills (**2015**).

Additionally, 55% said they "*would be interested in attending other training sessions*". These sessions included budgeting, business planning, marketing, customer care, quality control, premises, staff hiring and development. (**Fig 1.3**)

Figure 1.3 Profile of Learners by Ethnicity
(Source: Community IT Course Evaluation June-August 2015, London)

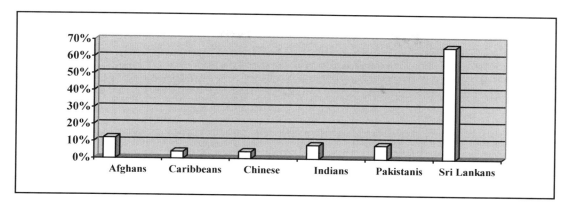

Remittances

South Asian groups are utilising remittances to improve the lives of families, other relatives and friends. The money transfer trade is lucrative and it provides significant revenue for countries in South Asia such as **Afghanistan** totalling $7billion or 3% of GDP (**2013 estimates**).

As an important source of capital, remittances can be used to securitise against future economic and financial situations. There are also primary and secondary uses of remittances for:

- Daily needs;
- Personal debts;
- Ceremonies and other festivities;
- Healthcare;
- Housing and land issues;
- Investment and business deals;
- Savings; and
- Other requirements.

On the whole, remittances make up between one and twenty-nine per cent of South Asian countries' domestic revenue. (**Fig 1.4**)

Different sources are used to remit funds; namely traditional banking institutions, Money Gram, Western Union and related money transfer channels. Transfers are channelled via mobile devices and the *'hawala system'*, the latter of which is faulty because of poor record-keeping systems in Afghanistan (**2013**) has explained in some detail, the way how the remittance trade is accounted for (**Table 1.1**).

Figure 1. 4   Currency Value of Remittances Reserves
(Source: IMF, World Bank Development Indicators and staff estimates, 2013)

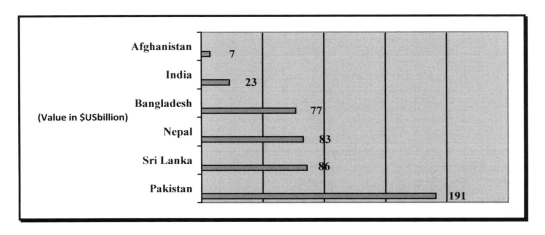

Table 1.1 Overview of remittance sending costs

Sender Country	Recipient Country	Service Provider	Amount	Cost
Netherlands	Afghanistan	ABN Amro, SNS Bank, Rabobank, ING Bank, Money Gram Western Union	EUR 100.00 EUR 100.00 EUR 200.00	EUR 15.00 EUR 55.00 EUR 17.00 EUR 20.50
Australia	Afghanistan	Western Union	AUD 100.00 AUD 200.00	AUD 10.00 AUD 25.00
Canada	Afghanistan	Western Union	CAD 100.00 CAD 100.00	CAD 12.00 CAD 20.00
Germany	Afghanistan	Western Union	EUR 100.00 EUR 200.00	EUR 14.50 EUR 19.00
United Kingdom	Afghanistan	Western Union	GBP 100.00 GBP 200.00	GBP 2.90 GBP 5.90
United States	Afghanistan	Western Union	USD 100.00 USD 200.00	USD 12.00 USD 15.00

(Source: Siegel et al., 2010; Western Union, 2013a-f; also Migration and Development Brief 24, April 13 2015, The World Bank).

Enterprising Afghanis

In September 2015, Sabir Zazai who arrived in the West Midlands from the conflict in Afghanistan, wrote a timely [online] article entitled, *'How migrants enrich our communities'*. Essentially, his editorial piece captured the self-determination and collective enterprise spirit of Afghanis against the backdrop of the 'social integration' challenges they face. Zazai's comments particularly, on the presence of, and the input of migrants to the British economy, are worthy of inclusion here.

"The growth of migrant-run businesses is happening across the country. You can find food from around the world. There are Kurdish, Afghan, Turkish and African food outlets, barber shops and bakeries. Many migrants especially those arriving through forced migration routes, are entrepreneurs and self-starters who can contribute to urban regeneration" **(2015)**.

When Afghanis find it difficult to access mainstream employment opportunities, they tend to seek different options. One alternative is doing low-waged part-time 'piece work' as a way of dealing with exclusion from the labour market **(Rutter, Cooley, Reynolds & Sheldon, October 2007)**.

The other is setting up businesses to plug gaps in goods and services. This has implications for growth prospects since owners often refer to a lack of technical assistance and business support. The issue of cultural sensitivity is said to be lacking too among agencies tasked with offering support to ethnic entrepreneurs from diverse backgrounds; be they cultural, economic, faith, social and other persuasions.

For the purposes of this chapter, we sampled 150 companies and social firms altogether. The principal aim was to understand and learn more about the organisation and performance of the British Afghani enterprise landscape.

Food and Hospitality

Aside of migration, conflict, social problems and other challenges affecting Afghans, few studies have captured essentially, the resilience of this community. The development of coping strategies by this group for dealing with discrimination and prejudice, remains largely unknown to the British public.

The Anatomy of British South Asian Enterprise

By trading in goods and services in this country, Afghan entrepreneurs are demonstrating their willingness to integrate into British society. Their success at developing various commercial firms and social enterprises is perhaps too, a noble act of succeeding against the odds.

However, it is the burgeoning food and hospitality sector that has been their initial path to enterprise success. Food businesses are dotted around the country, with firms comprising restaurants, take-aways, 'cash-and-carry', supermarkets/mini-marts and department retail stores.

They operate as single entities, partner-type firms and family-owned businesses, underpinned by cultural, ethnic and faith-based practices. Segments of the food and hospitality sector are visible in English Regions as well as Wales, Scotland and Ireland (**Figure 1.5**).

Figure 1.5 Mini-cases of Afghan Restaurants in Britain

Seven brothers of the Esmailzadah family who fled Afghanistan during the 1990s and 2000, opened the restaurant, '**Seven the Fusion Kitchen' (2009)** in London. Family members have a 'division of labour-type' approach to the business – 'tending to the bar, managing and supervising behind the scenes and in the kitchen; and sharing the washing-up' ('**Seven Afghan brothers open East Sheen restaurant'** *Your Local Guardian, 6 June 2009).'* Notably, other restaurants in the capital have business prefixes such as '*Afghan', Khyber', 'Pakhtoonkhwa', 'Charsi'* and '*Ferdow*s'.

In the Midland Counties, Afghan eating houses like the popular **Khan Saab Chef Village,** the **Taste of Namak Mandi and Taste of Khyber** are located in Birmingham. In Coventry, the **Zeenat Kebabish Restaurant** is described as the '*Best of Afghanistan food in the West Midlands'* by reviewers (**14 October 2012**). It employs over a dozen staff and operates alongside Kurdish, Turkish and African food outlets, barber shops and bakeries.

According to some diners, "*in terms of ambience, do not expect it (Zeenat) to be plush as it is styled on cafes in Afghanistan. Best items are mixed grill comprising a variety of meats including chicken tikka. Afghanistan eating is communal. Quality and quantity is good. The waiters are friendly and service is fast. They do not rush one to leave the restaurant after the meal.*"

There are other dining establishments with the common registration titles, '*Khyber';* many were established in the early part of this century. The **Khyber Pass Restaurant** in Scotland is popular with customers as one observed: "*With a thick and minimal Masala with more and more flavour as one makes one's way down the Karahi, the dish just gets better and better as one consumes the mandatory half-kilo.*"

The **Afghan Village** also known as the Village Curry House, is known for Glaswegian and visitor/tourist attractions.

Ireland has a variety of ethnic restaurants such as the **Afghan Grill House**. Customers describe it as an '*absolute delicious take-away,'* and '*a hidden gem.'* Others praise the business as a '*great*

value for money, plenty of free parking' and the food is delivered on time.' (https://www.yelp.co.uk/search?cflt=afghani&find_loc=Dublin) Undoubtedly, Afghan restaurateurs pride their success on:-
(a) The range of Middle Eastern and South Asian popular dishes;
(b) Varying spices between hot and mild, to meet different ('palates') tastes;
(c) Improving quality customer service;
(d) Maintaining a competitive (affordable) pricing strategy; and
(e) Creating a family-communal and friendly atmosphere for staff and customers.

Segments of the food and hospitality sector also include supermarkets, convenience stores, department stores and cash and carry. These outlets stock a selection of traditional consumer goods for communities as diverse as Indian, Pakistani, Sri Lankan, Bangladeshi, Malaysian, Nepali and South African. In our business sample, we discovered that Afghan firms had an estimated market share of over 20% in the food and hospitality sector.

Creative Industries

In 2010, one of Afghan's designers, Zolaykha Sherzad, gave a 'contemporary edge to traditional Afghan style' (**BBC, 2010**) after setting up **Zarif Designs (ZDs)** in 2004. The aim was to provide employment for skilled women who couldn't obtain work. It was also another way of Sherzad connecting with her ancestral home. *"It was not just going and helping, I think it is also something that I wanted to search my own identity and my own culture."*

About 60% of the company's employees are women, with 90% of products marketed across international capitals like Dubai, London, New York and Paris.

The performing arts segment influences popular culture as well. The film industry has a rich and varied genre with titles such as *Afghanistan, the Lost Truth (2003)*, *Khakestar-o-khak* (2004) along with *Bolbol and Cry in the Fog (2005)*.

Activities showcase Afghani traditions along with informing and educating mass audiences through cultural knowledge transfer. Although English Language fluency is a [functional literacy] challenge, Afghanis utilise different media to access information on current affairs in Britain, Afghanistan and around the world.

Data showed that Afghanis from diverse cultural, ethnic, faith and language backgrounds particularly, utilised sections of the mass media (print and audio-visual including the internet). Information also emphasised that Afghans recognised the information, educational and entertainment value of the media overall. (**Table 1.2**)

Table 1.2 Information Channels Outcomes
(Source: Afghan Mapping Exercise, IOM, February 2007, London

Channel	% Outcome
Television	• 71% listened to English programmes.
Radio	• 71% listened to radio in Dari/Pashto and 43% in English languages.
Newspapers	• 81% Afghanis viewed newspapers as vital information sources. *
Language	• 15% listened to radio in other languages.
Leaflets	• 43% preferred to consult leaflets in English; 49% in other languages.
Internet	• 80% used the internet and 20% were unable to access it.
Telephone	• 50% preferred to use their landline and 10% mobile phones.
Word of Mouth	• Just over 57% relied on this medium via family or friends.

*Notes: * 82% of Dari and 80% of Pashto -speakers read newspapers and 85% viewed TV - **Al Jazeera, Ariana Afghan**. 42% described the internet as informative. 15% used calling cards to communicate with families and friends abroad.*

Other creative forms
These consist of music and the theatre, followed by [media] journalism and literature. Lyrical productions are done in Persian and Pashto languages with compositions depicting the 'life and times' of ordinary folk. Some plays even reflect the English version of the Shakespearian experience through dramatic scenes of survival, love and intrigue.

Third generation Afghani **Hila Mayvand**, is a qualified television producer and broadcaster. She referred to her initial challenges while working in mainstream (audio-visual) media. "*I felt like doors were continually being shut on me and I just couldn't get anyone else to take a chance on me. I'm thrilled to have this opportunity – at last – to prove myself and begin my career in television*". (**http://creativeaccess.org.uk/interns/why-be-an-intern/an-intern-story-hilay-mayvand-at-mentorn-media**)

Another group of British-born Afghanis are making impressive strides in these creative segments; namely,
- Documentaries and film-making.
- [Acting in] Hindi films and
- [Compiling] poetry, other literature as well as taking part in visual arts.

In Ireland, Afghanis organise annual festivities to showcase their art, literature, music, theatre, religion, architecture and other artistry. This is indicative of their determination to ensure that Afghan creativity is mutually shared with diverse communities.

Healthcare

An essential business and professional sector for South Asians in general. Described as *'refugee doctors'* **(2014)** or *'professional refugees'*, Afghanis who are health and medicare specialists, end up working as volunteers, serving in much lower ranking jobs and not accorded the respect or recognition their occupation deserves.

In 2002, it was reported that Iraqis made up 30% and Afghanis18% of all 'refugee doctors in Britain' **(BBC, 2002)**. In 2013 there was 'public support for Afghan interpreters' **(2013)** many of whom are useful to healthcare and other essential public services. A leading executive of Refugee Action spoke out in support of Afghan interpreters' settlement in Britain:

"We call for a fully-funded support programme to aid the relocation, resettlement and successful integration of Afghan interpreters and their immediate family members in the UK. ………….. Like all individuals seeking asylum in the UK, Afghan interpreters deserve to be treated with dignity and respect." **(http://www.britishfuture.org/articles/public-support-asylum-for-afghan-interpreters/)**

Another media report published insights into the 'high expectations' vis-à-vis the spate of 'low expectations' by professionals. Below is one such experience by an Afghan health professional:

Locum

A 30-year-old male who worked as a doctor in Afghanistan, is a healthcare assistant. His English is flawless but yet he failed the [British] medical exam thrice. He is working as a locum phlebotomy, taking blood for testing. *"To become a doctor, you have to study for six to seven years. For phlebotomy, you just have to complete a four-day course. I know that it is only temporary"* **(2014).**

Afghan-qualified healthcare specialists – matured and young altogether – lamented the way they were treated by public health authorities when seeking healthcare jobs. Their country's medical qualifications were not recognised, more so, their skills versatility such as linguistic dexterity and cultural experiences.

Consequently, doctors, nurses and allied health professionals usually seek alternative employment in transport, food, construction and other sectors, to eke out a living. This situation affects the confidence, self-esteem and well-being of some Afghan males who feel demeaned by the way they're treated by health officials.

Still, the route towards becoming a fully-trained medical doctor in Britain is dependent not solely on levels of technical competency or occupational proficiency. Being able to communicate with clarity, precision and professional courtesy, are also essential ingredients in healthcare and similar occupations dealing with 'life-threatening' (emergency 'at risk') situations.

In the face of such challenges, a female Afghan doctor, working in the healthcare sector and who had experiences similar to her male counterparts, cautioned that,

"Doctors should not be worried about doing another job like mini-cabbing, pizza delivery etc., yet they should have financial support and every opportunity should be given to them to concentrate only on medicine other than anything else" **(2006)**.

Despite obstacles, British-based Afghan health/medicare specialists are achieving distinction though it is largely unreported or appear to be of little news value. A female Afghan doctor who came to Britain (2002) to join her husband, was fluent in English. Her primary medical qualifications from abroad were rejected by the authorities, but she persisted with her studies.

During that time, I found the Refugee Council's health professionals programme very useful. I was helped in so many ways from exam preparation classes, to financial and moral support. I would stay at the Council studying until the building closed and the help I had finding work experience – a clinical attachment was invaluable" **(2013)**.

A Legacy

While Afghanis' movement towards self-reliance and group power, remains a work in progress, they have advanced with institutional-building, as illustrated in **Fig 1.6**.

Figure 1.6 Association of Afghan Healthcare Professionals-UK
(Source: http://www.afghanhealthcareprofessionals.co.uk/)

The Association of Afghan Healthcare Professionals –UK is a professional, non-political and non-profit organisation established in March 2011. Its aims include:

- Assist with the education and training of healthcare professionals of Afghan origin in the UK.
- Work in co-operation with other medical and charitable organisations in the UK and Afghanistan.
- Organise seminars, workshops and on-line educational activities in order to promote up-to-date clinical and scientific awareness.
- Contribute to the reconstruction and development of Afghanistan healthcare sector.

The association is represented by specialists in key segments of healthcare such as: general practitioners GPs), registrars, psychiatrists, surgeons, gastroenterologists, pharmacists, dentists and bio-scientists, to name a few.

Members of the Management Committee are responsible for ensuring that statutory obligations and general commitments are met. Individual members have practices in London, Southeast, Midland Counties, Scotland and other UK Regions. A sub-committee system is integral to the overall organisational structure. Led by eminent healthcare specialists and practitioners, the main 'working' groups are:

a) *The Education Committee* includes GPs and surgeons.
b) *The Media Committee* consists of bio-scientists and GPs.
c) *The Fundraising Committee* comprises GPs and others.

From the evidence presented, an estimated 30% of females and 70% males make up this professional health body. Women have roles in leadership, 'administration', 'young professionals', 'women and family' as well as 'programme officer' responsibilities. To its credit, the association exemplifies gender inclusion and social integration within its operational ambit.

As far back as 2002, it was reported that 18% of all 'refugee doctors' in the country were of Afghan heritage. It means that there are scores of highly qualified and experienced health/medicare specialists and practitioners, representing this section of British South Asians. One notable feature of the association, is the emphasis on '*integration into the British society.*' Linkages with similar groups to enhance 'refugees' and 'migrant-settlers', is a symbol befitting inter-agency working across sectoral boundaries.

Significantly, Afghanis also demonstrate innovation in key segments of the health and social care sector. The following examples are a distillation of strategic routes health professional-entrepreneurs are pursuing in terms of excellence.

❖ **Dr Waheed Arian** is a clinical radiologist and specialist registrar. He helps UK doctors assist their Afghan colleagues to save human lives using internet and smartphone technology. "*I wanted to be able to offer world-class medical knowledge we have here in the UK to their most seriously-injured patients*" **(2015)**.

❖ **Dr. Zarghuna Taraki** received an award for her achievements as a breast surgeon. At the time of writing, she was the only female Afghan surgeon in the UK, with successes in this competitive field. "*Being a doctor I feel it is my duty to help those who are in need; may it be in a medical sense or just by raising awareness of an issue*" **(2014)**.

❖ **Dr Tahmina Weda** is a foundation doctor qualified in Orthopaedic Science. As founder of WEDA Ltd **(2015)**, her goal is to, *"to bring together leaders in the fields of trauma surgery and orthopaedics to encourage and inspire the next generation of surgeons"* (**http://www.trauma-orthopaedics.org/#!team/c24vq**).

❖ **Dr Hala Fadhli** is a dermatologist in Wales working in partnership with **Displaced People in Action** to help 'refugee' and 'asylum' doctors to pass exams they need to work in the UK (**Table 1.3**). He teaches medical courses for doctors who are from Iraq, Libya, Afghanistan, Iran and Liberia among other countries. *"They are all qualified doctors in their own countries but to practise in this country, they have to pass medical exams"* **(2013)**.

Personal Care

From Southall in London and Soho Road in Birmingham to Narborough in Leicester, ethnic business segments in the personal care sector are visible. Business proprietors from nationalities such as Afghans, Kurds, Indians, Pakistanis, Polish and Sri Lankans among others, provide a range of goods and services to a wide cross section of customers **(2016)**.

On Soho Road, owner Jalal founded **Amani Designer Tailor (ADT)** 10 years ago. His firm is reputed to be one of the city's well-known tailoring establishments. In competing with other fashion designers, ADT creates products using fabrics suitable for all 'style-wearers'; be they 'Asian', English or other customers. Afghan-born Jalal is keen on growing the business but said that lack of funding was affecting this strategy.

"We need funds to invest in machinery and equipment as well as expand into more spacious premises. Our customers have grown over the years –both loyal and new ones. The current economic situation makes it difficult to expand as quickly as you want to, but we have been around for some time and we will do whatever we can to make the business continue" (**2016**).

In spite of the current situation, Jalal asserted that the long-term goal of ADT is to maintain proper customer care and offer high quality 'finished' products and services at affordable prices.

Opposite ADT, is another personal care venture, **Aman's Jewellers**, founded by Jasbeer Singh Kapoor (<u>https://www.yelp.co.uk/biz/amans-birmingham</u>). – **See Fig 1.7**

Figure 1.7 Aman's Jewellers
(Source: Interview with Jasbeer Singh Kapoor, Birmingham, West Midlands 22 August 2016)

The firm specialises in all kinds of imitation jewellery, with product range consisting of:
- Bridal set and accessories to match.
- Kalleere from any magazine or from photo-matching personal outfits.
- Groom jewellery.
- Sikh turban material and matching accessories.
- Additional jewellery and accessories including necklaces, bangle and pandal sets.
- Artificial wedding bouquets. (**Aman's Jewellers Brochure, August 2016**)

Kapoor recounted the Afghanistan conflict and explained survival strategies used to counter 'life-and-death situations.' His enterprise endeavours are a testament to his Sikh faith and belief in the continuation of an 'enterprise destiny'

"Many of us chose business because we could not take part in the political system of the country. When I came to Britain, I wanted to continue doing business to help the community. So when I started the jewellery venture, my aim was to make it work for a long time. One of our promotion strategies, is 'buy one and get one free' which helps increase sales. We plan to add to our existing premises so that it we can become one of the largest fashion jewellery retailers in the country. Other plans are to have a proper financial plan, recruit additional sales and marketing staff, produce a company newsletter, set up a special Facebook account for customers, develop proper marketing intelligence systems and tap into local and overseas markets. We have customers from all backgrounds who buy from us."

The retail company receives numerous customer reviews such as these. *"The fashion covers such a broad spectrum of vintage, old-school, bohemian and modern styles,"* **female customer**. *"There is nothing more effective to complete an outfit than accessorising it with*

> *jewellery. Prices are actually decent and there are items in here that are definitely affordable. Members of staff are well-mannered,"* **a young customer observed.**

In evaluating the Afghani personal care sector in London and the Midland Counties particularly, these success factors stood out: -

a) Knowledge of the fashion market including its accessories segments.

b) Recognition of 'spousal' cultures and behaviours on style-appearance.

c) Duty of care to customers from diverse backgrounds.

d) Informal networking across personal care and creative industries sectors.

e) Strategies to manage the effects of recession on consumer spending.

Gender Dimension

Females also have a visible presence in segments of the personal care sector. Hossay Momand is founder of the award winning **Yllume Limited** (2009). The firm creates skincare products for global markets including large department stores like Fenwicks. As an entrepreneur who 'oozes' innovation, the British Afghan explained her desire to maintain proficiency in a reputable mainstream-type business.

"I spent years in research and development working closely with my formulator. I was determined to make a breakthrough because I knew it would change the cosmetic landscape. The business is the result of research development in working together with one of the most established laboratories in Germany, the UK and Japan to bring you cutting edge scientifically, advance skincare from within" **(2014)**.

British-based Afghani women also showed leadership of organisations that inspired, advocated and promoted gender inclusion and tolerance. Their (incremental) success was evident in groups where high levels of patriarchy existed.

Leicester Afghan Women Forum Limited and **Women for Afghan Women UK** were founded in 2015 to deliver services in the interest of Afghan and other minority ethnic women affected by gender discrimination and other types of prejudice. The key characteristics of female-led Afghan enterprises include: -

- Prioritising women's concerns and general interests.
- Encouraging young Afghanis (aged 20s-40s) to be directors.

- Emphasising the importance of skilled and culturally sensitive entrepreneurs.
- Operating diverse commercial firms and social enterprises across Britain.

Transport & Logistics

*"Walking on London's streets, one could easily find people who spoke Farsi. In the north and west of the city, about 70% of **taxi drivers** are either Afghanis or Iranians. So it didn't take me long to meet many fellow Afghans, and be introduced to their restaurants, eateries and associations"* (**2009**).

*"Through my work with migrant communities, I have seen many examples of successful businesses helping others in the local community. These migrants are our bus drivers, our **taxi operators**, the teaching assistants helping to support your children and the nurses who help you and your families"* (**2015**).

In the absence of any credible data on Afghanis in the transport sector, the above examples illustrate owners' engagement with this vital sector. We sampled about half a dozen firms that had a substantial mix of either travel agencies including cargo shipping, and or taxi/mini-cab services (**Fig 1.8**). These segments were found to be no less different from other South Asian firms and ethnic industry operators overall.

Taxi Services

Operators manage cabbing services throughout the length and breadth of the country. These firms are male-dominated since the majority of men are forced to seek alternative employment because of labour market discrimination.

Figure 1.8 Selected area-examples of the Taxi Trade

In **London,** a male Afghan spoke about his experience after fleeing his country to seek refuge in Britain. His initial plan was to become a doctor but later changed his decision to study engineering. When he arrived in Britain, he was forced to become part of the taxi-driving 'business.

"Because of the children, I needed a job with flexible hours. In 2007, I took out a loan, bought my car. It's OK. Customers are generally fine, but sometimes they get stressed.
I miss Afghanistan. I've been back, and when I arrived I cried and when I left I cried. I hope things change. I never expected to end up doing this."
https://www.theguardian.com/uk/2009/mar/07/cabbies-taxi-stories-work

A **Brighton** university study reported that Afghanis worked in kitchens, shops, take- aways, security guards and labourers. *"Approximately 80 Afghanis are registered taxi drivers,"* the study explained. **(Afghan Migrants in Brighton 2011, Community University Partnership Programme, University of Brighton, England)**

Nottingham Afghan taxi drivers relate stories that are similar to their 'cousins' in other parts of the country. Many of them who are in the transport trade 'claimed asylum' during 1996-2001. Now UK citizens, a small but significant group of men are plying their cabbing trade in the East Midlands Region. According to one expert view,

"Taxi-driving is a reputable 'profession' in keeping with Afghan and Pashtun acumen in transport economies in Kandahar, Quetta, Pesha-war, Karachi, and Dubai. Some progress to more profitable ventures, transporting second-hand trucks from Europe overland to Afghanistan. For others without basic English or literacy, taxi-driving is an impossible dream. Acquiring a licence is difficult". **(Journal of the Royal Anthropological Institute 20(3) June 2014)**

Afghan-qualified drivers could earn lucrative sums [of money] according to the hours worked and the volume of passenger 'traffic' generated. There were examples cited of labourers cum taxi drivers who invested in properties in both Afghanistan and in England (more especially in English suburbs).

Industry competition including yearly increases in motor and other forms of travel insurance premiums, are problematic for small operators in the taxi or cabbing sub-sector. But for now, it appears that hundreds of Afghanis will continue with this type of self-employment as a viable option rather than to 'face' alternative unemployment or joblessness.

Travel Agencies

The troubles in Afghanistan have not prevented nationals in Britain from setting up firms to provide much-needed services to customers; be they business visitors, tourists or other class of travellers. Travel agencies are popular with Afghanis in London and the Southeast. They usually provide services ranging from flight bookings, excursions, cargo shipping and money transfers to other logistical services.

Ariana Travel Limited was established in 2003 and is now a million-pound business. Its owner, Yasi Ahmad, was born in the mid-1970s and has grown the business over the years. The firm is a specialist in travel to Afghanistan and the Middle East. It works with major airlines such as Virgin Atlantic, Emirates, Gulfair and collaborates with Skyscanner, a global travel search site, to offer 'lowest prices' and the most 'convenient flight times' for customers travel needs **https://www.skyscanner.net/airline/airline-ariana-afghan-fg.html**.

UK Afghan Travel Limited was set up in 2015 as a sole proprietor firm. The business has numerous customers who travel on 'business' and for 'pleasure' (leisure). Travel agents usually woo travellers to tour historic cities in Afghanistan such as the '*capital Kabul, Buddhist sites, mountain villages, lakes and ancient forts*' (**2014**).

Social Enterprise

Over the past 10 years, Afghanis have followed the examples of other ethnic communities by establishing social firms to either complement or augment existing commercial businesses. These have dual legal status viz., limited companies and charities or not-for-profit entities (referred also as non-governmental organisations -NGOs).

Their structural composition varied from community groups, voluntary agencies and faith groups to professional associations and networks.

This sector's vibrancy is manifested across England and other UK regions. In the main, social enterprises are managed by a 'Committee' or 'Board-type' structure or structures.

Additionally, these enterprises are overseen by professionals, community activists, volunteers and a coterie of advisors, benefactors, supporters and others interested in the common good.

Like their British South Asian counterparts, Afghanis are in the 'businesses' of corporate social responsibility (CSR). The adage, 'helping those less fortunate than ourselves' seem to be a principled focus of their entrepreneurialism, especially when operating businesses within disadvantaged communities.

Commitment to helping and supporting worthy causes in Afghanistan, is also a vital consideration in this evolving industry. Sector activities with the highest priority include: -

- Information, advice guidance.
- Education and training.
- Women and youth welfare.
- Healthcare.
- Student affairs.
- Networking Partnerships. (**Table 1.3**)

Table 1.3 Major Social Enterprises within the British-based Afghan Community

Organisation	Set up	Purpose
Derbyshire Afghan Community Association	2006	Promote the welfare and benefit of the Afghan community in Derby.
Afghanistan and Central Asian Association	2000	Promote British values and integration among the refugee community.
Afghan Students Association UK	2006	Promote the importance of education within the Afghan community.
British Afghan Women's Society	2001	Support and empower Afghan and other UK refugee women and youth.
Association of Afghan Healthcare Professionals UK	2011	Education, training of healthcare professionals of UK-based Afghan. Professional standards, reconstruction and development of Afghanistan healthcare sector.
Afghan Aid	1983	Provide skills training and tools Afghanis need to help themselves, families and communities.
Afghan Association of Paiwand Ltd	2008	Maintain Afghani cultural identity and pass on the community's rich heritage to the next generation in the UK.
British Afghan Chamber of Commerce and Industry (BACCI)	2012	Promoting bilateral trade, investment and economic co-operation between Afghanistan and the UK.

(Source: Independent survey of Afghan organisations, July-August 2016, England

Enterprise Clusters

Over the past 20 years, there have been discussions and explanations of ethnic business development and success in Britain and elsewhere.

Several reasons have been advanced to determine the ability of minority ethnic entrepreneurs to overcome personal, industry and societal challenges.

Some of the more plausible reasons given are: -

- The lack of English Language fluency, variations in education and skills sets, labour market discrimination and stifling mobility (**1994**).
- The conventional 'push-pull' factors that tend to attract discriminated minorities to opt or choose enterprise start-ups to maximise advantage and improve their social status (**1990**).
- The importance of '*productive diversity principles*' has been alluded to by Chavan and Agrawal (**2002**) although this view doesn't necessarily considers the linguistic dexterity, cultural experiences and the innumerable networks ethnic entrepreneurs command.

Much of the above theories and views on the rationale for enterprise clusters have been tested and validated throughout this book including this chapter on *Afghan Enterprise*.

Evidence was obtained from face-to-face interviews, discussions with enterprise networks, observations at business incubation centres and the availability of business directories - both print and electronic.

Spatial Distribution

In almost every UK Region, there are ethnic business clusters, comprising a variety of commercial and industrial (heavy/light) companies and social enterprises. Importantly, the Afghani firm sector has 'concentrated' clusters in major UK city-regions such as:

- Southall (London).
- Brighton (Southeast).
- Coventry and Birmingham (West Midlands).
- Narborough Road and Nottingham (Leicester).
- Bournemouth (South West).
- Leeds, West Yorkshire (Yorkshire & Humber).
- Manchester (North West).
- Glasgow (Scotland).

In London, there was access to scores of Afghan companies particularly in Southall. In sampling 100 small to medium sized enterprises (SMEs) there was clear evidence that owners are contributing to local wealth creation and more [**Fig 1.9**].

Figure 1.9 Afghan SME Development in Southall, London
(Source: Meeting with Manager Charles House, Southall, London September 2016)

Approximately 95% of the 100 businesses in Charles House, a huge industrial facility, were owned predominantly by Afghanis. The research revealed some very interesting trends: -
- Most of the units had a tenancy schedule of 1-2 years (**2015 estimates**).
- The presence of firms dated back to 2008 (**2015 estimates**).
- Director-owners were of different faiths -Hindus, Muslims Sikhs and other believers.
- Loose-partnership' working is a vital 'resilience' strategy for all owners.
- Over 80% of the firms had non-Afghan or English business titles or signage.
- A total of 72,086 sq. feet of businesses space was calculated (**2015 estimates**).
- Gross rentals were estimated at £1,614,164 (**2015 estimates**).
- There were 7 individual industrial block units.
- The average net worth for each firm was £23,659.
- Average cash in bank per firm £20,810 (sampling of just over 30% of firms).
- An estimated 90% of firms are retail, wholesale, food, mobile tech and other sectors.

Challenges and Opportunities

All Afghani entrepreneurs – commercial and social – expressed the downside of the troubles in Afghanistan and the implications for families especially the younger generation. The quest to maintain a sense of identity, renewed confidence and trust in their abilities, plus meandering a different cultural and social terrain, are all imposing challenges for 'new arrivals' to Britain.

Then there is the labour market dilemma; that is, finding work in the absence of little or no qualification. Despite their multilingual prowess, the lack of English fluency is hampering some of the most hard-working and conscientious Afghans.

This situation is also affecting their endeavours towards gradual integration. Members of the third Afghani generation are also grappling with this challenge, but are demonstrating increasing levels of education attainment, as this chapter illustrated.

In many respects, Afghani women are taking specialist English courses as a first step towards pursuing vocational training to find either employment as workers or hopefully, set up enterprises in their respective disciplines. Until now, like their male counterparts, females have little help with starting a business.

Almost all Afghanis interviewed or surveyed, lamented the absence of *'technical assistance'* and *'enterprise support'*. The dissolution of over 60 firms (with no reason or reasons given), according to Companies House 2012-2014, was a typical example of the pressures on existing and new entrepreneurs at the time.

Surviving against intense competition is hinged on owners' enterprise instincts coupled with their alliances with ethnic, co and inter-ethnic firms. Much support for the Afghani business sector is also derived from communities –ethnic and mainstream inclusive. Lacking institutional help is inhibiting the orderly growth and development of firms even in spite of the resilience shown by an overwhelming number of Afghani business [cluster] owners. **Table 1.4**

Characteristic Features

As evidence shows, Afghanis who are operating commercial and social firms possess a variety of skills and degree of competencies that are not often considered in mainstream studies. Much of the research is focused on migratory trends, (English) language problems, health issues and inability to integrate into British society.

Table 1.4 Market variable for the sustainability of Afghani-owned Firms
(Source: Interview and surveys of Afghan Enterprises, July-September 2016)

Sector Challenges	Market Opportunities
Education and Training: no reliable data on Afghani attainment levels exist.	Second and third generation Afghanis are making strides in attainment levels including vocational training.
Remittances: are traditionally used for personal needs and requirements.	Creation of a micro-finance fund to support small incubator firms for young Afghani potential entrepreneurs.
Food & Hospitality: few Afghanis are engaged in the food production segment.	Experienced restaurateurs should sponsor food & hospitality apprenticeships for the young unemployed.
Creative Industries: limited information and data on Afghanis in this vital sector.	Creative firms should collaborate with other groups to promote (British)-type Afghani culture.
Health & Social Care: 18% of Afghan refugee doctors are part of the NHS.	Professionals in this sector should boost the national campaign for a greater fusion of health and social care.
Personal Care: dominated only by a few firms.	Existing firms should promote products and services locally via public & community agencies.
Transport & Logistics: Afghan men dominate a percentage of this trade.	Afghan taxi owners should form a national association to help and support industry operatives. Travel agencies should invest more in

	adventure, leisure and cultural tourism.
Social Enterprise: little is also known about the corporate social responsibility of Afghans.	Social groups should sponsor programmes for young people – male and females- as a means of encouraging them to be engaged in social entrepreneurship as a viable career option.
Overall Sector Challenges: high business rates, lack of enterprise support, little or no financial strategy, limited sales & marketing staff, poor links with business organisations, low return on investment among other issues. (**Source: Interviews with Print it & Telecom, Mr. Toiletry Ltd, 3 Angels Ltd, 8 September 2016, Southall, London, England)**	Industrial units and other such entities should offer relevant technical assistance and appropriate enterprise support for Afghan and other ethnic firms. A percentage of revenue from tenancy charges can be used to [routinely] evaluate the organisation and performance of firms. Since businesses contribute to wealth creation, statutory agencies should demonstrate a greater sense of economic and social fairness.

Conversely, the presence of Afghanis in key UK regions demonstrate quite clearly, their determination to be inclusive. There are numerous reasons for this fact; namely: -

- Their *innate* ability to adapt to friendly and hostile environments as their history attests.
- Unique levels of *linguistic dexterity* evidenced by multiple language speakers –Arabic, English, European (German and Russian) and South Asian dialects.
- Inherently enterprising with a '*can-do*' attitude.
- Strong *family ideals* and cultural traditions that drive success.
- Well-networked with a high level of *corporate social responsibility* attached.
- Dedicated towards working in *partnership* viz., informal alliances.
- The *dynamics* in Afghani cuisine versatility, faith-based practices, artistry, creativity, altruism and related human-centred values.
- *Self-determination: "I had limited English when I arrived, I worked hard to get established and rebuild my life"* (**2016**).

Interestingly, while researching the enterprise activities of Afghanis, other South Asian businesses persons including those from the Indian community, gave their views on the increasing self-employment rates amongst British-based Afghanis.

Parag Bhargava who manages one of the most successful firms that straddles between 'business and the professions' and the 'creative industries', observed that the challenges faced by Afghanis gave them the impetus to set up businesses. He considered such challenges as a reflection of the pattern of many ethnic firms in the West London sub-region.

"Since December 1972 when the business was established by my mother, there have been lots of developments. Though our main problem is limited finance, we plan to advertise in local newspapers and radio and update our company website. We have diversified into the African and Caribbean community market with the launch of African and Caribbean Partners as of October 2010. It is true that members of the Afghani business community are not given the type of credit they deserve. Like other South Asian entrepreneurs, Afghanis are making a real economic and social contribution to the London regional economy. We ought to celebrate and publicise their input along with other ethnic businesses' overall contribution to the wider British economy" **(Interview with Suman Marriage Bureau, London, September 2016)**.

Veteran engineer Dr Sarindar Singh Sahota OBE, also commented on the emerging strategies that Afghanis are using to sustain their businesses while helping to sustain regional economic landscapes.

"Afghanis are setting a fine example to other South Asian firms by involving their families in all aspects of the organisational-business value chain. In doing so, they are reinforcing the importance of succession planning as an integral part of the small firm sector's strategy for further development and growth" **(Interview with Dr Sarindar Singh Sahota OBE, West Midlands, August 2016)**.

Conclusion

This chapter focused on the gradual rise of Afghan entrepreneurship in Britain today against the backdrop of persistent challenges facing this ethnic group. In many respects, members of the second and third generation have blended their culture, faith, customs and other traditions with British values.

Indeed, attempts at social integration are important since it provides a further stepping stone towards making a valuable contribution to local and national development.

Afghans, like other minorities, take great pride in history and are demonstrating unique creativity and innovation by participating in an array of self-employment ventures. This fact was illustrated [in this chapter] by the evidence of countless achievements in commercial start-ups and the establishment of social enterprises across the British Isles.

Whether unskilled or having a profession, Afghanis of all age groups are making their activities around enterprise development count, in key business segments and industry sectors. An important element in their migratory transition, was the fusion of commercial and social enterprise. Examples cited in this chapter, illustrated the intrinsic and extrinsic value of complementing business ventures with social-type activities.

Notwithstanding the differences between older and younger Afghans, there are real attempts to bridge the generation gap. Sections in this chapter highlighted the mushrooming of local groups including non-governmental organisations (NGOs) and other charities, in various parts of the country.

Strategically, this meant that many Afghanis were serious about social entrepreneurship as both an act of self-reliance and group power. Through positive action, they firmly believe that social enterprises are beneficial for those who are deemed unskilled, poor, powerless, uneducated and jobless as well as those lacking confidence and trust in public officials.

It should be noted that this chapter was inspired by the founder of Community Education Academy of Leadership (CEAL), Harminder Kaur Bhogal. As a long-time business partner, she is impressed by the progress that Afghanis(especially those of Sikh faith) have made in Britain.

"Not many people know much about this section of the South Asian community. This book will certainly help to publicise their endeavours in areas of culture, economic, faith and social development. Quietly, they are making their mark in communities within London, the Midlands and other parts of Britain. Even though they represent layers of diversity, their faith-belief system is often seen as one-dimensional because little is known about their struggles —both past and present. In our line of work, we have witnessed the continued efforts made by Afghanis to fit into local communities. This fact has been borne out by the increasing academic successes of young Afghan learners, described as 'new arrivals' in Britain. This is indeed a true testament, if not revelation of Afghans' determination to realise their potential and real talent" (**2016**).

Chapter Notes

Afghan Nationality
The majority of Afghan-born residents in the UK were between 30-34 years of age. GCSE and A-Level language exams were offered in Persian from 2000 and 2002 respectively (*ICAR Population Guide: Afghans in the UK*, July 2010).

The UK Afghani population was estimated at 57,000 (2013), 81,000 (2014) and 76,000 (*Office for National Statistics* 2015).

Status
The Home Office reported on the status of refugees coming to the UK. Matters included were 'length of time spent in the UK' , 'previous occupation of refugees employed and self-employed', 'emotional health' and 'types of support needed' (July 2010).

Entrepreneurship
Irish institutions also conducted 'rare studies' on migrant entrepreneurship including those of Afghanis: 'The Experience of Migrant Workers in Ireland' in *The Other View*, Issue 14. Bell, K Jarman, N and Lefebvre, T (2004) *Migrant Workers in Northern Ireland, Belfast:* Institute for Conflict Research, p6.

Remittances
The issue of remittances by Afghanis globally, was also addressed by the International Organisation for Migration (IOM) in a report entitled, *Afghanistan Remittance Overview and Trends* (2013). Other institutions looked at this trend – Rynecki, S (2013): 'The Future of Mobile Money in Afghanistan', *USAID Impact Blog*, 22 May, http://blog.usaid.gov/2013/05/the-future-of-mobile-money-in-afghanistan/ (accessed in June 2013).

Opportunities
Most of the Afghanis interviewed in Southall said "it was very difficult to set up businesses in the UK" because of a lack of technical assistance and enterprise support" (Interviews, August 2016). Quite noticeable, were hundreds of enterprises owned by this section of the South Asian community. Industries included media, household items, retailing, warehousing, fashion and textiles, food and drinks, 'cash and carry' firms.

Web Links

www.southasianconcern.org/

http://en.wikipedia.org/wiki/British_Raj

Afghan Mapping Exercise, IOM, February 2007, London.

https://www.yelp.co.uk/search?cflt=afghani&find_loc=Dublin

http://creativeaccess.org.uk/interns/why-be-an-intern/an-intern-story-hilay-mayvand-at-mentorn-media.

www.theguardian.com/2014/mar/08/professional-refugee-lawyers-doctrs-minimum-wage-uk.

http://www.britishfuture.org/articles/public-support-asylum-for-afghan-interpreters/

http://www.afghanhealthcareprofessionals.co.uk/.

http://www.trauma-orthopaedics.org/#!team/c24vq.

https://www.yelp.co.uk/biz/amans-birmingham.

http://blog.usaid.gov/2013/05/the-future-of-mobile-money-in-afghanistan/.

https://yllume.co.uk/about-us/ & YLLUME Skincare launches Exclusively at Harvey Nichols Dubai, 14 January 2014.

https://www.theguardian.com/uk/2009/mar/07/cabbies-taxi-stories-work.

https://www.skyscanner.net/airline/airline-ariana-afghan-fg.html.

Selected References

Sudeshna Sen: How Gujaratis changed corner shop biz in UK, *The Economic Times of India, 8 January 2013*

ONS 2011; 'The equality impacts of the current recession', Equality Human Rights Commission P178, England Autumn 2009.

Ram, Monder and Jones, Trevor: Ethnic-minority businesses in the UK: a review of research and policy developments, 1 March 2007).

Diversity? It's a question of profit, Business Sense, November 2012; Jones et al, 1992; Phizac Klean, 1990; Ram and Smallbone, 2001).

Clark, Ken & Drinkwater, Stephen 2007, Self-employment, Small Firms and Enterprise P75).

Hussain, Javed Ethnic entrepreneurship in reverse in the UK, Birmingham City University, West Midlands; and Dhaliwal, Spinder, Silent contributors, Asian Female Entrepreneurs and Women in Business.

Fielden, S L., Dawe, A J. *"The Experiences of Asian Women Entering Business Start-up in the UK."* Cheltenham: Edward Elgar, 2005).

Vertovec, S. (2007): Super-diversity and its implications. *Ethnic and racial studies* 30 (6) p: 1024-1054.

Ram, M and Smallbone, D. (2003) 'Ethnic minority enterprise: Policy in practice' (Editorial) *Entrepreneurship and Regional Development,* 15 (2):99-102).

National Asian Business Association's Evidence, House of Commons, September 2010.

Ethnic minority small businesses by Turnstone Research and Consultancy Ltd, February 2004.

Altinay, Levent and Wang, Catherine L. (2009) "Facilitating and maintaining research access into ethnic minority firms" Qualitative Market Research: *An International Journal, Vol. 12 Issue*: 4, pp.367 – 390).

VOLERY, Thierry (2007). "Ethnic Entrepreneurship: a theoretical framework", in: Léo-Paul Dana (ed.). *Handbook of Research on Ethnic Minority Entrepreneurship. A Co-evolutionary View on Resource Management*. Cheltenham – Northampton: Edward Elgar Publishing, pp. 30–41).

Brah, Avtar: 1996 *Cartographies of Diaspora*, Routledge: London, pg241.

EU SMEs in 2012, European Commission September 2012.

Global Entrepreneurship Monitor, Rebecca Harding 2005: Mascarehas-Keyes, 2007b:10.

Krishen, Ram: Kashmir and Partition of India, *Seema Publishers*, New Delhi India 2001.

SAARC Annual Report 2012.

Vindawho? Chicken tikka masala knocked off top spot by Chinese stir-fry as Britain's favourite dish, Suzannah Hills, *Mail On Line* India, 23 January 2012.

Big Better Business, Department for Business, Innovation and Skills, January 2011; New Ethnic Minority Business Communities in Britain.

Sepulveda, Leandro; Syrett, Stephen and Lyon, Fergus (2008): *Challenges of Diversity and Informality for the UK Business and Policy Frameworks*, Middlesex University, November 2008.

Importance of Remittances to South Asia, World Bank 2008.

Basu, Anuradha and Altinay, Eser (2002): *The interaction between culture and entrepreneurship in London's immigrant businesses*, Henley Business School, University of Reading.

'The Experience of Migrant Workers in Ireland' in *The Other View*, Issue 14.
Bell, K Jarman, N and Lefebvre, T (2004) *Migrant Workers in Northern Ireland, Belfast:* Institute for Conflict Research, p6.
Coventry Refugee and Migrant Centre, 4 September 2015;
https://coventry.cityofsanctuary.org/2015/09/04/how-migrants-enrich-our-communities.

International Organisation for Migration –IOM, 2007).
ONS, 2013.

ICAR Population Guide: Afghans in the UK, July 2010.

Jones, S (2010): Afghans in the UK. *Information Centre about Asylum and Refugees (ICAR) Population Guide,* http://www.icar.org.uk/12709/population-guides/afghans-in-the-uk.html accessed June 2013.

Afghanistan Remittance Overview and Trends (2013). Other institutions looked at this trend – Rynecki, S (2013): 'The Future of Mobile Money in Afghanistan', *USAID Impact Blog,* 22 May 2013

Home Office, Migration Statistics Unit 2010.

'The History and Current Position of Afghanistan's Hindu and Sikh Population', *Centre for Applied South Asian Studies*, retrieved 24 December 2014.

The National Centre for Language 2009.

ONS 2015.

The Afghan Muslim Community in England, Department for Communities and Local Government, London, April 2009, p34.

Rutter, J., L., Reynolds, S., & Sheldon, R [October 2007]: 'From refugee to citizen: 'Standing on my own two feet', a research report on integration, 'Britishness and citizenship', Metropolitan Support Trust and the Institute of Public Policy Research, London.

Bloch, A [2002]: 'Refugees' opportunities and barriers in employment and training', Research Report No. 179, Department for Work & Pensions, London) also Jones, S [2010]: 'Afghans in the UK', ICAR Population Guide, July 2010.

'The Afghan Muslim Community in England: Understanding Muslim Ethnic Communities', Change Institute, Department for Communities and Local Government, April 2009.

HICK Project Evaluation Report, Community IT, September 2015.

IMF, World Bank Development Indicators and staff estimates, 2013.

Siegel et al., 2010; Western Union, 2013a-f; also Migration and Development Brief 24, April 13 2015, The World Bank.

Rutter, J., Cooley, L., Reynolds, S., & Sheldon, R. [October 2007] –'From refugee to citizen: 'Standing on my own two feet' A research report on integration, 'Britishness' and citizenship', Metropolitan Support Trust and the Institute of Public Policy Research, London.
http://www.refugeesupport.org.uk/documents/RS_ReportOct07.pdf.

BBC News, 14 October 2010.

The Guardian.com, 8 March 2014.

Migrant and Communities Refugee Forum Report, London 2006.

Refugee Council, 7 August 2013.

BBC, 28 November 2002.

The Guardian, 10 May 2013.

Manchester News, 31 December 2015.

Afghan Women Support Forum, London February 2014.

Exam help for refugee doctors,' WalesOnline, 31 March 2013.
Hall, M. Suzanne; King, Julia and Finlay, Robin (2016), 'Migrant infrastructure: transaction economies in Birmingham and Leicester, *London School of Economics,* February 2016.

Jones, Trevor; Ram, Monder; Li, Yaojun; Edwards, Paul and Villares, Maria, Institute for Research into Superdiversity *IRIS WORKING PAPER SERIES,* NO 8/2015, University of Birmingham.

Reza Mohammadi, *The Guardian* 10 May 2009.

Sabir Zazai, Coventry Refugee and Migrant Centre, 4 September 2015.

Afghan Migrants in Brighton 2011, Community University Partnership Programme, University of Brighton, England.

Journal of the Royal Anthropological Institute 20(3) June 2014.

MailOnline, 29 December 2014.

Independent survey of Afghan organisations, July-August 2016, England.

Boyd, R. L. (1990): Black and Asian self-employment in large metropolitan areas: a comparative analysis`, Social Problems, vol. 37, no. 2: pp 258-274.

Brockhaus, R. H. (1982): The psychology of the entrepreneur, in: Kent, C., Sexton, D. L., Vesper, K. H. eds., Encyclopedia of Entrepreneurship. Prentice Hall, Englewood Cliffs, NJ.

Slevin, D. D. and Covin, J. G. (1992): Creating and maintaining high performance teams, in Sexton, D. Kasard, J., eds, The State of the Art of Entrepreneurship. Coleman Foundation, PWS, Kent, Boston, MA.

Sroosh Kouyhar, Social Integration Officer, *Coventry Refugee and Migrant Centre*, West Midlands, England, June 2016.

Chapter 2 Thriving Markets for Bangladeshi Traders

"The customer is King and my business is about bringing people closer" – **Zaman Telecom**.

Introduction

This chapter looks at the Bangladeshi community's economic contribution to Britain by exploring their rise from working class migrants to owners of commercial and social enterprises. Perceived as one of the most deprived minorities due to low education attainment levels, poor take up of mainstream services, spatial distribution as well as cultural and English language fluency problems, Bangladeshis have risen to these hurdles by engaging in niche markets. By the end of this chapter therefore, readers will learn the following: -

- Bengalis migration from Bangladesh to Britain;
- Their cultural and social value systems;
- Their industry sector contribution to the British economy;
- Their attitudes to business and industry; and
- The challenges faced and opportunities they have in the 21st century.

Origins

Like other South Asians who migrated before and after the 20th century, Bangladeshis first came to Britain as migrant workers – originally as *lascars* or cooks in the 19th century from the predominantly Sylhet Division (north-east of Bangladesh). After the partition of India in 1947 and the resultant conflict, hundreds migrated to the UK in the 1970s. Initially, most came to London and later, others made their way to other English regions. Over 50% of Bangladeshis reside in London/Greater London with a sizeable number located in East London.

Bangladeshis make up 447,021 or 6.1% of the non-white population, with numbers increasing since the 1960s (**Table 2.1**). An estimated 8,000 live in Wales, Scotland and Northern Island combined. Although they came to Britain to take up low paid jobs in small factories and the textiles trade, when the 'Indian restaurant' concept became popular, hundreds of Bangladeshis opened cafes. They have set up over 17,000 businesses (**2012 estimates**) in London and other UK regions.

Table 2.1 Growth in the number of Bangladeshis in the UK
(Source: The Emigrant Bangladeshis in the UK and USA, Ministry of Expatriates' Welfare and Overseas Employment, February 2004)

Year	Population	+% (average)
1961	6,000	-
1971	22,000	+266.7%
1981	64,561	+193.5%
1991	162,835	+152.2%
2001	283,063	+73.8%
2011	447,021	+58.0%

Deprivation Indicators

Educationally, Bangladeshi pupils' A-C GCSE pass rate varies between 56% and 88% plus for boys and girls respectively. (**Table 2.2**) Educational 'distributions' are not perfectly comparable across ethnicity and countries involving South Asian groups in general. For instance, nearly 60% of Bangladeshis have college degrees, compared to 30% in the UK
(**2010**). Members of this group also have persistent high levels of unemployment or worklessness (Notes on this) and at the time of writing, the ratio for men and women was 20:24 (**ONS 2011:2012**).

Social housing is also a problem with many families living below the poverty line thereby confirming the notion that Bangladeshis suffer more from multiple disadvantage than any other group in Britain.

However, second and third generation Bangladeshis have bucked the trend by moving into professional careers, as (medical) doctors, information technology specialists, teachers and business persons, to name a few. As events have shown over the past decade or so, the enterprise tradition remains a key to this group's success.

Table 2.2 Attainment of 5 or more A*-C GCSE Grades by key minorities
(Source: Department for Education, June 2015)

Pupils by ethnicity (Boys)	2008	2009	2010	2011	2012	2013
White (including British)	58.5%	64.7%	71.2%	76.85%	78.25%	78.55%
Indian	74.3%	78.8%	85.0%	87.6%	89.3%	88.6%
Pakistani	52.7%	61.2%	69.8%	77.4%	79.9%	81.0%
Bangladeshi	**56.0%**	**65.5%**	**72.0%**	**79.4%**	**82.9%**	**81.5%**
African	53.5%	65.7%	71.6%	79.1%	80.5%	81.3%
Caribbean	46.9%	56.4%	64.2%	72.2%	75.3%	76.3%
Chinese	80.9%	84.1%	87.6%	90.6%	91.9%	90.9%
Other Ethnic Groups	49.8%	60.%	65.9%	73.9%	76.6%	79.3%

ALL BOYS	59.1%	65.8%	71.9%	77.0%	79.8%	79.6%
Pupils by ethnicity (Girls)	**2008**	**2009**	**2010**	**2011**	**2012**	**2013**
White (including British)	66.65%	72.1%	78.2%	82.55%	85.05%	84.85%
Indian	82.7%	85.8%	89.7%	92.8%	93.1%	93.6%
Pakistani	64.0%	72.0%	78.4%	84.1%	85.6%	86.4%
Bangladeshi	**68.9%**	**73.8%**	**79.9%**	**86.2%**	**87.6%**	**88.4%**
African	87.6%	91.2%	92.3%	95.0%	94.2%	95.2%
Caribbean	60.8%	69.9%	76.2%	82.6%	83.9%	84.5%
Chinese	87.6%	91.2%	92.3%	95.0%	94.2%	95.2%
Other Ethnic Groups	62.5%	68.4%	77.3%	84.1%	82.8%	85.6%
ALL GIRLS	68.2%	73.9%	79.5%	84.0%	86.3%	86%

(Notes: The above figures show the steady progress of young Bangladeshis over the past five years. Despite multiple advantage, female Bengali students are competing quite favourably in the education attainment rankings when compared to both white and other minority ethnic learners).

Enterprising British Bangladeshis

Most studies indicate that South Asians have higher business ownership rates relative to mainstream. Bangladeshis participation rates in economic development tend to increase when education and other demographic changes occur **(2010)**. Those who excel academically and professionally have a 'positive effect on employment' patterns including business start-ups.

Overall, British Bangladeshis enterprise success is reflected by the young generation's interest in academic and professional attainment. This fact is borne out by their choice of subjects - business finance, administration, mathematics, law, media, science and technology. English students form the bulk of the 'learners' population' compared to minorities including Bengalis, who're under-represented within higher education institutions.

Nevertheless, figures showed the nominal, but varied increase in the number of Bengali 'accepted applicants', registered to pursue higher education courses during 2007 and 2012. **(Fig 2.1)**

Figure 2.1 British Bengali applicants, 2007-12

- 2007- 3,249 (0.9%)
- 2008 – 3,705 (0.95)
- 2009- 4,040 (1.0%)
- 2010 – 4,308 (1.0%)
- 2011 – 4,685 (1.1%)
- 2012 – 4,821 (1.2%) - 24,808 students pursued higher education.

(Source: UCAS Ethnic Group 2007-2012)

While higher education remains a necessity, there are other 'push-pull' factors attributed to Bangladeshis efforts towards competing in the labour market (including enterprise participation); they encompass:

- Perceived Opportunities (64.4%);
- Perceived Capabilities (23.6%);
- Fear of Failure (72%);
- Entrepreneurship as a Good Career Choice (73%);
- High Status to Successful Entrepreneurs (100%); and
- Media Attention for Entrepreneurship (49.3%).

(Source: Global Report, Global Entrepreneurship Monitor 2011)

Self-employment

Much research has been done to determine self-employment rates by ethnicity in the UK. For example, in 2011 it was estimated that over two million minorities were categorised as 'employees' and 'self-employment' segments accordingly. A comparison was made between 'disadvantaged' groups versus mainstream. From an ethnic standpoint, approximately 310,034 business owners were listed in the 'self-employed' category; that is, 6.4% of all entrepreneurial activities and/or 13.9% of overall self –employment by ethnicity (**Table 2.3**).

Table 2.3 Employees/Self-employment by key UK Ethnic Minorities
(Source: Urwin, Peter: Self-employment, Small Firms and Enterprise, The Institute of Economic Affairs, Britain 2011)

Ethnicity	Employee	Self employed	% Self employed
African	285,654	18,416	9.6%
Bangladeshi	**107,264**	**17,205**	**13.8%**
Caribbean	232,271	18,416	7.4%
Chinese	98,964	22,448	18.5%
Indian	569,363	76,980	11.9%
Pakistan	211,553	79,214	27.2%
Nepali	50,000	271	2.6%
Other Asian *	220,356	26,523	10.7%
Other	362,109	50,832	12.3%
Grand Total	**2,087,534**	**310,034**	**6.4%**

*Notes: * 'Other Asian' refers to Afghans and Sri Lankans*

Statistics for Bangladeshi business owners pointed to their ability to compete in specific markets on the basis of knowledge and reach. Data also showed their lowest business ownership rate among other British South Asians. Against the backdrop of their low 'employee' productivity, they have compensated this by securing the third highest business ownership ranking for UK minority ethnic groups altogether.

The above indices also show their tenacity to compete in specialist markets. For instance, Bangladeshis have an estimated 7,200 restaurants across the British Isles. Owners invest in enterprise diversity by setting up multiple business segments within the food and hospitality industry (**Fig 2.2**).

Figure 2.2 Mini-cases of the British Bangladeshi Food Trade

Bangladeshis own over 80% of the UK curry industry. The Bangladesh Caterers Association (BCA) was formed in 1960. About 2.5 million diners visit Bengali-owned restaurants. Brick Lane was nominated the curry capital in 2012.

BCA presented special awards to 11 restaurants along with 9 young chefs. *"It gave us an opportunity to present our demands on importing skill manpower from Bangladesh for development of the 4 billion pound curry industry. We expect the government to come up with solutions to our existing problems"* (**BCA 2012**).

Iqbal Ahmed who heads **Seamark Plc**, built the Manchester-based business on seafood companies. Awarded an OBE (2001) for services to international trade. Muquim Ahmed of **Cafe Naz** group of restaurants and property investments, is a campaigner for a national "curry university" to train the unemployed in the 'spicy arts'. Wali Tasar Uddin of **Britannia Spice (Scotland)** is a recipient of the Scottish and British Curry Awards and owner of several food businesses. He's a former Director General & Chairman of the Bangladesh British Chamber as well as executive member of the European Bangladesh Federation. He was awarded an MBE in 1995 for his services to race relations. Atique Choudhury is proprietor of London restaurants - **Thai YumYum**, the **Japanese Oishii** and the **Mexican Mercado**. He is interested in more apprenticeships for aspiring restaurateurs and is a sponsor of Hackney Empire and the Asian and Oriental School of Catering (Hackney College).

(Source: Export Potential for Bangladeshi Products to British Curry Industry, BCA 2012)

The Bangladeshi curry industry contributed £4.5 billion to the British economy and created 100,000 jobs for people in this sector (**2011**). The food and hospitality sector offers owners the chance to exhibit their passion for foods whilst sharing cultural practices. Indeed, Bangladeshis' enterprising spirit is further manifested in a moral obligation to support materially, family, friends and their ancestral home, as the growing money transfer trade attests.

Remittances

Remittances have multiple economic and social benefits for Bangladeshis. Money transfers help to maintain healthy foreign reserves which are vital, as was evidenced during 2010-11 when Bangladeshis remitted $US11.65 billion. The contribution of this 'financial enterprise' from the UK is particularly significant as it represents around 8% of overall transfers received by Bangladesh (**Table 2.4**).

Total transfers from the UK during the financial year 2010-11 stood at $US 890 million, with the UK being the 5th largest source of remittance after Saudi Arabia, USA, UAE and Kuwait.

Table 2.4: Remittances inflows to Bangladesh from the UK Update to 2013/2015

Period	Amount (in $US millions)
2000-2001	55.70
2001-2002	103.31
2002-2003	220.22
2003-2004	297.54
2004-2005	375.77
2005-2006	517.39
2006-2007	886.90
2007-2008	896.13
2008-2009	788.85
2009-2010	827.25
2010-2011	889.60
2011-2012	987.46

(Source: Bangladesh High Commission, London 2012)

As subsequent chapters illustrated, other South Asians contribute to the money transfer trade even at the height of the prolonged recession. Being true to form, Bangladeshis have used faith and cultural traditions to secure market advantage as their contribution to segments of the creative industries demonstrates.

Creative Industries

They are several personalities making their mark, either as individuals within the Bangladeshi community and/or 'national treasures' in the wider British society. Much of these achievements are evident within the mass media, music and films along with publishing and allied literature segments.

Bangladeshis hold prominent positions in the media with up to five television channels competing with various multimedia agencies and institutions – both mainstream and minority in character. Presenters include Ajmal Masoor, Kanan 'Konnie' Huq, Lisa Aziz, Rizwan Hussain, Tasmin Lucian-Khan, Abdul Choudury and Faisal Islam (**Fig 2.3**).

Figure 2.3 Mini-cases of British Bangladeshi media practitioners

Ajmal Masroor is an Imam, television broadcaster and politician. He came to Britain when he was nine, went back to Bangladesh briefly and returned to Britain as a teenager. He presents his own shows on the *Islam Channel* and is also a panellist on Channel 4's programme, *Shariah TV* and appeared on major news channels – the *BBC, CNN* and others as a commentator on various issues.

Konnie Huq is a Cambridge University economics graduate and TV presenter with an outstanding filmography career. She is the longest female presenter of the *Blue Peter* series, breaking a *Guinness World Record* by pinning 17 *Blue Peter Badges* on fellow presenter, Andy Akinwolere's shirt. Huq made her debut on the *BBC Asian Network* in the 'Asian Network Report' programme series. She is involved in a host of charity activities including the British Red Cross.

Rizwan Hussain is a barrister, TV presenter and an international humanitarian worker. He is also a former Hindi singer and a law lecturer. He performed under the brand name "Sargam" (1990s) and produced popular albums such as *B-Boy*, with a UK 'Asia' chart hit single. He has also done charity stints in Africa, Bangladesh and elsewhere.

Tasmin Lucia-Khan is a journalist/television presenter. She holds an Oxford degree in politics, philosophy and economics and has worked with mainstream channels including *BBC Three, BBC News* and *ITV News*. She hosted talk shows interviewing personalities such as former US President, Bill Clinton and other high-profile events - the *BCA and Scottish Asian Business Awards,* the *Basis Soft Expo* and an HIV/AIDS Conference, held in Dhaka (200). The media star was nominated for *'Young Achiever of the Year'* (2008) by the Asian Woman Awards for Excellence.

Faisal Islam is a 1970s-born Cambridge economics graduate whose work in the print and electronic media has earned him prestigious awards. In 2000 and 2010, he received awards for excellent reporting on business trade and financial market issues, *Young Journalist of the Year* (2006), *Broadcast News Journalist Award* (2007), Business *Journalist of the Year'* and a prize for *Best Broadcast Story*. He was named too as the *"Broadcast News Reporter of the Year"* (2009) by the Work World Foundation. , for his "excellent writing" by converting "abstract economics" for total accessibility whilst "informing viewers in a compelling and original way."

Music

Another sub-sector of the creative industries owned by the Bangladeshi community is music with songwriters, bands and producers, ruling the roost. They **include Bilal Shahid, Farook Shamshar, Lucy Rahman, Kishan Khan, Nazeel Azam** and **Zoe Rahman** who earned the '*Musician of the Year'* in the early part of this century.

Western influences have impacted on South Asian music especially Bhangra similar to how African, Caribbean and other musical cultures have fused or 'borrowed' from other styles to recreate authentic genres or musical art forms (**Fig 2.4**). According to British-born Bangladeshi, **Idris Rahman**:

"From our parents, we got into the Western Classical music, later on jazz and Reggae. We just got influenced by our surroundings and we are very open to new styles of music. We also listened to Bangladeshi popular music from our cousins in Bangladesh but that's about it. We were always more influenced by English and a whole variety of styles, since we were born and brought up in the UK. We don't speak Bengali" **(2007)**.

Figure 2.4 Mini-case of Bangladeshi music websites

There are scores of musical websites managed by Bangladeshis aged 25 plus. These sites have titles featuring the 'Bangla' prefix nearly half a dozen times. As dotcom links, they specialise in genres such as:-

- Hindi music
- Bangla music
- Drama serials
- Movies
- Music videos
- Telefilms
- Download of other artistic material and musical products.

There is also a dedicated **Bangla Community Online Radio Station**, broadcasting 24 hours daily and complemented by '**MyBangla Music'**. Along with their music, composers link teaching, television presenting with related professions.

Theatre

There are outstanding performers such as **Nazim Choudury** screen writer and actress known for her critically acclaimed radio play *Mixed Blood* in 2006. Sadik Ahmed's short film *Tanju Miah* (notes on what this means) was selected as the first Bangladeshi film in the Toronto Sundance and Amsterdam film festivals in 2007.

Another popular film was *The Last Thakur* which opened at the London, Dublin, Mumbai and New York and other film festivals. Playwright Tanika Gupta MBE won a media award for her BBC 2 play *Flight* in 1998. She won the Arts and Culture Award in 2003. Her play *The Waiting Room* was staged by the Royal National Theatre, winning the John Whiting Award in 2000.

Artists Akram Khan MBE, Kamiz Ali Reza Wahid MBE and Ruhral al- Alam, are all icons in their own way. Khan is a multiple award-winner including the *Distinguished Artist Award* at the International Society for the Performing Arts 201. In August 2000, he launched the Akram Khan Company and produced his first full-length work, *Kaash* in collaboration with Anish Kapoor and Nitin Sawhney, at the Edinburgh Festival.

Literature

In this creative sub-sector, Dr Ghula Murshid, Monica Ali, Rekha Waheed and Tahima Anam are all specialists, ranging from journalism, media production to novels and storytelling genres. In particular, Ali stands out, as the author of the famous *Brick Lane*, *In the Kitchen* and the *Untold Story*.

As a visiting professor of Creative Writing at Columbia University, Ali is former chair of the 2011 Asian Man Booker Prize and a member of the Advisory Council. At the time of writing, she was chairing the judging panel of the Royal Society Winton prize for science writing and judging the Guardian First Book Award.

Other literary works include non-fiction produced by eminent persons; namely Mustaq Hussian Khan, professor in economics, the School of Oriental and African Studies (SOAS), University of London. His ground breaking work focuses on the economies of poor countries with notable contributions in the field of institutional economics and South Asian development. There are agencies that have been set up to promote the artistic and cultural endeavours of the South Asian community (**Fig 2.5**).

Figure 2.5 Case Study of Sampad

The West Midlands-based **Sampad** or South Asian Arts Development (2011), was founded to promote the appreciation and practice of diverse art forms of Indians, Pakistanis, **Bangladeshis** and Sri Lankans, although not exclusively. Activities include exhibitions such as *Dancing about Sculpture,* professional development based on leadership and artist workshops, international partnerships and the celebration of the 150th anniversary of Rabindranath Tagore as well as a digital map of cultural activity produced by 123 volunteers. As a highly creative modern entity with a turnover in excess of £600,000, Sampad has experienced directors and staff combined coupled with private and public institutional funders, supporters and partners. According to director Paili Ray OBE, *"During the Cultural Olympiad and London 2012 Festival, we championed the use of digital technology through the provision of practice-based training and participatory arts experiences, and continue to develop Sampad as an exemplar organisation for South Asian arts"* (**Annual Report, Sampad 2012**).
In its quest for excellence, the organisation contributes to cultural regeneration and social cohesion by integrating children (aged 7-12 during school holidays), women and diverse communities into its overall creative development programme.

Publishing

British Bangladeshis operate various media firms; weekly newspapers, journals and bulletins to fill gaps in national and international markets, Bangladesh inclusive. Since the 1980s these publications have attracted diverse audiences (**Fig 2.6**). Corporate sponsors including advertising from local businesses help bankroll newspapers and other print media.

Figure 2.6 Mini-cases of major Bangladeshi Newspapers in Britain

- **Bangla Post,** aimed at British Bengalis as a platform to engage in discourse, debate and highlight concerns excluded from mainstream media; circulation 48,000.
- **East End Life,** Tower Hamlets Council's free community weekly newspaper; read by residents and firms. Includes special sections with stories in Bengali and Somali.
- **Janomot Bengali,** first weekly Bengali paper published outside Bangladesh. Modernised British-Bengali journalism, reflective of the views and aspirations of

> Bangladeshis; readership 20,000.
> - **Notun Din,** Bengali news weekly, founded in 1987; reflects the views and aspirations of the British Bangladeshi people and others living overseas. Readership 11,700.
> - **The Potrika** weekly newspaper was established in 1977. It provides 'neutral coverage' of British Bangladeshi communities in the UK and worldwide. Readership 50,000.
> - **Surma,** Britain's largest Bengali newspaper, celebrated 30 years (2010). Sold in supermarkets and retail units in Britain. Circulation 100,000 plus.
> - **The Bangla Mirror** only English Language weekly newspaper aimed at British Bangladeshis, linking their ancestral home(s). Features news, lifestyle and health/sports, advertisements, anniversaries and obituaries.

(Source: http://www.solidbangla.com/bangla%20newspapers%20in%20uk.html)

Two other influential publications complement newspaper titles; namely the '*British Bangladeshi Power 100*' (**2011:2012**) and the 'British *Bangladeshi Who's Who*' (**2008:2012**). These publications listed hundreds of personalities involved in business and the professions along with civic groups across gender and age categories.

In his congratulatory remarks, former Mayor of London, Boris Johnson, said *"I am pleased to see Bangladeshis making their mark in every sphere of endeavour and getting the recognition they so richly deserve. In business, the arts, media, literature and financial services, to name a few, Bangladeshis are making a vital contribution to the capital's economy and society"* (**2011:2012**).

Health and Social Care

Members from the minority ethnic community have contributed (and still are) to the NHS with valuable inputs into the medical sciences field. Bangladeshi doctors are a small but growing contingent of specialists dedicated to healthcare advancement.

Estimates suggest that around 150 countries are represented on the UK medical register with 1,619 or 0.6% of Bangladeshis registered as doctors with the same number-ratio operating clinician levels 1 and 2. This is out of a total of UK 168,334 GPs and allied media specialists. **(Fig 2.7)**

Qualified migrants worked with the NHS for over 60 years with perspectives on geriatric medicine during the NHS formative years. Here is an extract of a Bengali doctor's experience with the health service in the last century:-

"I think the main reason, is that the geriatricians had a hard, heavy, clinical work load and had little time left to do other extra work, like research, publications and in terms of giving awards these other aspects were given more importance than the guy who was providing the sort of a bread and butter service, working hard from morning till evening.

I think that's the main reason really. Maybe old schoolboy ties and that sort of thing can play a part – **(1967)** (www.open.ac.uk/hsc/_assets/GeriatricMedicineFindings.pdf)

Figure 2.7 Number of South Asian doctors
(Source: General Medical Council July 2015, England)

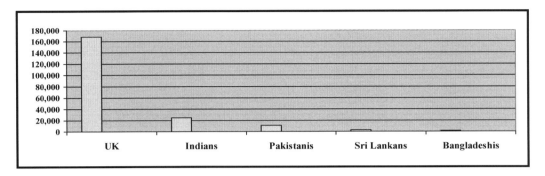

Career choices for Bangladeshi medical students are a combination of personal preferences and the desire to be professionals in clinical and related hospital sciences. It was estimated in 2006 that about 1% of Bengali practising physicians - almost 20% of medical graduates - migrated to other countries such as the UK. Their major subspecialties were *medicine, surgical, obstetrics and gynaecology plus allied forms of preventative medicine* (**Fig 2.8**).

Both genders in the British Bangladeshi community are excelling in medicare. **Professors Andy Miah, Ghulam Sarwar** and **Tipu Zahed Aziz** are accomplished scientists in ethics, technology, Islamic Studies and neuroscience respectively.

Dr Gulnahar Mortuza is a Pan-European scientist involved in developing proteins for the cellular cycle process. Her work at the National Institute of Medical Research contributed to the understanding of diseases; namely HIV and Leukaemia. Her work has been published in the prestigious journal, *Nature*.

Figure 2. 8 Example of a comparison of career choices
(Source: Advances in Medical Education and Practice 2011/12, University of Bradford, UK)

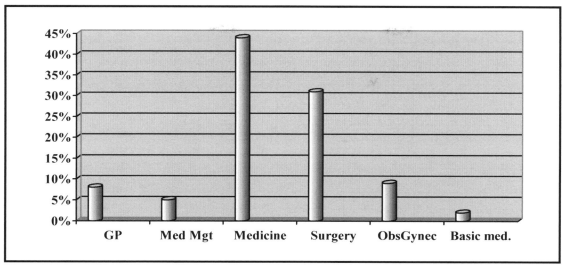

Notes on the abbreviations: **GP**- general practice, **Med Mgt** – medical management, **ObsGyne** – obstetrics and gynaecology, as well as **Basic med** – basic medicine.

Care Sector

Demographic changes such as an ageing population have created enterprise opportunities for minorities in the care sector. In particular, busy lifestyles result in many South Asians unable to take care of their elders as their tradition dictates.

Firms are segmented along private, local government-sponsored and or social enterprise-type lines. These entities are registered as *'old age and nursing homes'*, places for *'dementia, old age and physical disabilities'* and *'other specialist care services'* (**2011**).

Owners have a statutory responsibility to ensure that there is a balanced staff ratio that includes relevant ethnic representation for those who are caring for diverse 'resident-clients'. As the profile of **Careworld London Ltd** attests, Bangladeshis are making a positive difference to this vital 'human' industry **(Fig 2.9)**.

Figure 2.9 Case Study of Careworld London Ltd

Ayub Khan is Managing Director of **Careworld London Ltd** as well as **Careworld Community Hub**. He acquired a Registered Manager Award in 2004 from the Care Quality Commission (CQC) to confirm his professional status in the health and social care sector. Careworld London is a domiciliary care agency that primarily works with disabled people of Bangladeshi/Asian origin. The agency offers services for adults and children.

The focus is to support people to maximise their independence within the local community by using a person-centred approach. Khan is an advocate of people's empowerment especially supporting people who are at the margins of society.

"To empower the wider community, we need first to help those individuals that need support first. Therefore we need to first deal with marginalisation at the individual level so that we can address an individual's exclusion from meaningful participation in society. This is what the Careworld brand is about" (**Source: Health & Social Care,** *British Bangladeshi Who's Who* **2012).**

He holds a Master's Degrees in business management from Bangladesh and the UK. He was a board member and trustee of the Bangladeshi Parents and Carers Association (BPCA) 2005-2009.

Politics

The past two decades have witnessed Bangladeshis involvement in areas of local government and the legislature. **Baroness Manzila Uddin** is a Life Peer and the first Muslim and South Asian to sit in the House of Lords. **Murshad Quershi** is a Cabinet Member of the Greater London Assembly. **Syeda Amina Khatun** MBE is a deputy leader of the Labour Council in Sandwell, the first Bangladeshi woman to be elected in the Midlands (1999). Others include **Rabina Khan** who stood as an independent councillor for Bromley-by-Bow and Cabinet Member for Tower Hamlets. In 2006 at the age of 23, she became the youngest ever elected councillor in the country. Of course, they are prominent Bangladeshis who are unsung achievers in their own right (**Fig 2.10**).

Figure 2.10 Case Study of A distinguished internationalist

Dr Halima Begum works with the British Council with a particular focus on partnerships and collaborations, producing the Global Education Dialogue; that is, shaping the UK-ASEAN Knowledge Partnership.

She previously worked with the Department for International Development (DFID), the Centre for Civil Society, a think-tank at the London School of Economics, and at Action Aid in London, where she helped launch the Global Campaign for Education, a civil-society movement working to end the global education crisis.

She worked on large-scale programmes, covering a £50 million education sector programme in Nepal, £200 million programme in Bangladesh, through to overseeing UK government's bilateral education assistance to Pakistan, rising to £650 million. Helped create the Global Partnership on Education, world's single largest funding platform for education reform to relieve 67m out-of-school children into education.

She holds an MSc in International Relations (with distinction) and a BSc in Government and History from the London School of Economics, and she later completed a PhD from the University of London. Dr Begum has presented at numerous international conferences and high-level meetings, including annual Global Education Partnership global governance meetings 2003-07.

Bangladeshis have marginal seats (about 1%) in the UK Parliament, but nearly 100 local councillors mostly from the Labour Party, with a few from other political parties. Thus much lobbying is needed to recruit more minorities (South Asians inclusive) to serve in diverse areas of public life. Such a fervent campaign is necessary for these statistical reasons: -

- Only 0.9% of minority ethnic women are local authority councillors.
- 5.7% of minority ethnic women represent public appointments.
- 3.5% are Non-executives of National Health related bodies.
- 3.1% are Chairs of Local NHS Boards.

(Source: Government Equalities Office Factsheet, 2010)

Business and the Professions

Second and third generation Bangladeshis are making inroads into this sector that consists of banking finance, market research, consulting, accounting and related professional services. Members of this ethnic group represent other minorities (10%) in England who maximise opportunities in this sector when compared to 2% to 3% for other UK regions (Wales, Scotland and Ireland).

Recent estimates (2012) suggested that Bangladeshis accounted for 19% in the fields of accounting, financial, legal and related business professions **(2012).** They have shown demonstrative sector skills, with an increase of 6% in this sector from 2002. The banking sector is an artery for all transactions and some of this is facilitated by Sonali Bank Limited, a Bangladesh subsidiary of the same name **(Fig 2.11)**.

Figure 2.11 Profile of the Sonali (UK) Limited

The Sonali Bank (UK) Ltd was incorporated (2001) to provide excellent, faster and efficient services to members of the Bangladeshi community. It is regulated by the Financial Services Authority (FSA) with a total of 51% of the shares held by the Bangladesh Government and 49% by Sonali Bank Ltd, Bangladesh. The specific aims of this institution are:
(a) To help the UK Bangladesh community involved with the development of the Bangladesh economy through the remittance of foreign exchange and Trade finance;
(b) Provide niche banking service to the UK Bangladeshi community; and
(c) Provide access to the London financial market for the banking and corporate communities in Bangladesh.

Apart from banking services, Sonali has a remittance service for UK customers, along with a (similar remittance) telephone service for Bangladeshis in Europe. The institution has 6 UK offices and provides expatriate Bangladeshis with banking services and facilities, with offices in London, East of England, Midland Counties, Yorkshire and Humber and the North West respectively.

(Source: http://www.sonali-bank.com/index.php)

Legal Services

This segment of the PBS sector is also popular with British Bangladeshis with many young, highly qualified members of this community emerging as influential litigation specialists/advocates. A study of 152 British Bangladeshi students (**2011**) revealed that after medicine (49%) which was a popular choice, many students favoured law (9%), engineering (7%), teaching (7%) and accountancy (7%). When their interest in law was actually translated into Bar pupillage, Bangladeshis had less than 1%. This was further evidenced by the 129 minority ethnic individuals who succeeded in their legal studies during the periods; 2009/10 and 2010/11.

Figures during the same period for those 'self-employed' at the Bar by 'gender and ethnicity mix', also made interesting reading as **Table 2.5** illustrates. Overall, males fared better than females although they both excelled in their respective law degree courses.

Table 2.5 Sample of Self-employed barristers by gender and major ethnicity matrix
(Source: The General Council of the Bar of England and Wales, November 2012)

Ethnicity	Women	%	Men	%	Total	%
White (4 UK Regions)	2,970	74.87%	7,039	82.16	10,009	78.50%
Indian	120	2.92%	168	1.96%	288	2.27%
Pakistan	51	1.24%	107	1.25%	158	1.25%
Bangladeshi	**16**	**0.39%**	**32**	**0.37%**	**48**	**0.38%**
Chinese	23	0.56%	11	0.13%	34	0.27%
Other Asian	64	1.56%	91	1.06%	155	1.31%
African	68	1.66%	94	0.98%	180	1.32%
Caribbean	80	1.93%	70	0.81%	150	1.37%
Other ethnic group	16	1.18%	10	0.65%	26	0.89%
Total	**3,408**	**86.31%**	**7,622**	**89.37%**	**11,030**	**87.56%**

Fashion and Textiles

Increasing consumption patterns amongst minorities have propelled Bangladeshis to develop products and services to meet diverse customer demands. Entrepreneurs **Ruby Hammer, Parvez Ahmed**, **Ahfaz Miah**, and **Tommy Miah** trade in the personal care sector to complement existing businesses or develop niche market segments to boost revenue streams. They have extended their range of sectors - from clothing and textiles manufacturing to food among other trades (**Fig 2.12**).

The first ever *British Bangladeshi Fashion Week* (BBFW) held in late 2012, showcased versatile designers of Bangladeshi heritage – exhibiting traditional and modern 'garment/jewellery ensemble'.

Founder and Chair of the BBFW event, Fokrul Hoque, said:

"The very first British Bangladesh Fashion Week is a platform for aspiring and renowned British Bangladeshi fashion designers to bring their creations to the forefront of the International fashion calendar. Not only is this a great opportunity for designer-makers to showcase an array of ethnic fashion to the mainstream fashion industry, but it also provides vital networking amongst key figures within the creative sector as a whole" **(2012)**.

Figure 2.12 Leading icons in the British Bangladeshi fashion business

---

Ruby Hammer MBE is an internationally-acclaimed fashion and beauty make-up artist, columnist and co-founder of **Ruby & Mille (1998)**, and co-founder and director of **Scarlett & Crimson (2009)** cosmetics brand. Born of Bangladeshi parents in Nigeria, the economics graduate collaborated with Mille Kendall to create the cosmetics brand which is sold exclusively in Boots nationwide. Hammer has worked on photo shoots for fashion magazines - *Vogue, Elle, Red, Harpers and Queen, Bazaar and Marie Claire*. She has been invited to launch products and advise on new looks and train personnel for Estee Lauder, Clarins, Clinique, Aveda and Revlon. Apart from the teen cosmetics range, the versatile beautician launched the cosmetics beauty gifting range – **'Ruby Hammer Recommends' (2011)** exclusive to Debenhams. Organisers of the British Asian Fashion Awards presented Hammer the *'Outstanding Individual Award'* for her contribution to fashion industry.

Harun Pasha's **Pasha Razzo** is a modern British company that creates contemporary clothing, Ahfaz Miah who founded **The UKAY Group Limited** in 1978. As a certified mechanic, he used his technical skills to set up a clothing business to cater for the needs of 'Asian' communities. He has since set up the **UKAY International Saree Centre** and the first Bengali-owned 22 carat gold jewellery shop, **'UKAY International Jewellery'**, branding it as the first such company to trade in Britain, Europe and America.

(Source: Bangla Stories, 2012 & British Bangladeshis Who's Who 2012)

Transport and Logistics

Since the mid to late 20th century, minorities have founded companies in this sector. With their enterprise flair, Bangladeshis have a slender market share of roughly 3% and growing, in transport and logistics. Owners are keen to satisfy market demands especially for those travelling to and from South Asia as well as other popular destinations, globally.

Publishers, caterers and social activists are at the helm of travel agencies in the British Bangladeshi community. Through direct contacts, owners have influenced consumers/travellers to invest in ethnic travel agencies across Britain.

Their distinctive competence lies in affordable prices for cargo shipping, low cost airfares and convenient, multi-packaged tours for traveller-tourists en route to 'back home' destinations.

Sayed Chowdhury's **United Airways** firm has played a vital role in encouraging expatriate Bangladeshis to get involved in the airline trade. His company operates in the Middle East and North Africa, Nepal, India and all domestic Bangladeshi routes. Monir Ahmed's **JMG Air Cargo** has a higher traveller market share, with more than 60 UK agents. Its mission is *'making cargo services cheaper, but also quicker to consumers to achieve a major share in the market'* (**Monir Ahmed Interview, The Bangla Mirror Group 2012/2013**).

Information Technology

Bengalis particularly those of British (born) heritage, have entered into traditional fields once the preserve of mainstream. Both male and female are optimising the use of modern technology to access various commercial, industrial, professional, civic and social enterprise opportunities.

Business owners and professionals combined, are benefitting from highly successful careers and increased market share in their respective companies. The majority of firms are built on quality customer care, recruiting culturally sensitive staff and continuous improvement to a range of 'dedicated' services to meet changing market demands (**Fig 21.13**).

Figure 2.13 Mini-case of Zamir Telecom

Head of **Zamir Telecom**, M Naufal Zamir, established his London-based firm in 2004 and six years later, had a turnover of £11.2 million that was set to double a year later, according to the firm's estimates. As a professional lawyer, Zamir is determined to differentiate his company from others; *"the customer is king and my business is about bringing people closer"*. More than 50% of consumers are (personal) referrals.
The company has a strong diverse workforce, blending expertise with experience in the telecoms

field. This strategy has enabled Zamir Telecom to expand its UK market share whilst extending services to European, Middle Eastern, American and more recently African markets (notably Kenya and Sudan). Services such as SimpleCall have allowed the company to secure a substantial stake in the ethnic market, with the owner keen to offer services to a much wider consumer audiences.

(Source: Interview with M Naufal Zamir, The Bangla Mirror Group 2012/2013)

The Gender Equation

As part of the national discourse, minorities have been subjects of 'rehearsed' themes on *immigration, race, discrimination, prejudice, faith-based* issues among others. Whilst minorities recognise that discriminatory practices will remain challenges, they also feel that despite this age-old scourge, their contribution to British society should be acknowledged.

It is against such a compelling background that Bangladeshi women like both their South Asian 'cousins' and other minorities, are forging ahead with ground-breaking enterprise initiatives that still astound much of British society.

Several of these inspirational women have been profiled in various sections of this book, as a testament to their relentless pursuit of excellence whilst giving further credence to female [ethnic] entrepreneurship.

Hundreds of well-educated Bangladeshi women are successful in public and civic life. They maximise opportunities in sector areas as diverse as the creative industries, education-training, healthcare, fashion-textiles, business professional services and community affairs cum social enterprise.

In doing so, they have exemplified the achievement-factor of minority ethnic women despite personal, familial and/or traditional labour market barriers. They have also developed resilient strategies to realise competitive advantage in goods and services. **(Fig 2.14)**

Figure 2.14 Mini-cases of female leaders in the British Bangladeshi Community

Media- Lisa Aziz is a public broadcaster for over 25 years, mostly with the BBC. She writes for mainstream print media and heads the fundraising department of a global media charity.
Legal - Barrister Dilruba Qureshi is a specialist in Immigration, Employment and Family Law; she manages the international annex of **Temple Court Chambers**.
Politics - Rushanara Ali is a Bethnal Green Labour MP, elected in 2010. Prior to being elected, she was the Director of the Young Foundation and developed Language Line, a company to help people with language problems to have equal access to public services.
Arts - Shamin Azad and Shahin Badar are artists. Azad is a bilingual poet, storyteller/ writer whose work consists of Bangladeshi and European folklore. She published novels, short stories,

essays and poems in English and Bangla. Badar is an award-winning singer-songwriter featuring Arabic, Indian and Bengali musical genres.

Education – Shaida Hasant Husain is an academic, a teacher, an artist and social worker combined; had stints in Libya and Zambia.

Business and the Professions – Dr Nazia Khanum is founder of **Equality in Diversity**, an international management and research consultancy. She has served as an equalities specialist throughout England and is a fervent campaigner for the 'ideals of democracy and humanitarianism'.

(Source: Interview samples from the Bangla Mirror Group, 2010-2013)

Social Enterprise Sector

Over a third or 35% of British Bengalis are involved in some form of social enterprise activity. This is used to complement different commercial interests – whether in the provision of goods or services. The functions of ownership, management and direction of these social entities are important from the point view of the corporate social responsibility often associated with large mainstream companies rather than ethnic SMEs.

They tell stories of entrepreneurs who believe in industry, but with a social conscience founded on community activism. Importantly, business leaders and civic entrepreneurs profiled in this section are operating enterprises across the UK including London and the Home Counties. Not only are they serving ethnic communities but also sections of mainstream society. **(Fig 2.15)**

Many are either self-funded or receive grant aid or donor support from various public, trust and or private sector agencies and institutions. For the most part, Bangladeshi-owned social enterprises provide different types of services – some of which resemble those of mainstream. They include (among others):-

- Information, Advice and Guidance – 25%;
- Culture and Social Welfare – 15%;
- Women's Affairs – 5%;
- Social Housing – 5%;
- Education-Training – 3%;
- Professional Associations – 10%; and
- Enterprise Networks – 37%.

(Source: Analysis of British Bangladeshi social enterprises, England 2012/2013)

Figure 2.15 Mini-cases of British Bengali Social Entrepreneurs

Civic Affairs – Faruque Ahmed is founder of **Polash Sheba Trust**. A recipient of numerous awards; his contribution is acknowledged in books, magazines and newspapers in Britain and abroad.

Social Welfare – Apart from being an executive member of the Bangladesh Caterers Association in Britain, M. A. Munim served as acting Director of the **Consortium of the Bengali Association.**

Industrial Relations – Doros Ahmed is a founder member of the **Bengali Workers Association.**

Business Network – Mohammed Ali is a member of the **British Bangladesh Chamber of Commerce**. He is also President of the **Development Council for Bangladeshis in the UK.**

Legal – Muhammad Abdul Kalam (at the time of writing) was the General Secretary of the Society of Bangladeshi Solicitors (UK) and member of the Balagonj Samitte UK.

Migrant Representation – Nijam M Rahman is the founder of the Bangladesh Overseas Social Society (BOSS). He is also active in other civic organisations, locally and nationally.

Philanthropist – Dr Wali Tasar Uddin MBE is an award-winning restaurateur who was honoured with a Lloyds *Lifetime Achievement Award.*

He has raised over half a million pounds for Bangladesh and British charities and was awarded honorary degrees from Heriot-Watt, Queen Margaret and Napier Universities. He is a Director of the Council of Foreign Chambers of Commerce in the UK and a founder member and Director of Britain in Europe.

Business Location

'Location, location' is today's mantra for business success; it determines a firm's success or alternatively, under-performance because of poor quality premises and the area in which firms operate. From all indications, Bangladeshi business owners' overall success attributed to choice of location as evidenced by the geographic spread of firms across the UK Regions.

Principally, members of this ethnic group feature in largely 11 industry sectors in London, the Midland Counties, the North West, East of England, South West, Northern Island, Scotland and Wales respectively. By applying both business and market intelligence (formal and informal), owners can position or reposition their firms to suit customer needs.

This chapter highlighted glimpses of the movement from start-up and growth to the develop phase of commercial firms and social enterprises and the premium owners and their directors placed on location. Spatial distribution or geography is very important to the potential growth and development of any firm and this has been exemplified by both Bangladeshi men and women.

Table **2.6** below illustrates the major UK regions locations where business and social firms are operating from. It also points to the different industry segments operated by thousands of Bangladeshi owners and directors of firms across the country.

This table was formulated, using information and data contained in case studies, interviews, anecdotes and reviews of literature obtained from mainstream and private sources including minority ethnic communities' publications.

Similar to other chapters, it is hoped that this section of the book will enable readers to have a better understanding and appreciation of the importance and relevance of location, as an essential ingredient in the overall business development matrix.

Table 2.6 British Bangladeshi Business Ownership by Location

Major Location	Principal Industry Sector
London	Food, retail, IT, transport and logistics, creative industries, social enterprise, health and social care, manufacturing, engineering, construction, business and the professions services, media.
South East	Retail food, creative industries, social enterprise, social enterprise, business and the professions, and media.
East of England	Food, retail, education, social enterprise, business and the professions.
West Midlands	Education, retail, social enterprise, business and the professions.
East Midlands	Food and hospitality, transport and logistics, business and the professions, social enterprise, training, health and social care.
North West	Media, the creative industries, social enterprises, food and hospitality.
Scotland	Food and hospitality, social enterprises, business and the professions, education and training.
Wales	Food and hospitality, retail, transport and logistics, manufacturing, training and social care.
Northern Island	Healthcare, education and training, food retail.

Challenges and Opportunities

Throughout this chapter, the focus has been on the sector performance of British Bangladeshi business owners. Like other chapters that profiled five other South Asian business groups – Afghans, Indians, Nepalese, Pakistanis and Sri Lankans – this section summarises key challenges affecting British Bangladeshi-owned industries.

The idea is to analyse briefly some of the fundamental challenges affecting owners by business segment and industry representation. By examining these issues, readers will also be able to appreciate the real value-add minority firms bring to the British economy.

This approach is followed by attempts to put forward reasonable but workable solutions in the form of market opportunities according to the particular industry situation. Much of the information in this sub-section is also obtained from textual analysis in each industry sector and business segment of this chapter.

Irrespective of composition and size, every firm has its fair share of problems, limitations and drawbacks since that is the nature of business operations – be they commercial or social.

Apart from market forces, trends in the political climate, investment priorities and other statutory changes to the economy, can have a positive or negative impact on both emerging and existing firms in any economy.

The focus therefore of **Table 2.7** is to evaluate Bangladeshi firms' performance and to show how owners can maximise advantage in the UK domestic and overseas markets respectively.

Table 2.7: Challenges and Opportunities for British Bengali firms

Sector Challenges	Market Opportunities
Politics/Public Life: Bangladeshis make up one-sixth of the British population but only about 3% of members of the legislature (**Tables 2.8 and 2.9**).	They can maximise advantage of their current position in local government areas to build greater influence to widen participation in public life.
Education/Training: Only a third of young Bangladeshis have done well in college/university education.	More young people especially boys, could be helped via selective mentoring that focuses on key subjects matching abilities and talents of young learners.
Self-Employment Rates: These are still relatively low for Bangladeshis living in poorly resourced city areas.	Increased business owners' sponsorship of industry sector-based training to support the 75% of Bengalis who regard entrepreneurship as a 'good career choice'.
Creative Industries: Bangladeshis lifestyle is influenced by British traditions including creative influences.	Existing artists and cultural producers can use their unique influence to fuse Bengali culture with British creativity to offer innovative products and services.
Medicare Sciences: Practitioners represent less than 1% of all minority ethnic doctors on the national medical register.	Medical specialists can sponsor or organise mentoring programmes for the 40% of Bengalis favouring medicine as a career choice.
Social Care: Firms operating in this sector have a low market share compared to the domiciliary and respite care of ethnic communities.	Businesses can optimise care sector markets by researching further into learning, physical disabilities as well as service-users demanding 'assisted living' support provision.
Business Professional Services: About 1% of Bengalis are involved in the operation of law firms and related business professions.	Advocates can facilitate the expansion of community-based legal services to cater for the 9% of young 'hopefuls' who are keen on practising law, along with excluded groups who need such a service.
Transport and Logistics: Aside of Mela and traditional religious festivities, few firms are involved directly in the provision of tourism services.	Operators can explore the possibility of entering commercial markets for [allied] festival, cultural and adventure tourism to complement yearly Mela and other festivities.

Public Representation

Following the 2015 General Election, there are about 41 'non-white MPs' elected to the House of Commons, 6.3% of all 650 members of the legislature (**2016**). **Tables 2.8 and 2.9** highlight the number of MPs and Peers in the British Legislature.

Analysing minority ethnic representation in politics is problematic because ethnicity is both sensitive and difficult to define according to the House of Commons (**2012**). For the most part, Bangladeshis are represented at Local Government levels with scores of councillors in London, the Southeast and other UK regional constituencies. Yet in the national legislature, there numbers are less than 10%. Only 7% are MPs and 3% are Peers.

Table 2.8 A sample of Minority Ethnic MPs in the House of Commons
(Source: Minority Ethnic Members of Parliament, June 2015)

Ethnic Group	Male	Female	Total
African	7	1	8 (19%)
Bangladeshi	**1**	**2**	**3 (7%)**
Caribbean	2	2	4 (9%)
Chinese	1	-	1 (2%)
Indian *	4	3	7 (17%)
Pakistani	8	2	10 (24%)
Sri Lankan	1	-	1 (2%)

Notes: the % total has been calculated using the 41 ethnic MPs as a baseline figure.

Table 2.9 A selection of Minority Ethnic Peers, House of Lords
(Source: House of Commons Library Briefing Paper, 4 March 2016)

Ethnic Group	Male	Female	Total
African	3	1	4 (7%)
Bangladeshi	**1**	**1**	**2 (3%)**
Caribbean	3	2	5 (9%)
Chinese	-	1	1 (1%)
Indian *	16	4	20 (39%)
Pakistani	3	4	7 (13%)

Notes: the % total has been calculated using the 51 ethnic Peers as a baseline figure.

Conclusion

In this chapter, it emerged that despite perceived disadvantage of one sort or another, British Bangladeshis are excelling in business and the professions. Similar to other South Asians, Bengalis have applied cultural, faith and social traditions to establish successful firms in Britain. Through community activism, they have set codes of ethics or conduct to become the third leading ethnic business group nationally.

As part of the SME sector, owners operate within a legally defined environment with more than 80% of their companies formally registered with over 10% having sub-units or mini-branches of either in their locality or elsewhere. As is customary with ethnic firms, owners have direct contact with 'home countries' either through birth or heritage background. This allows them to trade in dual or multiple markets thereby spreading 'the risk' associated with having low-income markets.

A major focus in this chapter, were owners desire to create vertical and horizontal linkages via distribution and supply chains across ethnic/inter-ethnic as well as mainstream sources. These links helped firms to develop informal market intelligence systems which further informed and guided business decisions in terms of customer segmentation, type of produce, pricing strategy as well as supply volume.

Generally whilst Bangladeshis operate mostly within ethnic communities in London, judging by their consistent growth in the food, retail, business and professional services and other low entry barrier markets, there are indications that third generation entrepreneurs will favour expansion into co-ethnic as well as mainstream consumer markets. Not only will this bolster Bangladeshi businesses, but it will also help to redefine the notion of diversity within the broader minority entrepreneurial context. The next chapter will examine '**Global Trends in Indian Entrepreneurship**'.

Notes

Attainment Levels

Aside of social deprivation and economic exclusion indices, third generation Bengalis have increased education attainment levels from nearly 60% to nearly 80% for boys. For girls, the ratio is between 68% and 86% during the years 2008 and 2013.

During 2004-2013, there were significant improvements in 5 or more A*-C Grades for minorities including Indians, Bangladeshis and Pakistanis especially (DfE (2014). GCSE and *equivalent attainment by pupil characteristics in England 2012.2013 (SFR 05/2014).* Strand, Steve Professor: 'Ethnicity, deprivation and educational achievement at age 16 in England: trends over time', *Department for Education,* June 2015.

Self-employment

Greater support is needed for Bengali firms so that the enterprise formation rates of this community could be boosted beyond the 13% plus level (Institute of Economic Affairs, Britain 2011).

Restaurant Trade

Brick Lane was (and still is) described as London's '*Curry Capital*' (2004) because of the varied Bengali-owned food and hospitality firms. The notion of rebranding the area as '*Banglatown*' was explored by Tower Hamlets Council in 2005. This idea was first mooted by Abu Sahid in the 1980s – "Banglatown - What the People Think", *Asian Herald* (London), November 23-30, 1988, 6.

Feedback

Some writers and reviewers reckoned that 'customers found curry houses attractive because they were cheap, filling, informal and opened late – circumstances in which food quality often proved secondary" ("Shah Knows What's What," *Telegraph and Argus*, November 2, 1985.

Money Transfers

These represent a growing number of nationals contributing to vital inflows for their country. The scale of these was measured during 2000 and 2012 when between $US55.70 million and $US 987.46 million in remittances were received by Bangladesh.

Medicare

Qualified Bengalis make up less than 1% of the total number of doctors and other medicare specialists in the whole of the NHS. However, anecdotal evidence suggests that young professionals are involved in allied health and social care enterprises.

Business-Professions

Second and third generation Bangladeshis are bucking the trend by branching out into various 'mainstream' business professions. These include financial and legal services, market research, information technology, logistics, fashion and textiles as well as other growth industries.

Web Links

http://www.solidbangla.com/bangla%20newspapers%20in%20uk.html.

www.open.ac.uk/hsc/_assets/GeriatricMedicineFindings.pdf.

http://www.sonali-bank.com/index.php.

Selected References

The Emigrant Bangladeshis in the UK and USA, Ministry of Expatriates
Welfare and Overseas Employment, February 2004.
ONS Labour Market Survey 2011/2012.

DfE (2014). GCSE and *equivalent attainment by pupil characteristics in England
2012.2013 (SFR 05/2014).* Strand, Steve Professor: 'Ethnicity, deprivation and
educational achievement at age 16 in England: trends over time', *Department for
Education,* June 2015.

Farilie, Robert. Zissimopoulos, Julie and Krashinsky, Harry: The International
Asian Business Success Story? *University of Chicago May 2010.*

UCAS Ethnic Group 2007-2012.

Global Report, Global Entrepreneurship Monitor 2011.

Abu Sahid in the 1980s – "Banglatown - What the People Think", *Asian Herald*
(London), November 23-30, 1988, 6.

"Shah Knows What's What," *Telegraph and Argus*, November 2, 1985.

Urwin, Peter: Self-employment, Small Firms and Enterprise,
The Institute of Economic Affairs, Britain 2011.

'Export Potential for Bangladeshi Products to British Curry Industry', *BCA* 2012.

Bangladesh High Commission, London 2012.

Shams Bin Quader, Impact of the British Bangladeshi Musicians of London 2007.

'British Bangladeshi Power 100', *The Bangladesh Chronicle* 2011/2012.
British *Bangladeshi Who's Who* 'Bangla Mirror Group 2008-2012.
General Medical Council July 2015, England.

Advances in Medical Education and Practice 2011/12, University of Bradford, UK.

Dignity and respect in residential care: issues for minority ethnic groups, *Report to Department of Health* July 2011, University of Stirling.

Government Equalities Office Factsheet, 2010.

Proulx, Kerrie: *Fighting the odds, Runnymede Bulletin, Issue 365, Spring 2011.*

The General Council of the Bar of England and Wales, November 2012.

Ethnic Minorities in Politics and Public Life, *House of Commons*, March 2016.

Ibid, January 2012.

Minority Ethnic Members of Parliament, House of Commons, June 2015.

House of Commons Library Briefing Paper, 4 March 2016.

Chapter 3 Global Trends in Indian Entrepreneurship

"We have grown in stages, as we try to have zero wastage of money and where everything runs very smoothly" – **Southall Travel.**

Introduction

This chapter explores the strategies British Indian business leaders from different backgrounds are using to globalise their firms to compete in the marketplace of ideas, goods and services. Indians are among leading British ethnic and mainstream industrialists and social entrepreneurs. The fact that India is considered the largest democracy, lends itself to become the second largest global economic powerhouse after China. On completion of this chapter readers should be able to:

- Understand the migration journey of Indians to Britain;
- Learn about the problems they face in business and the professions;
- Understand their cultural and social values systems;
- Recognise the sector contribution of British Indians to the UK in general; and
- Be familiar with the challenges and prospects of this group in the 21st century.

Origins

During the 19th century, the East India Company brought thousands of Indian *lascars* or cooks, scholars and workers to Britain, most of whom settled down and married British spouses due to a lack of Indian women and partners [in Britain at the time]. The earlier Indians were mostly Guajarati and Bengali lawyers, doctors and other professionals. By the mid-19th century, over 40,000 Indians consisting of seamen, diplomats, scholars, soldiers, businessmen and students were resident in Britain.

Following the 20th century conflicts, workers mainly from the Punjab region arrived in the 1950s and 1960s. Hundreds of women found work in the foundries of the (English) Midlands and a large number of Indian Sikhs were employed at Heathrow Airport.

By the 1970s, a new wave of Indian migration followed; East African Indians with British passports entered the UK after their expulsion from Kenya, Uganda and Zanzibar. Many were already shopkeepers and upon arrival, they opened shops and other retail outlets in the UK.

Indians consist of 2.6% of the total population (**Source: ONS 2011**), with numbers increasing since the 1960s (**Table 3.1**). They make up one quarter of the total minority ethnic population with London having the largest concentration (542,857), followed by West Midlands (199,300), East Midlands (143,200), the South-East (178,900), North-West (109,700) and Yorkshire/the Humber (96,900).

In addition, the North-East (26,700) and the South-West (63,700) have lower numbers and fewer than 2% of Indians reside in Scotland, Wales and Northern Ireland combined. (**Fig 3.1**)

Table 3.1 Growth in the number of Indians in the UK
(Source: ONS England 2011)

Year	Population	+% (average)
1961	81,000	-
1971	275,000	+29%
1981	676,000	+40%
1991	840,000	+80%
2001	1,053,411	+79%
2011	1,400,000	+75%

Note: the percentages have been rounded for uniformity

Figure 3.1 The geographic spread of Indians in the UK

Major Regions	Numbers
London	542,857
West Midlands	199,300
East Midlands	143,200
Southeast	178,900
Yorkshire & Humber	96,900
South West	63,700
North East	26,700

(Source: Office for National Statistics April 2001 Census)

Socio-economic indicators

Educationally, Indian pupils have the highest attainment level compared to other UK learners, with girls having a GCSE pass rate at over 80% compared to boys 70% average according to the data of 2008-2013 (**Table 3.2**). Rates for unemployment or worklessness vary around 9% for matured and young British Indians –with a deprivation ranking of 13% for this ethnic group.

English housing statistics show that 25% of all minority households live in private rented accommodation; Indian families represent 8% of all 'social renters' compared to Caribbeans (45%), Africans (47%) and white households (14%) respectively (**2013**).

British Indians are among the most affluent in the country and with a high level of property ownership or material assets, they stand a better chance to invest in commercial, industrial and or even social enterprise ventures (**2007**).

Table 3.2: Attainment of 5 or more A*-C GCSE Grades by key minorities
(Source: Department for Education, June 2015)

Pupils by ethnicity (Boys)	2008	2009	2010	2011	2012	2013
White (including British)	58.5%	64.7%	71.2%	76.85%	78.25%	78.55%
Indian	**74.3%**	**78.8%**	**85.0%**	**87.6%**	**89.3%**	**88.6%**
Pakistani	52.7%	61.2%	69.8%	77.4%	79.9%	81.0%
Bangladeshi	56.0%	65.5%	72.0%	79.4%	82.9%	81.5%
African	53.5%	65.7%	71.6%	79.1%	80.5%	81.3%
Caribbean	46.9%	56.4%	64.2%	72.2%	75.3%	76.3%
Chinese	80.9%	84.1%	87.6%	90.6%	91.9%	90.9%
Other Ethnic Groups	49.8%	60.%	65.9%	73.9%	76.6%	79.3%
ALL BOYS	59.1%	65.8%	71.9%	77.0%	79.8%	79.6%

Pupils by ethnicity (Girls)	2008	2009	2010	2011	2012	2013
White (including British)	66.65%	72.1%	78.2%	82.55%	85.05%	84.85%
Indian	**82.7%**	**85.8%**	**89.7%**	**92.8%**	**93.1%**	**93.6%**
Pakistani	64.0%	72.0%	78.4%	84.1%	85.6%	86.4%
Bangladeshi	68.9%	73.8%	79.9%	86.2%	87.6%	88.4%
African	87.6%	91.2%	92.3%	95.0%	94.2%	95.2%
Caribbean	60.8%	69.9%	76.2%	82.6%	83.9%	84.5%
Chinese	87.6%	91.2%	92.3%	95.0%	94.2%	95.2%
Other Ethnic Groups	62.5%	68.4%	77.3%	84.1%	82.8%	85.6%
ALL GIRLS	68.2%	73.9%	79.5%	84.0%	86.3%	865%

(Notes: The above figures show the steady progress of young Indians over the past five years. Despite multiple advantage, female Indian learners are competing favourably in the education attainment rankings when compared to both English and other minority ethnic learners).

Enterprising British Indians

British Indians operate businesses in food and hospitality, creative industries, healthcare, business and professional services, manufacturing (especially fashion textiles), technology futures, travel and logistics sectors, as well as social enterprise. Their participation in public service 'enterprise including gender equality concerns, also signifies how far this group has developed since their settlement in Britain.

The Anatomy of British South Asian Enterprise

An early 21st century report stated that *"Indian companies have invested over £250 million in the UK and have created several hundreds of jobs. Almost all of the 50 Chambers of Commerce and Industry in the UK incorporate 'South Asian' units within their chapters"* (**2004**).

The first generation of Indian migrants were described as 'shop-keepers' because they owned 'corner shops' or retail units; some fully owned, franchising operations/and or family firms. Shahid Rasool (**2012**) explained that *"Asian business draws upon the family to help sometimes with reduced or no pay because they know it will benefit the whole family"*. **Madan Showan** who ran a successful electrical retail business (£160 million turnover), was forced into administration because of the recession. After his sons suggested a 'winning formula', Showan went behind the scenes and helped his children with their new venture (**2012**).

Having learnt from the experiences of elders, second and third generation British-Indians focused more on academic and professional development to improve performance in business and industry as well as the professions. (**Fig 3.2**)

Figure 3.2 British Indian applicants, 2007-2015

Year	Number	(%)
• 2008	14,256	(3.4)
• 2009	14,723	(3.3%)
• 2010	14,388	(3.2%)
• 2011	14,906	(3.3%)
• 2012	14,070	(3.5%)
• 2015	26,024	(4.9%)

(*Source: UCAS Ethnic Group 2007-2012 & The Higher Education Academy, 2015*)

The above chart illustrates the value British Indians attach to education and training, and though they're disproportionately represented in the overall student population, they have 'the highest proportion' in attendance for minority learners in further education.

Nevertheless while higher education remains a focal point, the following areas illustrate that different 'push' and 'pull' factors impacting on the Indian performance in the labour market (self-employment inclusive):-

- Perceived Opportunities (39%);
- Knowledge or skills for start-up (42%);
- Fear of Failure or risk taking (38%);
- Personality Traits for business success (60% plus);

- Business Optimism (66%); and
- Persistence (65%).

(Source: Global Entrepreneurship Monitor 2011 & Gallup Business Journal, 2013/2014)

Self-employment

Much research has been undertaken to ascertain self-employment rates by ethnicity amongst UK residents. Evidence in 2011 suggested that over two million ethnic individuals represented categories of 'employees' and 'self-employment' segments combined.

These rates also showed the comparison between 'disadvantaged' groups versus mainstream. Yet from an ethnic standpoint, approximately 310,034 business owners were listed in the 'self-employed' category; that is, 6.4% of all entrepreneurial activities and/or 13.9% of overall self –employment by ethnicity. (**Table 3.3**)

Table 3.3 Employees/Self-employment by key UK Ethnic Minorities
(Source: Urwin, Peter: Self-employment, Small Firms and Enterprise, The Institute of Economic Affairs, Britain 2011).

Ethnicity	Employee	Self employed	% Self employed
African	285,654	18,416	9.6%
Bangladeshi	107,264	17,205	13.8%
Caribbean	232,271	18,416	7.4%
Chinese	98,964	22,448	18.5%
Indian	**569,363**	**76,980**	**11.9%**
Pakistan	211,553	79,214	27.2%
Nepali	50,000	271	2.6%
Other Asian *	220,356	26,523	10.7%
Other	362,109	50,832	12.3%
Grand Total	**2,087,534**	**310,034**	**6.4%**

*Notes: In this instance * 'Other Asian' refers to Afghans and Sri Lankans especially.*

Statistics for the Indian group illustrate that despite restrictive practices, owners are still able to compete in niche markets they're familiar with and in the process, achieve commercial success. Effectively, **Table 3.3** identifies this ethnic group's fourth highest business ownership amongst all South Asians and other ethnic groups combined.

Moreover, the above indices reflect this ethnic group's tenacity to compete in niche markets. For instance, Indians have an estimated 5,476 restaurants - 'curries' being the most popular and chicken tikka masala perceived as a major British (national) dish (**Fig 3.3**).

The geographical spread of Indian-owned restaurants and takeaways represents too, a diversification strategy based on expansion into ethnic and non-ethnic markets plus the determination to main high quality cuisine in expanding the UK food and hospital sector.

In exerting their numerical strength, applying risk-taking strategies and developing ideas around niche markets, Indian entrepreneurs are competing in sectors that were once the preserve of mainstream companies. Even though the food and hospitality sector dominates much of enterprise activities, they have also maximised this industry to move into other business segments that have either less or easier barriers to entry. They include the creative industries, fashion and textiles, retailing and the professions.

Figure 3.3 Profile of the British Indian Curry Industry

The centuries-old Indian food tradition, transformed the ethnic cuisine including eating habits of diners within the indigenous population, many of whom have grown accustomed to different types of ethnic food. However, it was **Sake Dean Mahomed (aka Mahomet)**, a Bengali-Indian traveller who established the first curry house – the **Hindostanee Coffee House** in London (1809). He produced Indian dishes and provided entertainment goods and services for the 'nobility and gentry'. Mahomet filed for bankruptcy in 1812 although the restaurant carried on without him in some form until 1833.

Other eating houses that emerged in the 19th century included **The Shafi** (1911) owned by Mohammed Wayseem and Mohammed Rahim. Later, it was taken over by Dharam Lal Bodua and run by an English manager with employees such as Israil Miah and Gofur Miah who later operated their own establishments.

Subsequently, restaurants were opened in different parts of Britain: Abdul Aziz opened a café shop selling curry and rice in Birmingham 1945, with the **Darjeeling** being the first Indian restaurant in Birmingham. Rashid Ali moved from a café shop in London to Cardiff to open his own eating house. The first restaurant to open up north was **The Anglo Asian Ocean Road** run by Syed Lukman Ali.

The 1946-founded **Punjab** is the oldest UK-based North Indian Restaurant offering a distinctive Punjabi cuisine to diners. As a boy, Sital Maan earned pocket money working at the Punjab. By 1971, he bought the business from his grandfather. Customers from all over the world including famous actors - Martin Short and Raj Kapoor - dined consistently at the Punjab (*Source: http://blog.punjab.co.uk/uk%E2%80%99s-oldest-punjabi-restaurant/*).

As of 2012, British Indians owned over 5,000 restaurants and takeaways in the UK and although figures for the sector were estimated at £3.6 billion, Horizon Foods put it at £777 million. In 2002, Indian food in supermarkets alone was worth £600 million – 80% of which was ready-meal curries (**2012**). *Spice Business* (**Ibid**) reported that 2.5 million customers eat in roughly 10,000 restaurants employing 80,000 staff weekly. Indian food houses can be found in the following UK locations:

- London – 1250 (City of Westminster 132);
- South East – 1246 (Essex 179);
- The Midlands – 1090 (West Midlands 291);
- Northern England – 933 (West Yorkshire 156);
- South West – 407 (Avon 90);
- Scotland – 327 (Strathclyde 149);
- Wales -182 (South Glamorgan 35);
- Northern Island – 41 (County Antrim 21).

(Source: http://www.ukindianrestaurants.co.uk/browse_categories.php?id=5124

Remittances

The UK is a major sender of remittances which have various benefits for India. Money transfers help maintain healthy but vital foreign reserves, as stated in a 2012 World Bank report. The document revealed that India received $69 billion (£45bn, €53bn) in 2012 in remittances. The South Asian country benefited from unskilled migrants working in the oil-rich Gulf Cooperation Council (GCC) countries as well as skilled Indian nationals in the US and other high-income countries.

The declining value of the Indian Rupee and high interest rates on external deposits also helped increase the final figure. Remittances from Britain and Europe are particularly important because they average 19% of money transfers to India by overseas nationals. Generally, remittances contribute to just over 3% of the total Gross Domestic Product (GDP) of India's economy (**Table 3.4**).

Table 3.4 Remittances inflows to India

Year	Remittances (US$ billion)	Percent GDP
2000-2001	12.85	2.84
2001-2002	15.4	3.29
2002-2003	16.39	3.39
2003-2004	21.61	3.69
2005-2006	24.55	3.08
2006-2007	29.10	2.78
2007-2008	37.2	3.29
2008-2009	51.6	4.1
2009-2010	55.06	3.6
2011	63.8	3.4
2012	69.79	3.9

The Anatomy of British South Asian Enterprise

(Source: The World Bank and Migration Policy Institute, 2000-2012).

As subsequent chapters will show, other South Asians contribute to the money transfer trade even at the height of recessionary trends. Indians also use cultural and faith traditions to secure market advantage as input into segments of the creative industries illustrates.

Creative Industries

Similar to other South Asian/ethnic communities, British Indians are contributing to this sector via achievements in segments such as **media, music, film, publishing and allied literature.** Indians own 17 television channels (satellite and cable) -**2011 estimates**, with 5 others jointly-owned and MATV, British owned.

The most notable TV shows were *Goodness Gracious Me* and *The Kumars at No 42*, a talk show that featured actors Sanjeev Bhaskar, Meera Syal, Indira Joshi and Vincent Ebrahim.

Though the market share for Indian films is under 2%; it fluctuated between 2003 and 2010 (**Fig 3.4**). Thus the UK market share of Indian films by year and percentage is as follows: 2003 (1%), 2004 (1.1%), 2005 (1.5%), 2006 (1.8%), 2007 (1.6), 2008 (1.4%), 2009 (1.0%), 2010 (1.3%) and 2011 (1.0%).

A total of 63 films from India were released in the UK, compared to 107 films in 2006. The UK is the largest market for Hindi films with 52 including *Om Shanti Om* and *Namastey London* released in 2007. Box office figures showed that Indian films grossed £14.6 million, a reduction from £15.6 million (2006-07).

They are still popular with Indian and South Asian fans altogether. Still, although the market share for Indian films have experienced peaks and troughs, a total of 72 Indian films were released grossing £11.1 million (**2011**).

Figure 3. 4 A Snapshot of British Indian Film and Radio/TV Segments

Film companies such as **Eros International, Yash Raj Films, ADLABS Films and Artificial Eye**, are segments of the creative industries. In 2007 the amount of city-based screening of films was 80%, an increase of 44% from 2006 due to the growing number of multiplex cinemas dedicated to showing South Asia films. Roughly 80% of films were shown in London plus 20% in the East Midlands. By 2011, 30 films were released in Hindi, Punjabi, Urdu and other South Asian languages, grossing £13 million (**2007: 2012**).
Both Indian and UK governments signed an agreement in December 2005 to collaborate on 'creative, artistic, technical, financial and marketing resources' for future film and television productions. The agreement facilitates tax breaks offered by the UK government, provided that co-production meets the criteria of films qualifying as British.

Audio media is another communications segment including **Sunrise Radio, Sunrise Radio Yorkshire, Punjab Radio, Sabras Radio, Radio XL, SUPA AM, Raj Radio** and **Ambur Radio**. These media help the India diaspora to remain connected with their ancestral homeland. The most popular television channels are **Asia 1 TV, Sony TV, APNA TV** and **Namaste TV**. These focus on news events related to the diaspora and developments in India and South Asia overall.

Official TV programming for South Asians started in the 1950s with the Asia Club (**BBCTV, 1953-61**). Further diversity campaigns resulted in *Apna Hi Ghar Smahiye*/Make Yourself at Home (BBC1) and *Nai Zindagi, Naya Jeevan*/New Life (BBC 1968-1982).

Other programmes - *Look, Listen and Speak* (**BBC, 1977**) and *Parosi* (**BBC, 1978**) - were aimed at providing information on integration especially on food and dress (**Malik, 2002**).

In 1977 Gharbar/Household (**BBC, 1997-1987**) was launched to engage predominately 'Asians', to discuss health, marriage, housekeeping, hygiene and career advice issues. Nai Zindagi was relaunched as the '*Asian Magazine*' (BBC 1982-1987). Today South Asians including British Indians, also feature in popular sitcoms - *Eastenders, Coronation* Street and *Emmerdale* among others.

Music

In the past decade or so, *Bhangra* artists have cemented the UK as an international stronghold for traditional Indian music overseas. As an integral part of Punjabi music, Bhangra is popular with the more than 600,000 strong British Sikhs as well as other ethnic sections of musical Britain. Notable performances include **Panjabi MC, Rishi Rich, Juggy D, Jay Sean, DCS** and **Sukshinder Shinda**. The late award winning singer-songwriter, **Freddie Mercury** (born Farrokh Bulsara), remains a foremost figure in the British Indian music scene.

Other famous artistes include **Biddu**, producer of the disco hit, '*Kung Fu Fighting*' that sold 11 million records worldwide and **Apace Indian** (DJ Steven Kapur) whose pulsating '*Boom Shack-A-Lak*' featured prominently in the music charts in the early 1990's. **Jay Sean** whose parents settled in the UK from the Punjab region, is the first British South Asian solo artist to reach number one on the Billboard Hot 100 with his single, '*Down*', that sold over 4 million US copies, making "*him the most successful male UK urban artist in US chart history*" (**2009: 2011**). Other performers are **S-Endz** (Turi and Casey Rain) and BRIT Award-nominated Nerina Pallot. Rain is a member of the acclaimed UK rap alternative bhangra band, **Swami**. Artists utilise 'dedicated' websites and allied multimedia to showcase their works to sectional audiences (**Fig 3.5**). In recounting his US (artistic and cultural) experience, British Indian global superstar, Sean, said:

"It's just different for them (the Americans). I talk funny. They say, dude, we wouldn't expect you, a little Brit, to be signed to Cash Money. They love the fact that we're from two different worlds, and I love that as well." "I want to do my best to represent the UK in America and let people really understand that it doesn't matter if we're from a little

place. As long as you work hard and strive to do your best and make good music, and of course with a bit of luck, it is possible" **(BBC, 2009)**.

Figure 3.5 Major British Indian music websites

British Indian websites and related web links are dedicated to the promotion of Indian music to global audiences. Below are some of these resourceful links:-

- Milapfest;
- Asian Music Circuit / Museum of Asian Music;
- UK Top Hits - Bollywood Hindi Tamil Telugu Indian Music;
- British India Official Facebook;
- Bharatiya Vidya Bhavan UK Centre;
- The Darbar Indian Classical Music Festival;
- British Indian Music Discography; and
- British India.

(Source: Independent analysis of British Indian music web links, May 2013)

In terms of technology literacy, British Indians are engaged in almost every multi-media spectrum; namely the ownership of digital, telecasting, internet access and personal/mobile phones. The following indices show the effect they have on the British media technology sector:

- Highest take up of broadband -82%;
- Watching recorded TV and TV on demand (combined) – 71%;
- Spending more on 'mobile devices ' – 54%; and
- 'Refer to the Internet before making a purchase' -51%:

(Source: Communications Market Report, Ofcom & Mobile Magazine, August 2013).

Theatre

Over the last 30 years, British South Asians have developed a vibrant theatre as part of their contribution to the creative industries. Blending tradition with modern, they have developed uniqueness within the performing arts.

Officially **(2012 estimates)**, there were 12 theatre companies and one major arts organisation including **Tara Arts,** operating across England promoting South Asian art forms. These companies are managed by artists, cultural producers and assisted by creative-type volunteers. Funding is directed via grant-aid support, private donations, 'gift aid' or through a number of self-funding activities involving South Asian and other communities **(Table 3.5)**.

Table 3.5 Sample of major South Asian theatre arts companies

Name of Company	Year	Activities
Tara was set up by Jatinder Verma.	1975	Arts training, new writing and intracultural practice. Successes include *East is East, Strictly Dandia* and the *Trouble with Asian Men.*
Tamasha was founded by director Kristine Landon-Smith and actor/playwright, Sudha Bhuchar.	1989	Britain's foremost touring theatre company focusing on emerging and established artists from culturally diverse backgrounds.
Kali and Moti Roti were established by Landon-Smith and Bhuchar.	1990	Theatrical performances depicting traditional and modern genres, whilst allowing the flowering of talent across all generations, gender and cultural traditions of the 'Asian' diaspora.
Kali Theatre founded by Rita Wolf and Rukhsana	1991	Championing South Asian women writers. Over 75% of new plays by British South Asian female playwrights were presented by Kali.
Rifco Arts Watford Palace Theatre (formerly The Reduced Indian Film Company) founded by Pravesh Kumar who is Artistic Director.	2001	Develops, creates vibrant, accessible and high quality theatre that reflects and celebrates the modern British 'Asian 'experience.
Man Mela Theatre Company (taken from the Hindustani phrase 'entertainment of the mind') founded by writer-director Dominic Rai	1993	Young people and community audiences, especially those disengaged from the arts. A strategy to develop major themes on British South Asian experiences.

(Source: Graham, Ley and Dadswell, Sarah (2012): British South Asian Theatres, University of Exeter Press, England)

Young artists and cultural producers are very keen to express their talent using a range of media channels – either through theatre, music, poetry, dance and or other art forms. The level of fusion or 'cross-cover cultures that exist, impact tremendously on South Asian culture and traditions overall. Much of this can be observed from the different perceptions and lifestyles of the four generations of South Asian and other ethnic communities in Britain today.

The diversity of generational cultures and their appeal to the oft-repeated 'East meets West' culture clash, is indeed worthy of further exploration. For instance, emerging musical genres are responding to a new generation of 'beats, tempos or rhythms'. Thanks to technology innovations, young people have almost unfettered access to various art forms –in oral, written and dramatic formats. These tend to influence much of their lives as they try recreating new identities whilst tussling to maintain the traditions of their forebears. It is here that Indian and South Asian professionals are making a difference – to ensure that the essentials of their [respective] cultures remain intact (**Fig 3.6**).

Figure 3.6 Case Study of Sampad - South Asian Arts Development

Sampad or South Asian Arts Development was founded in January 2001 in Birmingham, West Midlands. It aims to promote the appreciation and practice of diverse art forms of **Indians**, Pakistanis, Bangladeshis and Sri Lankans, although not exclusively. Activities include exhibitions such as *Dancing about Sculpture,* professional development based on leadership and artist workshops, international partnerships and the celebration of the 150th anniversary of Rabindranath Tagore as well as a digital map of cultural activity produced by 123 volunteers. The arts agency has partnerships with artists, youth and community, coupled with education agencies.

As a highly creative modern entity with a turnover in excess of £600,000 (**2012 estimates**), Sampad has experienced directors and committed staff. It has numerous private and public institutional funders, supporters and partners. According to director Paili Ray OBE, 2012 was a momentous period for the arts organisation. *"During the Cultural Olympiad and London 2012 Festival, we championed the use of digital technology through the provision of practice-based training and participatory arts experiences, and continue to develop Sampad as an exemplar organisation for South Asian arts"* (**Sampad 2012**).

The organisation contributes to cultural regeneration and social cohesion by integrating children (aged 7-12 during school holidays), women and diverse communities into its overall creative development programme.

Publishing

From early Sanskrit texts through to contemporary English literature, Indian writers have produced materials across different literary genres. India is ranked third after the US and the UK in English language publishing, and it continues pushing boundaries with an increasingly young talented generation (**2011).**

Tishani Doshi is dedicated to writing (poetry (poetry/fiction), **Kiran Desai** (fiction), **Amit Chaudhuri** (short stories, poetry, non-fiction and fiction), **Sujata Bhatt** (young adult poetry) and **Amtiav Ghosh** (non-fiction and fiction). They take part in programmes that offer opportunities for cultural exchange in the UK.

The British Council sampled Indian writers in areas such as fiction, poetry, short stories, non-fiction and plays. The writers were aged 40 to 65 (born during the 1950s-1980s). In celebrating 75 years of cultural relations, the Council collaborated with the London Book Fair, to host '*a celebration* of *Indian writing'* (**2009**). About 50 publications were on show, depicting these themes:-

- *Definitive Classics* – ancient Sanskrit, metaphysics, poetry and Hindu philosophy.
- *Modern Masters* – writings on culture, history, travelogue and reflections.
- *Literary Champions* – fictional works on cultural language, political and philosophical issues affecting urban and rural India.
- *Here and Now-* narratives on faith, truth, love, romance, identity, alienation and family in the 21st century Indian metropolis.
- *A Woman's Voice* - linguistics, patriarchy, partition and the violence suffered by women, India's most influential women, class, colonisation and mythology.

Each theme was interspersed with these 'quotable quotes' from selected publications:

- "When words die out on the tongue, new melodies break forth the heart; and where the old tracks are lost, a new country is revealed with its wonders" – *Gitanjali* (1910).
- "Sometimes legends make reality, and become more useful than the facts" – *Midnight's Children* (1981).
- "It is an ancient and venerated custom to people in my country to start a story by praying to a Higher Power" –*The White Tiger* (2008).
- "She stared at the letter, then handed it back to me carefully, gripping with her fingers as if it were a plate heaped with food" – *Interpreter of Maladies* (1999).
- "So, how are the resources doing?' Bakshi said, swivelling on his chair. He never referred to us as people; we were all resources" – *One Night at the Call Center*. (2005).

British Indians also publish weekly newspapers, journals and bulletins to plug gaps in the South Asian and international markets. The aim of these publications, is also to satisfy the demands of various readership audiences across Britain **(Fig 3.7)**. Advertising revenue from mainstream corporations and ethnic firms help to underwrite the printing costs of these publications.

Figure 3.7 Mini-cases of Indian Newspapers in Britain

- ***Des Pardes*** (1965) is the most popular, widely circulated Indian Punjabi weekly newspaper in Britain and Europe; it was established by the late Tarsem Singh Purewal. It has a circulation figure of 150,000 copies.
- ***Asian Times*** (1983) first published by Hansib Publishing Limited, aimed at providing a platform for Asians to access news, features and other information on issues affecting their communities in Britain and home countries. The Ethnic Media Group now publishes this paper with a circulation of 7,000 copies.
- ***Eastern Eye*** (1989) first published by *The Guardian* and changed hands several times until January 2009 when the Trinity Mirror Group took it over, before a management buyout that resulted in the creation of the Ethnic Media Group (EMG). Eastern Eye is regarded as the authentic voice of British South Asians in the UK, with a circulation of

> 25,000 (**www.magazinesabout.co.uk/Eastern+Eye**).
> - *Asian Lite* (2007) founded by Anasudhin Azeez and dedicated to 'bringing back the missionary values of journalism'. It has a circulation of 35,000 copies (**www.ethnicnow.com**).
> - *Asian Trader* (1985) established as a bi-weekly, covering news, features and other information for convenience stores, newsagents, retailers and off-licenses. With a circulation of 48,800 copies, this publication is produced in Urdu & Gujarati, two South Asian languages not found in other such magazines. **http://www.amg.biz/index.php?page=Publications&id=4**
>
> British Indians produce other periodicals – in 'hard copy format' and online 'streaming'. Midlands-based Karam Singh is editor of *Manjit Weekly*, a newspaper that caters for Punjabi speakers in the UK and abroad. In keeping with technology trends, most South Asian media publications are on line, serving growing web audiences. (*Publisher's Note*: the above circulation figures represent 2013 estimates and therefore should not be construed as actuals).

British Indian Sikhs

Other literature depict Indian businesses and organisations from a faith-based perspective. The most recent, is the *Sikh Directory* (2011) aiming to make visible, the contribution of Indian Sikhs. According to the publishers,

"This is the very first directory of Sikh businesses and organisations in the UK in which we will have true visibility of one another, creating unlimited trading and networking possibilities. It is also a tribute to the skills, achievements and successes of the Sikh community in the UK and it also teaches people about the Sikh Dharam".
(**http://www.thesikhdirectory.co.uk/**)

The authors of another publication, '*The British Sikh Report*' (**2013**), said that;

"The BSR is a strategic document for the benefit of the British Sikh community, for use both within and the community and with Central and Local Government. The results from the BSR will have an impact upon funding decisions made in the future. It is also expected that the report will be used by corporations and Third Sector organisations when looking at issues concerning the British Sikh community" (**Ibid**).

The report also highlighted the migration of the first Indian Sikh –Maharaja Duleep Singh – who settled in Britain in 1854. It also touched on subjects namely lifestyle, gender, politics, religion, identity, health, family, equality, politics and labour relations. The data on employment demonstrated key indicators among Sikhs: a total of 375 job titles were associated with them, with 4.5% classified as 'unemployed/working', 58.2% in employment, 2.3% retired, 14.9% self-employed and 20.1% students. (**Fig 3.8**)

Figure 3.8 Employment Status of British Sikhs
(Source: Office for National Statistics 2012: The British Sikh Report 2013)

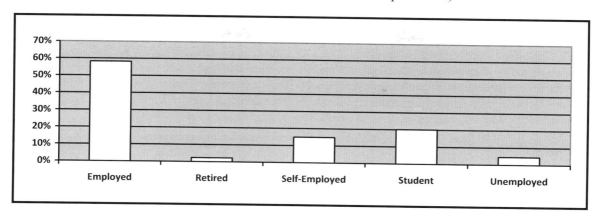

Note: If the figure of 14.9% for Sikhs' self-employment is anything to go by, then they would have an estimated 74.12% market share for British Indian enterprises overall. Most businesses can be found in food and drink, travel, business and the professions, the creative industries, health and social care, as well as the social enterprise sector respectively.

Overall attitudes

The focus on cultural diversity in the arts often escapes the attention of public institutions as it relates to minority ethnic groups' attendance, participation and attitudes. Yet minorities' general engagement in the arts should be acknowledged since this can help foster greater diversity of British Indians in the creative industries.

Over the past 10 years, the Arts Council of England has been analysing English audiences 'attendance at specific artistic and cultural events. Indians had the highest access rates for audio-visual media (84%) which included TV, video and DVD. Members of this community also showed a greater propensity for film (74%) as earlier evidence showed. Low attendance at crafts (13%), visual arts (14%) and theatre (19%) reflected their artistic and cultural interest. For instance, members of this ethnic group had the fourth highest rating (29%) for 'South Asian classical music' altogether (**Fig 3.9**).

Figure 3.9 Percentage of Indians attending artistic and cultural events
(Source: Focus on cultural diversity: Arts Council of England, December 2003)

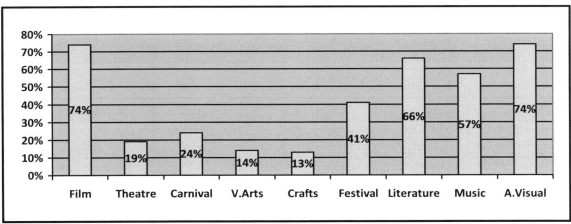

Note: The Arts Council of England survey showed an average of 42.4% Indians active in arts and culture. The London 2012 Olympics Festival was unable to evidence ethnic groups including South Asians 'participation in festivities. Although 11% of minorities were widely quoted, there was no definitive analysis on the actual participation of individual ethnic groups to this event.

Health and Social Care
Medicare Sciences

The state of medical education and practice in the UK is at an interesting phase. For the first time, the state analysed in depth, the diversification and changes resulting from the composition of medicare and health practitioners. The latest figures **(2014)** showed that Indian GPs represented 11.8% of all UK registered doctors. Members of this group make up 13% of all ethnic medical professionals. There were 31,617 Indian doctors in on the UK medical register (2005-2014). **(Fig 3.10)**

Indian GPs have worked with the NHS over 60 years, with Britain benefitting from the skills of migrant-settlers from ex-colonies. However, their career tenure was limited by hierarchies, as one consultant duly recalled: *"……my consultant, who was exactly like me, was a trained cardiologist and then when there were openings in geriatrics, he quickly moved into that area and said, 'Look if you want to go through the fast track up then this is a less crowded road. You could do geriatrics and you could do cardiology; it would be a good way rather than waiting in the queue"* **(1996)** (www.open.ac.uk/hsc/_assets/GeriatricMedicineFindings.pdf)

Figure 3.10 Number of South Asian doctors
(Source: General Media Council July 2015, England)

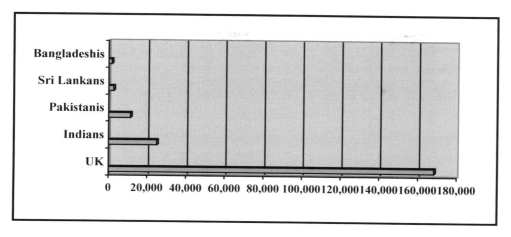

Career choices for Indian medical students are biased in favour of individual preferences and the desire to become clinical and hospital-centred (professional) scientists. An estimated 17,265 or 16% of all British Indian students chose key specialities, with electives being *medicine and dentistry, subjects allied to medicine and biological sciences.* (**Fig 3.11**)

Figure 3.11 British Indian medical science students 2010/11
(Source: Higher Education Statistics Agency Limited, England 2012)

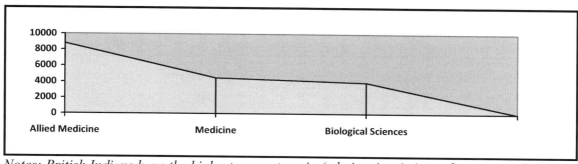

Notes: British Indians have the highest percentage in (ethnic minority) enrolment rates for these subjects: medicine/dentistry (11%), allied medicine subjects (3.9%) and biological sciences (2.7%).

Care Sector

Demographic changes such as a growing, aging population have created both commercial and social enterprise opportunities for ethnic communities in social care. Due to busy lifestyles, many South Asians are unable to take care of elders according to customs and traditions. As one family carer observed,

The Anatomy of British South Asian Enterprise

"Members of this generation have been born and brought up in a different country – the awareness isn't there or acknowledgement of the cultural needs, especially for those who have dementia. It's about honouring the person" **(2012).**

There is a significant trend in the South Asian residential care sector in which those with varying degrees of disabilities and others vulnerable or frail, lack adequate family support. Indian-operated care firms are segmented by private, local authority-sponsored and or have a Third Sector-type structure. These entities are registered as *'old age and nursing homes'*, places for *'dementia, old age and physical disabilities'* and *'other specialist care services'*
(2011).

In an effort to fulfil statutory requirements, value for money, meet customer demands and sustain firms, some operators have developed small respite (social) care units while others have opted for medium-care facilities to cater for diverse service-users. Several have a tendency to augment property portfolios to complement care homes so as to increase asset base whilst creating competitive advantage in the healthcare sector (**Fig 3.12**).

Figure 3.12 Case Study of Careworld London Ltd

Dr Chaitanya Patel, CBE is a businessman, philanthropist and Chairman of **Elysian Capital**, a private equity firm specialising in UK lower mid-market deals between £10m and £100m. He is also Chairman of the 2011-registered HC-**One**, a nursing home management company that manages many of South Cross' former homes.

He founded **Court Cavendish** and in 1996 set up **Care First**, the UK's largest continuing care company. Dr Patel remained as Chief Executive until it was taken over by BUPA in 1997. In 1999 he acquired **Westminster Health Care plc**, the largest publicly quoted UK healthcare services group, which then acquired Priory Hospitals in 2000. After a management buyout of the Care Home division in 2002, the business executive continued as Chief Executive of the **Priory Group**, the UK's largest independent specialist mental health and education services group. On the 5th March 2007 his management team resigned from Priory Healthcare.

Following the collapse of **Southern Cross Healthcare** in 2011 the business leader re-formed Court Cavendish as a consultancy and joined with the landlord company NHP (Nursing Home Properties) to form HC-One. Despite industry challenges, this savvy entrepreneur has developed different strategies to sustain his healthcare enterprise. These developmental actions are:

- A relentless focus on high quality service;
- Large-scale (investment) acquisition strategy involving over 30 companies;
- Advanced operational systems of governance;
- Integrated care services across elderly care, mental health and education;
- Building excellent management teams and investors; and
- Utilising international market leveraging techniques to increase asset portfolio.

Management is aware of the public concern about the role of the private sector in delivering NHS care. *"Making profits out of healthcare is still an emotional issue. This is compounded by*

> *a culture that is primarily inward-and-upward focused, delivering on short-term expediencies and bedevilled with organisational constraints. Public servants are left hugely frustrated and demoralised,"* stated Dr Patel **(Interview with *Society Guardian, 25 September 2002*).**

Business and the Professions

Historically, entrepreneurial activities within the South Asian community have been restricted to 'low profits and low growth industries such as retail and clothing' **(2001)**. However over the passage of time, there has been a decisive shift by members of the second and third generation who're pursuing higher education and professional training.

This approach has enabled highly successful business careers where owners are creating niche markets within segments of the Business and Professional Services (BPS) sector.

The most popular are accountancy and finance, travel and logistics, property development, energy and related services. British Indians have a market share of 17.3% in this highly segmented services sector.

Each year, information on highly successful companies including British South Asian businesses, is published. The aim being, to publicise the achievements of owners and analyse companies' capital assets vis-à-vis their net contribution to the economy. British Indian companies 'increased their wealth by more than a third in the past year despite the onset of the global economic crisis' according to one report **(2008)**.

The *Sunday Times* published a list of 10 of the wealthiest Indians in Britain, featuring various industry sectors. These companies are led primarily by first generation captains of industry in multiple sectors such as: manufacturing, telecommunications, energy, defence, real estate, transport and logistics, among others. They have a total market value exceeding £billions **(Table 3.6)**.

Table 3.6 Profile of the 10 wealthiest British Indian companies
(Source: Sunday Times Rich List, 18 August 2012)

Name/Market Value	Formed	Sector
The Hinduja Group -£12.5bn	1919	Automotive, financial services, oil/gas, media.
Arcelor Mittal - £11bn	2006	Steel and other metal products.
Vedanta Resources -£3bn	1976	Metals, oil and gas.
Essar Group -£2bn	1969	Steel, oil/gas, minerals, shipping and logistics.
Edwardian Group – 1.5bn	1977	Hotel and hospitality sectors.
Indorama Corporation -1.27bn	1976	Manufacturing (polyester and plastic).
Arora Hotels -£323m	1999	Hotel and hospitality sectors.
New Look -£270m	1969	Retail (clothing fashion) industry.
Eros International -£267m	1977	Film entertainment and general media products.

New Look Travel -£227m	1991	Travel (airline) sector.

The above table is indicative of the multiple industries founded by first generation Indians particularly, in their efforts to be financially independent and economically self-sufficient. The information also highlights other features that reflect the organisation and performance of these companies, as follows:-

- 90% of companies were established in the early to mid-late 20th century;
- 40% were founded during the 1970s-1980s recession;
- Growth acquisition strategy to increase market share and profits;
- Diversification as a tool for new product-service lines and locations;
- Owners' projection of corporate growth despite recessionary trends;
- Companies operate in global markets; that is, across continental-regions;
- Workforce diversity is a unique selling point and distinctive market advantage;
- Viable alliances with distribution and supply chains; and
- Organisational structures designed for relevant sector/business operations.

One of the most successful companies that emerged in the last century was the **B& M Retail Limited (Fig 3.13),** a conglomerate typifying model strategies for business expansion, customer intelligence and private equity investment for sustainable growth.

Figure 3.13 Case Study of B& M Retail Limited
(Source: http://www.bmstores.co.uk/about)

B&M Retail Limited is a retail chain of variety stores operating in the UK since 1976 and serving millions of shoppers. The company has moved from being a regional to a national retailer. From its first store in Blackpool, Lancashire, B&M has grown to over 300 stores and employs thousands of staff. It promotes top branded products at competitive prices to meet the demands of multiple customer segments who are driven by both tradition and modernity.
The business was started by Peter McAllister, a Croftfoot based entrepreneur and purchased by brothers Simon and Bobby Arora. The company has 21 stores with annual revenues of £65 million (**2012 estimates**).
The company grew significantly between 2006 and 2012, acquiring the Glyn Webb chain of DIY stores and converting them into its B&M Homestore format. Other acquisitions included Kwik Save, Woolworths and Au-Natural stores which are integrated within the firm's broader operational portfolio in other UK regions. B&M's philosophy is built on these principles:-
- Single point delivery for suppliers;
- Quick and clear decision-making;
- Value for money for leading brands;
- 30% of purchases are clearance sales; and
- Stores are in secondary retail locations that are accessible to consumers.
B&M has stores throughout England, Scotland, Wales and Northern Ireland.

Legal Services

This segment of the PBS sector is very popular with British Indians especially for young and highly qualified lawyers and solicitors. Out of a total of 15,581 persons, 374 Indians qualified for the bar according to the 'gender and ethnicity matrix'.

Men made up 209 and women 165, highlighting the fact that female participation rates in the legal profession has evolved especially within the British Indian community compared to other South Asians – Pakistanis with a total of 185 and Bangladeshis 58 (**2012**).

During the same period, figures for those 'self-employed' made interesting reading as **Table 3.7** illustrates. Overall, males fared better than females though both excelled in their respective law degree courses.

Table 3.7: Sample of Self-employed barristers by gender and major ethnicity matrix
(Source: The General Council of the Bar of England and Wales, November 2012)

Ethnicity	Women	%	Men	%	Total	%
White (4 UK Regions)	2,970	74.87%	7,039	82.16	10,009	78.50%
Indian	**120**	**2.92%**	**168**	**1.96%**	**288**	**2.27%**
Pakistani	51	1.24%	107	1.25%	158	1.25%
Bangladeshi	16	0.39%	32	0.37%	48	0.38%
Chinese	23	0.56%	11	0.13%	34	0.27%
Other Asian	64	1.56%	91	1.06%	155	1.31%
African	68	1.66%	94	0.98%	180	1.32%
Caribbean	80	1.93%	70	0.81%	150	1.37%
Other ethnic group	16	1.18%	10	0.65%	26	0.89%
Total	**3,408**	**86.31%**	**7,622**	**89.37%**	**11,030**	**87.56%**

Over the past decade, the Bar Council has been monitoring the ethnic composition of barristers by gender in England and Wales though statistics for Indians do not include para-legal services for clients who can ill-afford exorbitant litigation fees.

The Anatomy of British South Asian Enterprise

The Law Society has been assessing ethnic trends in the solicitor's profession **(2009 estimates)**. Official indices suggest that 11.4% of all 'solicitors on the Roll' are from minority ethnic groups.

Noteworthy, 16,611 **(ibid)** minority ethnic group solicitors have practising licences. The Law Society trends included:

- The number of minority ethnic solicitor practices in various UK Regions.
- The status of private practice solicitors by ethnicity.
- Ethnicity by size of solicitors firm.
- The ethnic gender of students enrolling with the Law Society.

Poor ethnic monitoring was prevalent in 2009 when trends showed imprecise information on 'Asian' solicitors comprising ethnic minority segments of the profession. Of particular interest, were the number of private practice practitioners (by ethnicity and the size of law firms).

Table 3.8 shows that just over half of all minority ethnic group solicitors (50.2%) work in firms with 4 or fewer partners, compared to 28.1% of their European counterparts.

Table 3.8: Composition of solicitors' firms by ethnicity

Ethnicity	Sole Practice	2-4 Partners	5-10 Partners	11-25 Partners	26-80 Partners	81+Partners
Caribbean	17.8%	40.1%	14.0%	8.3%	9.0%	10.7%
Asian (*)	**16.6%**	**37.1%**	**11.4%**	**8.1%**	**11.6%**	**15.1%**
Chinese	8.7%	20.0%	8.7%	9.3%	15.2%	38.1%
African	24.9%	44.5%	6.4%	4.1%	7.9%	12.2%
Other ethnic origin	11.2%	23.1%	12.4%	9.6%	16.4%	27.2%
All ethnic minority	15.9%	34.3%	11.0%	8.1%	12.2%	18.4%
White European	7.5%	20.6%	15.8%	13.3%	18.4%	24.5%
Unknown	10.4%	23.8%	12.8%	11.1%	16.7%	25.2%
Total	**8.6%**	**22.3%**	**15.0%**	**12.5%**	**17.6%**	**23.9%**

(Source: Trends in the solicitors' profession, Annual statistical report 2009, The Law Society, England).

Fashion and Textiles

India and the UK have had a unique creative relationship for centuries. The subcontinent's textiles, traditional products and designs are integral to British designs (**2011**). The rising influence and power of minority ethnic groups is a motivation and a catalyst for entrepreneurs to introduce different products and services for domestic and overseas markets.

Described as a 'flagship bridal magazine', *Asiana* incorporates bridal fashion, features, wedding planning and an essential wedding directory. At the time of researching this segment of the Indian creative industries, the print version of the magazine was ceased (2011) giving way to an online TV portal (**Ibid**).

Exquisite fabrics, luxuriously rich colours and intricate, hand-sewn embroidery are among the rich tapestry exhibited on catwalks at premiere fashion shows and other annual cultural festivals. These events depict a fusion of tradition and contemporary designs, and according to one observer,

"In a fusion of East meets West, many of the designers, from all over India were combining classic styles from their (Indian) heritage and culture with cutting edge shapes and forms. Designers have given us glimpses of opulence and colour that are incredibly vibrant for futuristic designs based around our time" (**2010: 2011, Londonist.com**).

Besides fashion exhibitions, since the last century, Indians have built iconic businesses in the garment industry to offer higher quality of goods and services, to satisfy the demands and tastes of [sophisticated], fashion-conscious customer segments (**Fig 3.14**).

Figure 3.14 Case Study of New Look, an iconic fashion company

New Look was founded in 1969 by Tom Singh and since then, the company has expanded to over 1,000 stores internationally, with a staff of 30,000. The group had a profit margin of £61m though sales fell heavily due to recession (**2012**). In February 2009, on the occasion of its 40th anniversary, the firm opened its first store in Russia. A year later, New Look opened its Scottish flagship store –covering 18,000 sq. ft. (1,700m^2). The largest New Look store in the world was opened in Ireland in November 2010.

The firm's core market is women (16-30 year old bracket), but in 2001, it diversified into men's clothing which has since been implemented in over 20% of the business chain. In 2007, New Look launched its first advertising campaign for three years and that same year, it used online advertising and launched its website. Apart from women and menswear, the firm has expanded also into the Generation 915 product line consisting of teens, kids, footwear, accessories, and lingerie, maternity, tall and Inspire (sizes 18-26). The company was ranked 32 among the list of 100 of the largest private companies in the UK (**2008**). The success of New Look is attributed to its unique strategy model based on:-

- A competent and experienced management team;
- Premises and locations that reflect volume 1,000 (**2010 estimates**);
- Globalisation of operations dozens of countries worldwide;
- Product development and segmentation in consumer retail markets;
- Investment in infrastructure and new product lines;
- Revamping stores format to broaden retailer's appeal to older shoppers; and
- New technology for shoppers to 'see the fit' without fitting rooms.

Singh who studied international politics and geography at the University of Wales; plans to expand into Eastern Europe and Asia, Russia and China. At the time of writing, he was head of the UK Advisory Council for the British Asian Trust, and remains active as a philanthropist and social investor, linked to Indian charity projects such as eye care, education and water (**2013**).

Transport and Logistics

In an industry depending on travellers with a lucrative global market of £2 billion (**2012 estimates**), British Indians have a small but significant market share of the travel logistics industry. In competing with other travel agencies at home and overseas, British Indian operators are constantly developing niche markets through repeat sales and customer loyalty.

Travel agencies and other logistics firms operate in London, the English Counties and other UK cities. Through contact with various communities, owners induce consumers to invest more in ethnic travel agencies. The distinctive competencies of firms are affordable prices for cargo shipping, low cost airfares and convenient, multi-packaged tours for tourists en route to 'back home' destinations.

One of the most successful British-based South Asian travel operators is **Southall Travel**, owned by Kuljinder Bahia. The firm is located in one of London's most vibrant ethnic communities, Southall which is described by many as '*Little India*'. It has a 'proud' reputation for providing quality services. (**Fig 3.15**)

Figure 3.15 Mini-case of Southall Travel – a corporate leader

Kuljinder Bahia founded **Southall Travel** in 1984 and since then, the business has developed within the travel mainstream market as a consolidator to the trade. The firm mushroomed from a £500,000 turnover in 1991 to the £240 million as of **June 2011**.

Bahia acknowledged that focusing on the basics is important to the type of sector. *"We are doing the same things we were doing 10 years back, it is just our volumes have gone up. We have a non-corporate approach that makes us competitive. We have grown in stages, as we try to have zero wastage of money and where everything runs very simply".*

Southall Travel is a major sponsor of cricket tournaments – the Indian Premiere League (IPL) tournament and the 2013 International Cricket Council (ICC) World Champions Trophy.

"For cricket fans this is one of the highest quality tournaments, exciting a worldwide audience,. It gives our brand premium visibility and asserts our position to our target audience as the number one flight and holiday firm for exotic travel" (**http://news.southalltravel.co.uk/press-release**).

Bahia asserted that other travel companies can emulate Southall Travel's success by securing niche markets thereby using them as a platform for growth - both in size and profitability.

The Gender Equation

National themes such as immigration, race, discrimination, prejudice and faith issues remain central to the national discourse on the presence of minority ethnic groups in Britain. In the face of adversity however, South Asian women are pursuing careers in business and the professions. Whilst the economic contribution of Indian women remains somewhat unclear, over the years, trends show that more are developing enterprises across different industry sectors.

Meena Patak of **Patak Foods** is a major producer of spices and chutneys. **Kamul Basram** is also involved in food manufacturing. **Bobby Dhillon** is in the property and luxury market. Along with her brother, she established a chain of London hotels. As one commentator observed,

"Behind the male façade, the oldest South Asian immigrant firms in Britain are run by inter-generational wives and daughters who play an important role, and are barely mentioned in the press" (**Thandi, 2006**).

Women are dominating the clothing industry from traditional Indian saris to modern fashions and complementary accessories (**Fig 3.15**). They have emerged from 'behind the scenes as helpers' to genuine fashion designers and entrepreneurs. Bhachu (**2004**) describes the impact of supply networks such as importers, local boutiques and designers, mini-bazars and home-based Tupperware-style sales.

The Anatomy of British South Asian Enterprise

Gender Attributes

The achievements of female entrepreneurs within the British Indians are signified by these sector (model) interests:-

- *Education* –promoting society's well-being via citizenship activities.

- *Creativity* – using art as a tool-booster for disadvantaged communities.

- *Employment* – helping 'unfortunate' learners to move into education and jobs.

- *Healthcare* – pioneering health services to combat social problems.

- *Food* – revolutionising city centre dining using a customer-centred approach.

- *Medicare* – specialism in cardiology, gynaecology and medicine.

- *Social Enterprise* – social investment opportunities for vulnerable families.

   (Source: Textual analysis of 100 leading British Indian businesswomen, June 2013)

On the occasion of the 2013 Asian Women of Achievement Awards, several persons were honoured for contributing to business, industry and the professions. Fifty-five (55) were shortlisted for 5 sectors: creative industries, business and professional services, healthcare, social enterprises, education and training (**Fig 3.16**).

Figure 3.16 Mini-cases of leading British Indian Businesswomen
(Source: The Asian Women of Achievement Awards, shortlist 2013)

- Jaya Chakrabarti founded **Nameless Media Group** in 1999 with an £8,000 investment. Years later, the business was valued at over £3 million and is one of the leading creative digital agencies in northern England including Orange, Dyson and HSBC. She is passionate about digital technology to empower and improve the quality of human lives.
- In 1987, Shaheen Bhatia and her husband converted an old grocery shop into a successful pharmacy, **P& S Chem Ltd** to pioneer essential health services in Essex. The business is a market leader in delivering services for persons suffering from drug addiction, teenage pregnancy and sexual ill-health. Locals are benefitting from Bhatia's initiative which has become a centre for community healthcare.
- Helen Dhaliwal founded the £2 million **Red Hot Buffet restaurant** brand (2012) in Nottingham. It is reputed to be the UK's fastest growing restaurant chain. The founder has helped revolutionise affordable city-centre dining by combining a person-centred approach, the best of world cuisines, motivated staff and formidable business acumen.
- Parvinder Kaur is the founder and manager of **Eternal Taal** (1999), a leading Bhangra entertainments team. With a love for music since childhood, Kaur's decision to take 'a quantum leap' in a male-dominated industry was both bold and innovative. She became the only female Dhol drummer perform on the biggest UK stages. She also teaches students this art form.

> - Shalini Khemka is chief executive and director of **E2E Invest Ltd** (2013), a non-profit organisation 'for entrepreneurs, by entrepreneurs' that seeks to formulate partnerships with entrepreneurial organisations and corporate institutions to promote enterprise activity. At the time of writing the Board of Directors included Virgin's Sir Richard Branson and Lornamead founder, George Jatania as well as Lord Karan Bilimoria, founder of Cobra Beer.
> - Sanju Pal is the founder of **Rural Indian School Enterprise (RISE-2009),** a charity set up to realise the potential and talent amongst 'unserved' children in India and the UK. Although she has a demanding consulting job at Accenture where she specialises in process transformation, Pal considers RISE an important facilitator of social services for young people. She is also director of the residents property firm, **2 Smyrna Road Limited** (2010).

Social Enterprise Sector

The South Asian population in the UK is strikingly pluralistic in faith, class, country of origin, sub-ethnicity, language, gender, social, economic, cultural and other creeds. Since this book is examining the Afghani, Bangladeshi, **Indian**, Nepali, Pakistani and Sri Lankan communities respectively, their diversity impacts on social entrepreneurship. Ventures comprise charities, volunteering and making contributions to 'good causes' (education, health, food, housing, science and so forth).

One example of corporate social responsibility, is the provision of food and clothing for the benefit of Buddhist, Christian, Hindu, Muslim, Sikh and other faith communities. Along with this, is advice, support and finance that South Asian networks – local, national and international – provide for each other especially within existing and/or emerging commercial, industrial and social firms (**Modood and Metcalfe, Werbner**).

The modern term 'Asian-ness', is used to partly describe South Asians' commercial flair, social dynamics and cultural modelling according to specific heritage status. This phrase was endorsed by then Tony Sarin, Chief Executive of the Asian Business Association who felt that in 20-30 years' time, there will "no longer be a need for an Asian Business Association" (**Sarin**) to promote solely Asian business concerns, as the barriers and distinctions would be less when 'Asians' integrate.

Against the background of limited information and or knowledge of South Asian business involvement in social enterprise activities in the UK, there are two schools of thought on CSR with regard to ethnic firms:

- One is that these businesses were originally 'sweat shops' often employing people below the minimum wage and exploiting workers by forcing them to work long hours. In this instance, such businesses cannot be regarded as being socially responsible.

- Two, the other argument is that CSR is integral to the average Indian/South Asian entrepreneur (as well as other ethnic groups –*the publisher's emphasis*), since businesses are set up to serve their respective communities. This is further boosted by imbedded cultural and religious traditions of giving back to society; for example with donations to build community facilities (**2003**).

In a survey of 32 South Asian enterprises (**2003**), most were involved in different types of CSR activity. They donated capital and time, worked with local institutions and encouraged skill development amongst their workforce. Though faith remains central to the engagement process including commercial activities, the CSR concept is relatively new to South Asian firms particularly.

However companies such as **Noon Products, Cobra Beer** and **Aimimage Camera Company**, are setting worthy examples as 'corporate social leaders' in their right. The activities of CSR-driven British Indian businesses should be acknowledged and celebrated as this book does (**Fig 3.17**).

Figure 3.17 Case Study of British Indian firms promoting CSR

- Lord Karan Bilimoria founded **Cobra Beer** in 1989 with a strategy of targeting Indian restaurants in London. The company employs over 50 people and has a turnover of 55 million at retail value (**2003 estimates**). The firm was chosen as a champion and role model for 'Asian' entrepreneurs, leading the way in CSR. The *Sunday Times* ranked Cobra in the Virgin Atlantic Fast Rack 100 and the list of Britain's fastest growing private companies in 1999. The company is involved with communities, academia, and the voluntary sector and government initiatives. Cobra provides its products free of charge to charity, cultural and sporting events, acknowledging not only the value-add to business, by increased visible and recognition, but emphasises the importance of public engagement.
- Dr Atif Ghani is founder of **Aimimage Camera Company** (1982), a provider of equipment for the film and television industry. The business has grown to include studio, equipment hire as well as post-production facilities. Projects include dramas and pop videos as well as children's programmes for the BBC. The *Land of the Mammoth* won the Emmy for Best Cinematography in 2001 as well as factual programmes such as *Cutting Edge, Horizon* and *Panorama,* won acclaim. Dr Ghani recognises the value of cultural diversity and feels that the company is obligated to support aspiring and talented young minority ethnic writers, directors and other technical personnel facing significant entry barriers in mainstream films and television productions.
- Sital Punja established **Sari (UK) Limited** in 2002; to produce clothing, accessories and soft furnishings from recycled saris. The aim is to 'recycle old saris into designer clothes and products, and use the profits to support women overseas' (**www.saricouture.com**). As a founding member of the Ethical Fashion Forum, Punja was shortlisted for awards including the *Daily Mirror's* Young Brit of the Year, *New*

Statesman's Edge Upstarts and *Eastern Eye* Asian Business Awards 2007. Sari's success is built on raising money for charities, reinvesting profits into the business, partnerships with communities in the UK and promoting sound environmental practices via the 'Save A Sari' campaign. *"The people giving their saris have input into which charities are supported and this is important. The sari has played a huge part in the lives of Indian women over generations and is a way to articulate their experience"*, Puna acknowledged. **(2008)**

Emerging Themes

The impact of the prolonged recession plus globalisation has offered members of the Indian diaspora opportunities to be engaged in the principle of giving. As indicated above, owners of firms are keen to contribute to good causes in their 'home towns'. They recognise their role as instruments for 'donor-advised funds' based on a successful 'microfinance-type operation' (**Sridhar, 2011**). From various indicators to date, British Indian firms have developed essential CSR themes such as these:

- Diversity in charitable motivations;
- Application of business principles to philanthropy;
- Types of religious/faith giving;
- Strategic leveraging of capital resources;
- Maximum utility of inter-ethnic networks;
- Contribution to international causes; and
- Partnerships across ethnic, community and religious pathways.

The Indian community's vibrancy is reflected by the reported 1000 organisations (**2003 estimates**) that constitute faith and allied organisations according to specific regional and ethnic affiliations. Faith and cultural identities are significant factors that help members to cope with discrimination and prejudice. This is evidenced by the hundreds of temples, gurudwaras, mosques and other religious centres that serve as a compass for cultural, educational, faith and other social activities.

Politics

Indian participation in British politics is legendary as Dadabhai Naoroji and Gopal Krishnan among others, exemplified. The former was a successful Parsi businessman, was elected to the House of Commons as a Liberal Member in 1892. Naoroji was followed by Sir Mancherjee Bhawangree, a Conservative 1895 to 1906 and Shapurji Saklatvala, Labour in 1922 and then again in 1924. In 1919, Sir Satyendra Sinha, created Baron Sinha Raipur, was the first Indian to be given a hereditary peerage. The late Lord Tarsem Singh King was the first Sikh to become a member of the House of Lords.

Since that period, there has been an increase in the number of Indians in the (British) legislature due to the 'accretion in economic strength, attainment of higher educational levels and enhancement in social status' (**2003**). Statistics on the number of minority ethnic groups in British politics vary from election to election.

Following the 2015 General Election, there are about 41 'non-white MPs' elected to the House of Commons, 6.3% of all 650 members of the legislature (**2016**). **Tables 3.9 and 3.10** highlight the number of MPs and Peers in the British Legislature.

Both public and private researchers have conceded that in many instances, trying to analyse minority ethnic representation in British mainstream politics is problematic because ethnicity is both sensitive [case] and difficult to define according to the House of Commons (**2012**).

Table 3.9 A sample of Minority Ethnic MPs in the House of Commons
(Source: Minority Ethnic Members of Parliament, June 2015)

Ethnic Group	Male	Female	Total
African	7	1	8 (19%)
Bangladeshi	1	2	3 (7%)
Caribbean	2	2	4 (9%)
Chinese	1	-	1 (2%)
Indian *	**4**	**3**	**7 (17%)**
Pakistani	8	2	10 (24%)
Sri Lankan	1	-	1 (2%)

Notes: the % total has been calculated using the 41 ethnic MPs as a baseline figure.

Table 3.10 A selection of Minority Ethnic Peers, House of Lords
(Source: House of Commons Library Briefing Paper, 4 March 2016)

Ethnic Group	Male	Female	Total
African	3	1	4 (7%)
Bangladeshi	1	1	2 (3%)
Caribbean	3	2	5 (9%)
Chinese	-	1	1 (1%)
Indian *	**16**	**4**	**20 (39%)**
Pakistani	3	4	7 (13%)

Notes: the % total has been calculated using the 51 ethnic Peers as a baseline figure.

Local Politics

Whilst the level of participation in the national legislature is low for men and women (the latter especially), the situation is different at the grassroot level. There are approximately 250 - 300 Councillors of Indian origin in the UK so much so that a group named the

'British-Indian Councillors Association' (BICA) was formed. Traditionally, Indians support the British Labour Party and at the last elections (**May 2015**), an estimated 65% plus voted for the Party.

A study of minority voters showed divergent views on issues such as migration, democracy, trust, the economy, opportunities for minorities and personal experience of discrimination
(**2012**). Minorities make up around 8% of the electorate so their views on national issues are vital (**Table 3.11**).

Table 3.11: Attitudes of Minority Ethnic Groups on key British issues
(Source: Runnymede Trust, February 2012)

Ethnicity	Spend rather than cut taxes	Don't send asylum seekers home	Improve opportunities for minorities	Non-whites are held back by prejudice	Give priority to minorities	Very or fairly dissatisfied with democracy
British	49%	39%	19%	-	1%	37%
African	43%	74%	75%	53%	36%	24%
Bangladesh	32%	43%	70%	41%	37%	20%
Caribbean	42%	59%	74%	58%	20%	49%
Chinese	-	-	-	-	-	-
Indian	**33%**	**34%**	**65%**	**40%**	**26%**	**25%**
Pakistani	33%	41%	71%	38%	28%	23%
Mixed	-	-	62%	54%	25%	52%
All MEGs*	+12%	-11%	70%	47%	28%	30%

*Notes: MEGs * minority ethnic groups based on selected themes for inclusion in this book. These reflect the representation of minorities on issues of societal concern.*

Business Location

Having a proper location is important for overall business development and growth as most of the Indian entrepreneurs demonstrated in every industry sector they are participating in. Location coupled with suitable premises can go a long way in determining the level of performance or under-performance of firms. Poor quality premises can affect the [customer-public] image and reputation of companies.

Principally, members of the British Indian business enterprise are actively trading in multiple sectors of business and industry in cites and conurbations across London, the Midlands and Home Counties as well as Ireland, Scotland and Wales.

Clearly, this wide berth of trading activity is indicative of owners, directors and managers' understanding of, and appreciation for suitable business locations in terms of convenience, product segmentation, quality service, customer care and various industry linkages associated with viable strategies for long-term growth (**Table 3.12**).

Table 3.12: British Indian Business Ownership by Location
(Source: textual analysis of firms by geographical dispersion, 2016)

Major Location	Principal Industry Sector
London	Food, retail, IT, transport and logistics, creative industries, social enterprise, health and social care, manufacturing, engineering, construction, business-professions and media.
South East	Retail food, creative industries, social enterprise, social enterprise, business-professions and media.
East of England	Food, retail, education, social enterprise, business and the professions.
West Midlands	Education, retail, social enterprise, business and the professions.
East Midlands	Food and hospitality, transport and logistics, business and the professions, social enterprise, training, health and social care.
North West	Media, the creative industries, social enterprises, food and hospitality.
Scotland	Food and hospitality, social enterprises, business and the professions, education and training.
Wales	Food and hospitality, retail, transport and logistics, manufacturing, training and social care.
Northern Ireland	Healthcare, education, training and food retail.

Challenges and Opportunities

Throughout this chapter, the focus has been on the sector performance of British Indian business owners. Like other chapters profiling the four other business groups – Afghans, Bangladeshis, Nepalis, Pakistanis and Sri Lankans – this section of the book summarises key challenges affecting vital sectors/segments of business, industry and the professions. It also offers pointers for sector growth and development prospects in emerging markets.

It is hoped that this information will help British Indian business owners to improve firm performance thereby linking it towards growth patterns in the UK as well as entry into overseas markets. **Table 3.13** thus identifies sector challenges and demonstrates how these can be overcome by relevant market prospecting and focus.

Table 3.13: Challenges and Opportunities for British Indian firms

Sector Challenges	Prospects and Opportunities
Education/Training: Students are underperforming by 10% in GCSEs and just around 5% in business and law degree courses.	Business owners including top notch Indian barristers/solicitors can support career advancement initiatives for the young, gifted and talented.
Self-Employment Rates: are still relatively low - 11.9% - for Indians compared to their vast entrepreneurial talent.	These rates can increase - over a sixth if start-up Indian firms are supported more. Companies can sponsor training and promote entrepreneurship as a 'good career choice'.
Creative Industries: The lifestyle of Indians is influenced by British traditions that also impact on creativity.	Artists and cultural producers can introduce creative products and services; for example more newspaper and book publishing (materials) on matters of concern to British Indians particularly.
Medicare Sciences: Practitioners represent 10.8% of the total UK medical register and just over 4% of minority ethnic groups are in the profession.	Current medical specialists should sponsor mentoring programs for the 15% of Indian students favouring medicine and allied sciences as their major(s).
Social Care: The market share for firms in this sector is quite low compared to the demand for domiciliary/respite care.	Businesses can optimise care sector markets involving learning and physical disabilities as well as service-users who need 'assisted living' support.
Professional Services: Only about 2.27% of Indians are self-employed barristers.	Advocates can facilitate the creation of law firms amongst the 6% of 'hopefuls' keen on legal studies.
Transport and Logistics: Only a few firms are in the travel agency trade, but owners' involvement in tourism services is almost unknown.	Current operators can expand their markets to include festival, cultural and adventure tourism thereby complementing yearly Mela, Diwali, Vaisakhi and other festivities. Leisure and sports-related events including annual cricket tournaments need consideration as key tourism packages.

(Source: textual analysis of issues affecting British Indian firms)

Conclusion

In this chapter, it emerged that despite perceived disadvantage of one sort or another; British Indians are excelling in business and the professions. Like their South Asian 'cousins' along with other ethnic groups, British Indian entrepreneurs apply cultural, faith and social traditions to establish successful firms. Through community activism, they have established codes of practice to become the fourth leading minority ethnic business group nationally.

Organisationally, owners operate within a legally defined structure with more than 80% of companies formally registered and over 10% of larger companies having subsidiaries or branches – nationally and internationally. As is customary with ethnic firms, owners have direct contact with their 'home countries' either through birth or heritage background. This allows trading in dual or multiple consumer markets thereby spreading 'the risk' associated (commercially), with low-income markets.

Of particular interest, was the need to be more socially responsible in business deals/dealings. Evidence show that members of the Indian community have this principle imbedded within business and social enterprise activities. Community Education Academy of Leadership (CEAL) has pioneered enterprise education in primary and secondary schools in response to youth unemployment which is further compounded by the prolonged recession. The Midlands-based charity (**2002**) recognised the fundamental link between enterprise and career development. The founder of CEAL explained the reason for pursuing this important mission;

"We are duty-bound to help disadvantaged, vulnerable and other 'at risk' communities whilst working with mainstream institutions to prepare children and young people for the future world of work. Some research suggests that only about 30% of parents, guardians and carers are satisfied with the way in which schools prepare children for future work. There is also evidence to suggest that in the Midlands, only 32% of vocational institutions offer quality career guidance and support to under-25s. That is why we need initiatives that match the needs of young people, their communities as well as the local labour market. Youth enterprise must remain a top priority rather than be limited to token gestures" (**2015**).

However, a major focus in this chapter, was the desire for owners to create vertical and horizontal integration linkages across distribution and supply chains, using inter/intra-ethnic and mainstream sources. These links are a boost to firms in their development of market intelligence systems which also help business decisions relating to customer segmentation, product-type, pricing strategy as well as volume. First generation Indian entrepreneurs tend to operate in London's almost exclusive ethnic community.

Nonetheless, judging by their phenomenal growth in food, retail, business and professional services and other low entry barrier markets, the second and third generation of British Indian entrepreneurs favour expansion into co-ethnic as well as mainstream consumer markets. Not only will this reposition this business community, but it will also help to redefine the notion of diversity versus super-diversity within the broader minority entrepreneurial context. In the next chapter, we will look at '**Nepalese Enterprise Dynamics'**.

Notes

Migration
Indians have a 9.4% share of the market for migrants 'by country, birth and nationality' in the UK (*The Migration Observatory*, University of Oxford 2014).

The Pioneer
Sake Dean Mahomed was born Sheikh Din Muhammad) 1759 in Patna, Bihar [then part of the Bengal Presidency]. His father belonged to the traditional *Nai* (barber) caste was employed with the East India Company. The young Sake learned business techniques from the making of spas and shampoos. Although his 1810 Hindoostanee Coffee House went bust due to financial difficulties, Mohamed became famous with the British. On 29 September 2005, the City of Westminster unveiled a plaque in honour of this pioneering Indian/South Asian entrepreneur.

Eating Out
The British Hospitality Association (BHA) reported that Britons spent £31 billion on eating out (2006) compared with approximately £7 billion (1981). The estimated value of the retail Indian food market stood at £493.8 million (Mintel). www.bha.org.uk/members-area/downloads/reports/

Value
The UK Indian foods market was projected to grow by 6% to reach a value of £524.6 million at current prices by 2011 (ibid). During 2012 and 2015, there were 9,500 'Indian' restaurants with London having 45.6%, the Midlands 16.4% and the North West 8.4%. This sector employs over 60,000 people.

History
Ex-colonials including English-Brits, dined at Indian restaurants during 1950s-1960s. The Manager of London's Shafi observed that, *"the Indian Khichris, Curries, Bombay Duck and Chutneys and other delicacies have become a regular must for Englishmen who had lived in India"* (*Where to Eat in London*, London, 1955, 65: 1960, 22).

Negativity

Yet some writers described Indian cuisine in negative tones- that it caused "dyspepsia', made you 'evil-tempered and tends to shorten your life". Other publications gave their own misconceptions of curry (Harvey, Day with the collaboration of Sarojini Mudnani, *Curries of India* (London, 1955), 8; Harvey Day, assisted by May Ewing, *Fourth Book of Curries* (London, 1964), 6.

Arts Creativity

The Arts Council of England researched the '*attendance, participation and attitudes'* rates of minority ethnic groups as part of its diversity agenda. Indians participation in the creative industries exceeded 70%. Over over 50% of British South Asians accessed 'Asian radio stations' ('*Focus on cultural diversity: the arts in England'*, *Research Report* 34, December 2003, Arts Council of England p78).

Growth Dynamics

A report confirmed that UK-based Indian companies had 'growth appreciation' rates of 10% and 23%. A total of 12 firms employed over 1,000 people in the UK. Businesses paid a combined corporation tax bill of £650 million – up from £500 million the previous year' ('India meets Britain: Tracking the UK's top Indian companies, *Grant Thornton India Tracker* 2016, pp3-5).

Pioneering Efforts

The Indian Workers Association (founded in the 1930s) is a pioneering body that represented the views of immigrant workers. It contributed to the improvement of conditions of work and service for new settlers, while collaborating with the British mainstream labour movement. In spite of formidable challenges, the IWA has continued promoting, economic and social development and more recently, facilitating cultural and heritage exchange activities.

Web Links

www.bha.org.uk/members-area/downloads/reports/.

http://www.thesikhdirectory.co.uk/.

http://www.bmstores.co.uk/about.

Londonist.com.

http://news.southalltravel.co.uk/press-release

www.saricouture.com

References

The Migration Observatory, University of Oxford 2014.

Where to Eat in London, London, 1955, 65: 1960, 22.

Mudnani, Sarojini : *Curries of India* (London, 1955), 8; Harvey Day, assisted by Ewing, May: *Fourth Book of Curries* (London, 1964), 6.

'Focus on cultural diversity: the arts in England', *Research Report* 34, December 2003, Arts Council of England p78).

ONS 2011

Office for National Statistics April 2001 Census.

Department for Communities and Local Government, February 2013.

Clark, Ken & Drinkwater, Stephen: *Ethnic minorities in the labour market: Dynamics and diversity*, The Joseph Rowntree Foundation, 2007.

Department for Education, June 2015.

Report on the High Level Committee on the Indian Diaspora, Ministry of Overseas Indian Affairs, India October 2004.

Bradford University 2012.

'Family ties help Asian businesses in the UK' Sanjiv Buttoo, BBC Asian Network, 12 January 2012.

UCAS Ethnic Group 2007-2012 & The Higher Education Academy, 2015)

Global Entrepreneurship Monitor 2011 & Gallup Business Journal, 2013/2014.

The World Bank and Migration Policy Institute, 2000-2012.

British Film Institute 2011.

UK Film Council, 2007: British Film Institute Statistical Yearbook, 2012.

Recording Industry of Association of America, June 2011 and Youngs, Ian (2009): *"British R&B star conquers America"*, BBC News 23 September 2009. Other

BBC September, 2009.

Communications Market Report, *Ofcom & Mobile Magazine*, August 2013.

Graham, Ley and Dadswell, Sarah (2012*): British South Asian Theatres, University of Exeter Press,* England.

'Publishing in India Today; Growing imports/Exports, Territoriality, Piracy and Digital', *Publishing Perspectives*, 7 July 2011.

Of glance and lotus hand –a celebration of Indian writing, British Council, April 2009.

Office for National Statistics 2012

The British Sikh Report, 2013.

Higher Education Statistics Agency Limited, England 2012.

Nijjar, Manjit Kaur: *Perspectives on ageing in South Asian families*, Joseph Rowntree Foundation, January, 2012.

Dignity and respect in residential care: issues for minority ethnic groups, Report to Department of Health July 2011, University of Stirling.

Society Guardian, 25 September 2002.

Smallbone D., Ram M., Deakins D., and Baldock R. (2001) 'Accessing Finance and Business Support by Ethnic Minority Businesses in the UK', Paper presented at a conference: 'Public Policy and the Institutional Context of Immigrant Businesses', Liverpool, 22-25 March.

Ramnarayan, Abhinav: *The Guardian* 19 November 2008.

Sunday Times Rich List, 18 August 2012.

Bar Barometer Trends in the profile of the Bar, November 2012.

The General Council of the Bar of England and Wales, November 2012.

Trends in the solicitors' profession, Annual statistical report 2009, The Law Society, England.

Narang, Suneha MA Student, *Fashion Marketing and Communication*, Nottingham Trent University 2011.

'Asiana Magazine ceases publication of its print edition', Asian *Fashion Blog*, 30 November 2011.

Indian Premier London Fashion Week 2010/2011.

The Daily Telegraph November, 2012.

Thandhi, Shinder S. (2006) Brown Economy: Enterprise and Employment, in Nasreen Ali, Virinder S. Kalra and Salman Sayyid Eds., *A Post colonial People: South Asians in Britain*, London, Hurst Publishers, p.211.

Bhachu, Parminder: 'Dangerous Designs: Asian Women Fashion the Diaspora Economies', h

Journal of Anthropological Research, Vol. 60, No. 4 (Winter, 2004), pp. 583-585, The University of Chicago Press. http://www.jstor.org/stable/3631153

Metcalf, H., Modood, T. & Virdee, S. (1996) *Asian Self-Employment: The Interaction of Culture and Economics in England,* Policy Studies Institute.
"Giving Something Back" – Social Responsibility and South Asian Businesses in the United Kingdom: An Exploratory Study, Centre for Social Markets, October 2003.

Social Enterprise Coalition, London, June 2008.

Sridhar, Archana: 'An Opportunity to Lead: South Asian Philanthropy in Canada', *The Philanthropist* 2011, Vol. 24, 1, p18.

The High Level Committee on the Indian diaspora in the United Kingdom, 2003.

Heath, Anthony Professor and Khan, Omar Dr: Ethnic Minority British Election Study, University of Oxford and Runnymede Trust, February 2012.

Attitudes of Minority Ethnic Groups on key British issues, *Runnymede Trust,* February 2012.

Interview with Harminder Kaur Bhogal, West Midlands, 1 June 2015.

Chapter 4 Nepalese Enterprise Dynamics

"We are definitely planning to expand the business" – **Quick and Easy Remittance**.

Introduction

This chapter examines the evolution of British Nepalese enterprise culture against the backdrop of cultural, ethnic and other socio-economic disadvantage. Many have excelled in business and the professions. Nepalese, similar to Afghanis and Sri Lankans, are classified as *'Other Asian'* and yet their economic contribution to British society is not adequately documented more so known. For the purpose of reader identification, the phrases *'Nepalis'* and *'Nepalese'* will be used interchangeably to refer to this South Asian group. It is hoped that on completion of this chapter, readers should be able to:

- Understand the migration journey of Nepalis to Britain;
- Identify British Nepalese businesses and the professions;
- Appreciate factors contributing to this South Asian group;
- Understand key trends influencing Nepali enterprise; and
- Recognise their enterprise challenges and prospects for the 21st century.

Origins

Relations between Britain and Nepal dates to the early 1800s when the British East Indian Company increased its presence in the Indian sub-continent. Prior to the 1940s partition of India, boundary disputes and raids into Gurkha areas had implications for Nepali society in terms of British relations (**2008**). Additionally, while the Indian-sub continent was being divided, Nepal's sovereignty was recognised and its independence preserved leading up to Britain cessation of independence to South Asia.

Nepal's exportation of military labour into the British army was also a turning point in relations between the two countries as the military prowess of the Gurkhas won Britain's pride and admiration. Coupled with this, was the growing recognition of Nepal (from the 1950s through to the 1990s) as an emerging nation-state. During this period, globalisation offered 'unprecedented opportunities for nations to embark on ambitious economic projects which needed foreign labour and Nepal was one of those countries to provide such labour' (**2012**). Since it had contributed to 200 years to Britain's war efforts, it seemed fair in the circumstances, those ex-servicemen particularly Gurkhas should be allowed to settle in the UK.

Similar to other minorities, Nepalis have evolved into accomplished businesspersons, professionals, engineers and allied technicians in Britain. They contribute to local development in inner-city areas, and as such, their endeavours must be acknowledged, as this chapter seeks to do.

Since the last century, UK census figures for Nepalis varied between 5,000 and 6,000 plus. Under the ethnicity classification, they are described as 'Other Asian' (**ONS, 2001**) but independent studies including those from the Centre for Nepal Studies UK (CNSUK), suggest a more sizeable population in the country (**2012**). Figures show between 60,000 and 70,000 plus Nepalis live in the UK. In an exhaustive study, the centre examined the geographical distribution, made a comparison of South Asian people and analysed the dispersion of Nepalese communities across the UK. These estimates confirmed that 96.2% of Nepalese live in England (with the South East having 44.6%), 1.8% in Scotland, 1.6 in Wales and roughly 0.4% in Northern Island respectively. (**Table 4.1 & Fig 4.1**)

Table 4.1 Estimated geographical distribution of Nepalis in the UK
(Source: CNSUK survey 2008; ONS 2005/2011)

Region/Country	Number	+% (average)
North East England	79	0.1
North West England	1,632	2.3
Yorkshire & Humber	1,648	2.3
East Midlands	757	1
West Midlands	2,407	3.3
East of England	2,309	3.2
Greater London	22,504	31.2
South East England	32,167	44.6
South West London	2,790	3.9
Scotland	1,312	1.8
Wales	1,130	1.6
Northern Island	299	.4
Total	**69,034**	**95.7%**

Note: the selected figures are adapted from the Centre for Nepal Studies UK or 'CNSUK' survey in 2008. The study was based on population samples in city-towns involving individuals and family units by gender, sexual orientation, residency, faith, birth place, family structure, employment, health, education and so forth.

Figure 4.1 Percentage of high concentration of Nepalese in UK Regions
(Source: CNSUK survey 2008; ONS 2005/2011)

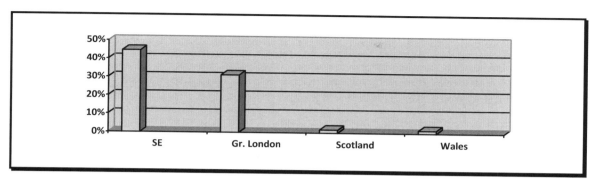

Note: Greater London/ South East of England have more than 75% of all Nepalis followed by an estimated 4% in Scotland, Wales and Northern Island respectively.

Socio-economic Indicators

Literacy levels among Nepalese vary from perception and self-claim to 'functional' reality. In 2001, literacy levels for Nepal for members of this group were considered 'very low' (over 60%) due to limited access to educational opportunities. By 2008, the authoritative CNSUK survey reported that 99% of Nepalis in Britain considered themselves 'literate'. This meant the ability to communicate in English such as being able to understand issues reported in print and electronic media.

However, the situation was somewhat different when it came to daily (social) interaction. The gradual increase in language services fuelled the notion that sections of the Nepali community had functional literacy problems. For instance, large numbers had difficulty interpreting information and data on health, welfare and other entitlements. This was prevalent among retired Gurkhas including spouses whose literacy and functional literacy skills were much lower than those highlighted in a 2008 study. Below are key indicators on the literacy levels of British Nepalese:

- Poor literacy skills;
- PhD;
- Bachelor of Arts Degrees;
- Master's;
- 'Grade or Years 1-6' level education
- A 'Level standards of education; and
- GCSE qualifications **(See also Fig 4.2)**.

Figure 4.2 Major literacy indicators of the British Nepalese population
(Source: CNSUK Survey 2008- 7,842 respondents)

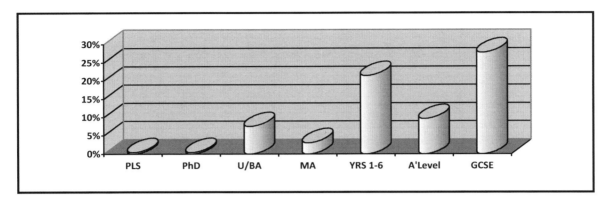

Notes to key indicators: PLS –poor literacy skills (0.4%); PhD – Doctor of Philosophy (0.4%); UBA –Undergraduate/Bachelor Arts degree (7.5%) ; MA –Master of Arts (3%); A' Level – Advanced Level
(9.6%) and GCSE – General Certificate of Secondary Education (27.8%).

Notably, (at the time of the 2008 study) 40% of Nepalis were under-15s and about 50% were of school age. On the one hand, fewer women (3.1%) were qualified at second/post graduate degree level than men (6.1%). Conversely, there was less gender disparity for those with school-level qualifications.

The contribution of British-based Nepalese, also involves understanding their faith, housing, professional training, employment and other trends. Members of this group have demonstrated self-determination which is indicative of progress in overcoming challenges in new environmental settings. The following variables are thus a reflection of the resilience shown by members of this South Asian community in Britain:

- 77% of Nepalis 'consume' English programmes in the media;
- 76% are 'trained' and professionally 'qualified';
- 73% migrated to the UK;
- 88% plan to 'buy a house in the near future';
- 75% are employed;
- 24% are active in education;
- 91% mix with 'people from different backgrounds'; and
- 90% celebrate 'cultural festivals' (**CNSUK 2008, p77**).

Enterprising British Nepalis
Prior to 2008, little was known about the economic contribution of British Nepalese who were continuously described as *'Other Asian'*. The 'working' ratio for Nepalis is quite

high with over three quarters described 'economically active'. This translates into over 50,000 Nepalis in the labour market, participating as business owners, professionals and civic/social entrepreneurs combined.

Data obtained by the CNSK showed that although less than 2.6% of Nepalis were self-employed or owned a business, there were 271 firms operating across 19 industry sectors **(2008 estimates)**. Food and hospitality segments such as catering, retailing and grocery-wholesaling are typical of this South Asian business community. Financial services, legal, real estate development, immigration and related areas are integral to business and the professions. Cabbing, driving and other associated services are part of the transport and logistics sector. Language translation and allied institutes represent segments of the education and training while entertainment, photography and various media are embedded within the creative industries sector (**Table 4.2**).

Table 4.2: Market share for key Nepalese small firm sector in Britain

Industry Sector	Market Share
• Restaurants/bars and cafes/cafes	45%
• Grocery (retail and wholesale)	8.1%
• Education institutes	6.3%
• Legal/immigration	5.9%
• Travel	5.9%
• Accounting, auditing and taxation	4.4%
• Media	4.4%
• Money transfer	2.2%

(Source: CNSUK Survey 2008)

Apart from serving local communities, these businesses contribute to inward investment inter alia skills development, employment creation, financial capital and the diversity dividend, a theory popularised in mainstream literature on ethnic entrepreneurship (Syrett and Sepulveda 2010).

Nepalis are using the academic and professional route to achieve enterprise stardom. In **Fig 4.3** below, the '*training and qualifications*' category illustrates that 79.2% of Nepalis are keen on medical careers, 59.7% engineering, 35.7% law, 23.7% social science and 14.3% are interested in education (teaching). Those who excel in these professions had a significant market share in business ranging from 2.8% to 21.4%.

Figure 4.3 Nepalese students in Higher Professions
(Source: CNSUK Survey 2008)

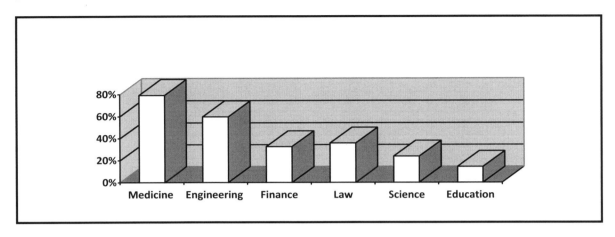

Trying to determine the impact of enterprise activities on the British economy by South Asian firms can be problematic due to a lack of information and reliable data. Yet, using the 2012 estimated figure of £25 billion as the total ethnic business contribution to the British economy, one can deduce that the 2.6% of Nepalese firms contribute to goods and services to the value of approximately £832 million per annum. Much of this derives from the 70 plus restaurants, takeaways and other food houses in English Counties and Scotland **(Fig 4.4)**.

Figure 4.4 Mini-case of the British Nepalese food sector

The Nepalese food sector consists of 82% of restaurants and take-ways altogether. The restaurant trade is complemented by groceries (retail and wholesale units) and convenience stores with a market share of 18%. The majority of businesses operate in town centres across London, Greater London, the South East of England, the Midlands, Yorkshire & Humber and Scotland.

Over 20% of restaurateurs have the names *'Gurkha'*, *'Kathmandu'* and *'Nepalese'* inscribed in their business names. In terms of identity, they represent both a country 'identifier' and heritage significance. Cuisine is made up of Indian, Nepalese and South Asian flavours to suit different various diners' tastes. Famous eating houses include the **'Great Nepalese'** (London), the **'Yeti Nepalese Restaurant** ' (Oxford), **'Namche Bazaar** (Manchester) –the UK's first Nepalese tapas bar restaurant   and **'The Gurkha Nepalese Restaurant** (Scotland). The Yeti in particular, prides itself in customer care and quality foods, as its online advertisement illustrates.

"We are a small family run business with a passion for excellent customer service and delicious foods. We want our customers to feel they are visiting a family home not a restaurant. Our food is based on healthy eating motto".(www.tripadvisor.co.uk/RestuarantReviews-Yeti). Other businesses consist of 'cash and carry' and 'convenience stores'. The unique selling point of the Nepalese restaurant trade is as follows:-

    a) Owners fierce pride in their heritage;
    b) Innovative recipes for special occasions;

> c) Simple and subtle blends of spices with distinct flavours; and
> d) Emphasis on refreshing menus and other cuisine to suit customer tastes.

Remittances

Money transfers help to maintain healthy foreign reserves (**2012**). Nepalese operate several 'money transfer' businesses including family firms in London, Greater London and Hampshire County. Most were established 2002-2011 onwards, offering 'financial intermediation' services (**2013**). As small asset companies, they benefit thousands of Nepalese and other nationalities keen to do business in the Indian sub-continent and elsewhere. (**Fig 4.5**)

Figure 4.5 Case Study of Quick and Easy Remittance Company

Yogendra Shrestha is Director of **Quick and Easy Remittance**, a company he established in 2010. A graduate from London Metropolitan University and Chartered Certified Accountant, his company is a partner of Himal Remit, has over 2,000 payment points in Nepal. His company's success lies in offering an easy money transfer service 'at a competitive rate'. In an exclusive interview with Nepalisamaj UK (2012), Shrestha, said he was inspired to buy-into the remittance trade after arriving in the UK 1996.

"Like other Nepalese residing here, sending money to Nepal through reliable sources and with less transfer cost was a matter of worry back then. There were very few mediums which were expensive, if not risky. The potential of the market triggered me to establish Easy Remittance to serve the Nepalese community who were in need of secure, reliable and fast money transfer service".

Although there are dozens of large companies such as Western Union, MoneyGram and WorldRemit, Shrestha explained that his firm's services are quite distinct from other remittance companies. The company invests in quality staff training to 'provide efficient and personalised service to all our customers'. A consistent pricing strategy is in place and this is possible through partnership with the Himalayan Bank Limited in Nepal.

Like most Nepalese-owned remittance companies, using the bank channel, Easy Remittance said that customers' use of unregistered companies meant it was difficult to offer competitive rates. 'People don't recognise the risks they are taking until and unless any incident occurs', Shrestha admitted. Despite industry and other challenges, the British-based Nepalese entrepreneur is confident about the future of Quick and Easy Remittance;

"We are definitely planning to expand the business. For now we are just focusing on the UK market. Due to the new rules and regulations for payment institutions, we still need more time to bring our business on the track smoothly. After that (process –the author's emphasis) we plan to expand in Europe. If everything goes as planned, we will definitely have few branches in the UK soon."

(**Source** http://www.nepalisamajuk.com/interview/919-hundi-is-the-only-problem-faced-by-all-of-us-regardless-of-so-much-of-awareness.html)

South Asian remittance inflows rose from 17% in 2005 to 27% in 2012 to shore up weak exports. They represent an important source of income for these countries' GDP: **Nepal** (24.7%), Bangladesh (12.2%), Sri Lanka (10.1%), India (3.7%) and Pakistan (5.7%). Although India received $US70 billion in 2013, Nepal's remittances represented the highest recipient as a share of its GDP.

Nepalese migrant workers are an important economic resource for Nepal with remittances accounting for nearly quarter of the country's GDP alone. Private capital plays a critical role for stabilising the region's balance of payments given the size of the area's current deficit. It covers daily consumption, repayment of loans, household property, education and capital formation (**2011 –see also Fig 4.6**).

Figure 4.6 Remittances inflows to Nepal 1993-2013

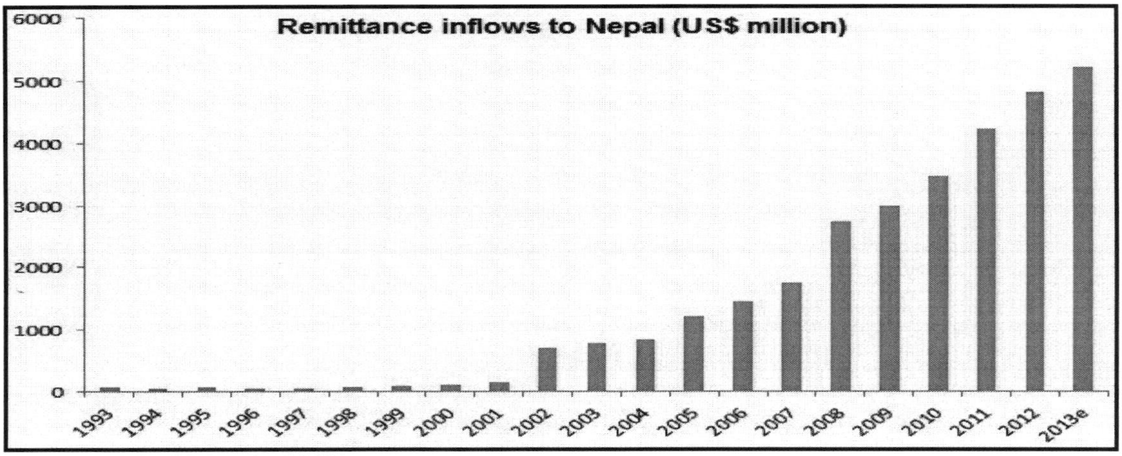

(Source: World Bank, 2012)

Creative Industries

Besides their religious diversity, Nepalis culture is imbedded in all aspects of business and industry. In spite of having a small market share in the creative industries, Nepalese dominate segments of **visual arts, film, print and electronic media**, along with other communications media. These creative elements help inform and guide the wider publics about the contribution of this section of the South Asian community to the British cultural economy.

Celia Washington established the **Kathmandu Contemporary Arts Centre (2007)** as a British charity to help raise funds for a similar facility in Nepal. Its mission is to offer Nepalis and other international artists opportunities to showcase their work and learn from other producers. Legend has it that Nepal's most profound expertise lies in its architecture. In the 13th century the Nepali architect, Arniko, travelled to Lhasa and the Mongo capital in Beijing, bringing with him the design of the pagoda, thus changing the face of religious temples across Asia. Veteran curator, Sangeeta Thapa, is also a founder/director of the KCAC and she explained the importance of the centre;

"Even today, Kathmandu, is a city that inspires artists around the world. Keeping this in mind, I feel that a Centre that brings together artists, musicians, writers and poets to a multifunctional space that reveres the past and at the same time is in tune with global trends and international artists, is essential to give a renewed vision and vigour to the contemporary art scene in Nepal. I am delighted to be working with Celia Washington"
http://www.kathmanduarts.org/Kathmandu_Arts/sangeeta.html

Another significant cultural edifice, is the **Gurkha Museum**, one of five such facilities established in Winchester (1973). It commemorates the service of Gurkhas to the British Crown since 1815. To safeguard this vital heritage, curators have conserved records and artefacts pertaining to the old Indian Army Gurkha Brigade, the post-partition Bridge of Gurkhas and the present Brigade of Gurkhas. Since the 1970s, the museum has been exhibiting the contribution of a section of Nepalese to Britain's war efforts – past and present. **http://www.cityofwinchester.co.uk/Museums/Military/Gurkha/gurkha.html** The motto of the museum typifies the Gurkhas' courage and resilience *"KAPHAR HUNNU BHANDA MORNU RAMRO CHHAA"* (It is better to die than live a coward).

The **Nepali Film Association UK (2011)** was established to bring together various talents to celebrate creativity. The company works with film companies, music producers, dancers and other artists to promote Nepalese heritage through the fusion of films and documentaries. The association was instrumental in promoting the movie *Dhanda*.

Added to the film segment, is **Nepali TV (2005)** created to provide quality language television programmes for the Nepalese diaspora. As the first channel of its kind, programmes are broadcast to over 1.2 million viewers across 60 countries and continents including the UK, Europe, the Middle East and some parts of North Africa.

Nepalese have also founded publishing enterprises – both online and paper-based publications - such as newspapers and so forth. These media give coverage to various cultural, economic, education, political and related issues affecting Nepalese - home and in the diaspora. **(Fig 4.7)**

Figure 4.7 Mini-cases of Nepali publishing houses

- Described as a 'great visionary', J.B. Tandon collaborated with Malmukund Prasad Joshi to publish the **Sagarmatha Times** *(ST),* first produced in the UK 1992. Initially, copies were hand written along with press clippings from Nepal. Later, an English edition of the magazine was introduced in the UK and Europe. The ST provides information and news on the Nepali community. The publishers are keen to use new technology to improve the magazine's quality. **www.thesagarmathatimes.com/**
- Nepali entrepreneur, Rajendra Kandel, founded **Europe Ko Nepali Patra Limited** (2006), to publish newspapers for distribution and sale across Britain and Europe. His co-director, Dr Chandra Laksamba, an academic researcher, is also a founding director of **Gurkha Voice & Gurkhali Aawaz Ltd**, incorporated in 2011.
- Businessman, Bijaya K.D. Thapa, established **Everest Media UK Limited** (2004) and published *The Voice of London ('Chautari')*. The paper's aim is to produce news, features and related current affairs in Nepalese language. Thapa acknowledged that it was *"hard to gather all the information, reports and news especially in a country like the UK in our Nepalese language"*. **http://www.nepalisamajuk.com/newsarchvbd.php?fldNID=48**
- One of the authoritative publications of this emerging South Asian community, is *Nepalis in the United Kingdom: An Overview* **(CNSUK, 2012)**. The publishers paid tribute to the all-round support given to members of this South Asian ethnic community, emphasising that the publication was dedicated to *"Nepalis, who as Gurkhas, dedicated their lives to Britain for the last two hundred years. The British public has demonstrated empathy, love and support for Nepalis in their pursuit of integration in the UK including their campaign for justice for the Gurkhas. For Nepalis and Nepali organisations in Britain who have painstakingly given information, labour and money for this study and other communities that helped to promote integration."* **(Ibid)**

Allied Creative Segments

The Arts Council of England's report **(2003)** on cultural diversity did not capture the versatility of arts and culture within the Nepalese community. Yet there is evidence to suggest that members are making strides in the creative industries. Many Nepalese aged 26 to 40 have exploited 'gap-opportunities' to establish creative segments - ranging from soft furnishings and portrait photography - to musical entertainment.

Sarmila Rai who is known for her accounting skills established **Namaskar Events Limited** in 2010. The business offers a flexible delivery, set up and collective service; hiring items and allowing clients to create self-displays or fitting chair covers. Namaskar's products include floral arrangement-designs, weddings, furniture and related services.

Since 2006, portrait photographer, Dipesh Gurung has headed **Rani Portraits**. Before arriving in Britain, Gurung lived in East Africa and America acquiring experience and professional training in linguistics. He is fluent in Nepali, Hindi, French, Kiswahili,

Gurung and English. As an accomplished guitarist, the Nepali's work consists of photo shoots in Asia, Europe and Africa.

With an impressive portfolio of clients, there is no doubt that Rani will continue building market share on 'professional wedding photography' and other services for key cultural and social events.

Sapan Kumari Rai created **Sapan Entertainment Limited** in 1992 with the aim of offering services around themed events; namely parties, weddings and special celebrations, Christmas & New Year fetes, charity programmes, as well as promotions and exhibitions. The business is renowned for its combined 'offerings' of live band and Karaoke music, pulsating sound systems and effective lighting systems suitable for clients from disparate backgrounds.

Other smaller firms such as **Vegas Sound House** and **Vision Sansar** have developed individual niche markets to meet the needs of Nepalis and other diverse groups in London, the Southeast and other regional counties.

The newspaper trade is supported by small technology enterprises engaged in providing computing, website maintenance and allied IT services for clients in London and the South East regions respectively. Indeed, by setting up creative firms, Nepalese are following the 'enterprise footprint' of other South Asian communities, by increasing participation in the arts thereby mirroring diversity and showcasing the integration of minority ethnic arts forms within a broader national cultural mix. Theirs too, represent the growing influence that global creative products have on the beliefs, and values of modern technology in Britain as a whole.

Healthcare Sciences

Nearly 80% of Nepali students are keen on the medical profession given that Gurkhas aged 60 plus experience ill health - hypertension, diabetes and obesity - to name a few (**2010**). Another study conducted by Casey (**Casey, 2010**) showed that young male Nepalis living in the Rushmoor area, had incidences of heroin use.

Other social determinants affecting the sections of this community include 'bullying and perceived risk of knife crime in their neighbourhoods' (**CNSUK, 2012**). These are followed by joblessness, poor information of access to essential public services and unwillingness to secure benefits because of cultural and language difficulties, especially involving women and the elderly.

As part of their attempt to seek broader representation in the healthcare profession, Nepalese formed networks mostly between 1985 and 2008. Two prominent organisations are the **Nepalese Doctors' Association UK** and the **Nepalese Nurses' Association UK** (**Fig 4. 8**).

Figure 4.8 Mini-cases of Nepalese Healthcare Associations

The Nepalese Doctors Association UK (NDAUK) was established in 1985 as a charity and opened to all Nepalese doctors residing in the UK. Although there are no exact figures, estimates suggest that there are hundreds of medical practitioners of Nepalese origin in Britain. The association aims to:

- Promote comradeship among Nepalese doctors in the UK;
- Provide a forum for regular meeting;
- Publish newsletter/souvenir brochures to exchange ideas, news and views;
- Contribute to the development of the health service in Nepal within our capacity;
- Sponsor charities in Nepal and the UK;
- Establish links with similar associations in Nepal and elsewhere; and
- Facilitate exchange of medical students and doctors between Nepal. .

Members of the NDAUK come from various medical and educational institutions across different UK Regions including London, Midland Counties, North West and Scotland. Specialities comprise anaesthesia, general practice, medicine, obstetrics, ophthalmology, paediatrics, psychiatry and surgery.

Another network, is the **Nepalese Nurses' Association UK (NNAUK)**; it was formed in 2008 and has around 1000 members. A significant number hold membership of the Royal College of Nurses (RCN).

Business and the Professions

British-based Nepalese firms have an average market share of 5% in business and the professions (BPS) trade. Services relate to security, financial (accounting, taxation and mortgages), and legal. Owners are committed to offering quality provision to their own community and non-Nepalese as well. Public information on these firms suggests that owners are diligent in researching markets to determine customer service-demands.

Other considerations are owners tendency to position or locate firms in areas where they can maximise advantage of complementary sectors in health and social care, travel and logistics, among others. In a random sample of about 25 BPS cluster firms, the findings revealed that:-

- 20% of firms provided 'freelance', 'premium' and other types of security services.
- 52% offered financial services across the board.
- 24% provided legal services viz., legal consultancy' to 'immigration.
- Firms had operations in London, Southeast, the Home Counties and Northern Ireland.

Social Enterprise

Social entrepreneurship is quite common amongst the British Nepalese community. Having a profound sense of social responsibility is important to both cultural and faith traditions. Besides Gurkha organisations, there are other organisations representing multiple concerns and interests of Nepalese. The following groupings reflect key professional and career segments of this segment of the British South Asian community:

- Society of Nepalese Engineers UK.
- British Nepali Lawyers Association.
- Britain Nepal Chamber of commerce.
- Nepal Business Association.
- Nepalese Highly Skilled Migrants Group.
- Nepalese Ex-Police Association
- Nepalese Financial Students' Association.

The **Greater Reading Nepalese Community Association** (GRNCA) is a registered local charity that was established in April 2008. As a reputable, pioneering organisation, it works with Nepalese communities including ex-Gurkha families by promoting cross-cultural understanding. The association's website stated that,

"The aims are integrating in the British systems and society in a meaningful way; by enhancing overall quality of life of its members and transforming to a happy, healthy and harmonious big society. Events and activities are primarily focussed towards educating and training, awareness raising, organising events, and providing necessary support and rendering advice services to vulnerable group of the society namely children, youths and elderly." (**http://www.grnca.org/aboutus.php**) The unique selling point of social enterprises amongst Nepalese can be captured possibly, in this way (**Fig 4.9**)

Figure 4.9 Unique Selling Point (USP) of British Nepalese Social Entrepreneurship
(Source: Nepalis in the United Kingdom: An Overview, pp 132-138)

In reviewing the work of professional organisations versus 'integration through organisational social capital', the Centre for Nepal Studies United Kingdom (CNSUK) highlighted these attributes of social engineering:-
- Community bonding to promote mutual trust, understanding and solidarity;
- A high sense of organisational mobilisation and activism;
- Building of a dynamic 'civic' virtue in society;
- Preserving diversity and staking out territory for multiculturalism;
- Pride in British Nepali nationhood;
- Dedicated to attracting more non-Nepali individuals and groups to cultural and social events;
- Mobilisation of bridging social capital to gain legitimacy and credence; and
- Using the 'Gurkha' settlement campaign as a 'positive force' for the good of civic society.

However, Nepalese also face increasing challenges in their attempt to sustain social enterprise activities. The CNSUK survey (**2008**) observed that nearly 20% were affected by unemployment, poor English Language skills and ill-health. Approximately 21% had security issues (fear of crime) and 30% had education issues relating to finding proper schools for children and level of parents' qualifications. Other issues were limited skills and employment training.

Business Location

Location is important for owners due to the spatial distribution of the Nepalese community coupled with 'other business relationships, social interests' and the type of trading environment. For instance, one entrepreneur when asked why he chose the Southeast for his business replied:

"I always wanted to return……...so we were constantly watching over –keeping an eye for opportunities in this area too. We are always aspiring to expand and continue our cause to bring Nepalese goods and services (author's emphasis) to achieve greater recognition"
(2012).

As is customary in preceding chapters, Nepalese also trade in goods and services across the UK. Invariably, whilst most of their community activities are in the South East Region or eastern England, they also operate in the Home Counties, Wales and Scotland. For Nepalese entrepreneurs therefore, geography is essential to both commercial and social enterprise development as the table below illustrates (**Table Fig 4.3**).

Table 4.3: Industry Sector by Business Location
(Source: textual analysis of Nepalese business-organisations by area profile December 2015)

Main Industry Sector	UK Regional Location
Business and the Professions	London, Southeast, Home Counties, Wales and Scotland.
Construction & Engineering	London, Southeast, Home Counties, Wales and Scotland.
Creative Industries	London, Southeast and Home Counties.
Food and Hospitality	London, Southeast, Home Counties, Wales, Scotland, Ireland.
Education & Training	London, Southeast, Home Counties, Wales and Scotland.
Health & Social Care	London & other English Regions, Wales, Scotland & Ireland.
Social Enterprise	London and other English Regions, Wales, Scotland & Ireland.
Travel & Logistics	London, Southeast and Home Counties.

Despite limited information in the public domain, it was still reasonably easy to access the contribution of British-based Nepalese entrepreneurs to the economy. Large bits of information (converted or translated into narrative and data) were obtained from online sources including the *'Lankan Times'*. Young business persons in particular, were opened to new ideas on profiling firms thereby creating greater access to goods and services produced by Nepalese. It was both fascinating and insightful, to observe the level of enthusiasm shown by officials of the CNSUK in 'volunteering' information on single firms, professional bodies and social enterprises in sectional areas of Britain.

Apart from the cultural and social dynamics of this South Asian group, attempts were made to cover vital commercial and processional sectors (of business and industry). Since they represent the crux of this book, case studies and their mini-versions were maximised to enable readers to access the actual contribution of Nepalese to the British economy.

Nevertheless, there are various challenges and opportunity-prospects for emerging British Nepalese entrepreneurial culture. This section highlights issues affecting firms in different industry sectors alongside of increasing chances in national and international trade markets as well as potential for further development and growth. There is no doubt that despite inevitable challenges, it is possible that business owners from all backgrounds can secure market advantage based upon strategic knowledge of the industry sector and segment they operate (**Table 4.4**).

Table 4.4 Challenges and Opportunity-Prospects for British Nepalese
(Source: textual analysis of firms and social enterprises, December 2015)

Industry Challenges	Sector Opportunity-Prospects
• *Business and the Professions:* approximately 100% of firms are in taxation, financial, money remittances and allied business services.	• The Nepalese BPS sector can secure market share by integrating financial, business and other such services with technical assistance and enterprise support for micro firms.
• *Construction & Engineering:* over 50% of Nepalese showed an interest in the 'engineering' sciences.	• Existing 'technical' practices should engage with young people who are pursuing studies in this field. This will help prepare them for enterprise start-ups.
• *Creative Industries*: little is known about the Nepalese community's annual festivals and allied creativity.	• CNSUK and other emerging ''centres of excellence' can use annual festivals to publicise the contribution of Nepalese artists and cultural producers to the British economy.
• *Food*: only narrow sections of mainstream and/or online media have been discussing Nepalese cuisine.	• Young Nepalese can be trained in food and hospitality to equip them with requisite skills. Efficient management of firms will help improve market share and enhance profits.
• *Education & Training*: less than 5% of Nepalese are educated at Higher/Further Education levels.	• Professionals should donate time-resources to help young Nepalese. Businesses can offer bursaries to improve attainment levels.

• *Health & Social Care*: 78.9% of Nepalese were keen to pursue medicine according to 2008 CNSUK Study.	• Medical practitioners should have viable internships at existing Nepalese practices or other establishments. Mentoring programmes for young Nepalese with the aptitude for medicare should be considered.
• *Social Enterprise*: 90% of Nepalese celebrate annual festivals, although these activities are limited to London or the South East.	• Annual events can be used to showcase the cultural and economic asset contribution of Nepalese social entrepreneurship. 'Acts' of social enterprise that impact on local, national, regional and international community 'markets' should be publicised widely.
• *Travel & Logistics*: 60% of firms are operating in this trade, but are limited to segmented spheres of operation.	• Thousands of Nepalese and other travellers are keen on the exotic nature of Nepal as a country. Tour operators can develop holistic services allied with environmental education, leisure and adventure tourism to facilitate competitive advantage.

Conclusion

This chapter examined in some detail, the organisation and performance of the newly-emerging British-Nepalese enterprise culture. Their contribution was analysed to the value of tens of millions to the British coffers. The Centre for Nepal Studies UK (CNSUK) gave the author permission to use elements of its authoritative survey (**2008**) to profile British-located Nepalese firms and enterprise organisations included in this chapter.

Newspaper clippings and other credible web-based sources were also used to capture owners' participation in key business sectors. Sample interviews were included on business owners and professionals to supplement information on key sectors that may not have been available for members of this particular South Asian segment.

A brief account of Nepal as a country and citizens' migratory trends to the UK especially over the last 10 years, were also discussed. The limitations placed on the author and other supporters due to sparse information and data-material on Nepalese business formation rates in Britain did not prevent a reasonable assessment being made of enterprise activities of this emerging South Asian group.

Interestingly, sections of the young British Nepalese community acknowledged this book by sharing individual and group stories on Facebook, LinkedIn and other social networking platforms. This type of enthusiasm is proof of the way in which South Asians generally, are optimising multi-media channels to discuss trends in their respective communities whilst trading in goods and services. In the process, they're constantly promoting individual and group cultural heritage(s) across mass market frontiers. In the next chapter we will examine '***The Durability of Pakistani Industries***'.

Notes

CNSUK
The Centre for Nepal Studies UK or '*CNSUK*' conducted a full-length study on the Nepalese immigrant population. This authoritative study covered community, culture, education, employment, immigration and a host of related issues of concern to this newly-established South Asian ethnic grouping.

Census Figures
The Nepalese population has varied over the years, from single-digit thousands to tens of thousands (Office for National (2011: CNSUK 2012). Much of this is due to the dispersion of 75% of Nepalese, ex-Gurkhas inclusive who live in England, especially the Southeast plus other UK Regions.

Literacy
Only about 28% of members from this South Asian (ethnic community) are educated at 'GCE' level. Just over 10% are qualified at 'undergraduate/postgraduate levels. Over half of all Nepalese are of school age; that is, under-15s.

Enterprising
Although mainstream statistics on ethnic firms exclude the contribution of Nepalese businesses, anecdotal evidence suggests that business-members from this community contribute an estimated £832 million per annum to the British economy. Much of this can be evidenced by the number of food companies, retail and wholesale firms including convenience stores, along with related businesses and the professions combined.

Remittances
During 1993 and 2013, Nepalese nationals' remittances contributed to 24.7% of Nepal's GDP (2012), the highest for all South Asian countries. Remittance inflows to the region were as follows: Afghanistan US$726 million, Bangladesh US$15,053 million, India US$71,000 million, Nepal US$6,229 million, Pakistan US$17,058 million and Sri Lanka US$7,202 million (2014). As a percentage of GDP, money transfers ranged from 3.5% to 28.8% for the 6 South Asian countries (Adapted from *World Bank Migration and Remittance Fact book*, October 2014 & 'Migration and Development Brief 24', *The World Bank*, April 13, 2015). .

Social Enterprise

An important feature of the British Nepali community, are the scores of agencies and quasi-institutions founded by professionals and lay persons. These enterprises consisted of engineers, students and ex-service personnel and various other [highly] skilled migrant groups including healthcare specialists (*Nepalis in the United Kingdom: An Overview*, Centre for Nepal Studies UK, pp132-138).

Web Links

www.tripadvisor.co.uk/RestuarantReviews-Yeti

http://www.kathmanduarts.org/Kathmandu_Arts/sangeeta.html

http://www.cityofwinchester.co.uk/Museums/Military/Gurkha/gurkha.html

http://www.nepalisamajuk.com/newsarchvbd.php?fldNID=48

http://www.grnca.org/aboutus.php

Selected References

Sims, Jessia Sims: *Soldiers, Migrants and Citizens – The Nepalese in Britain*, the Runnymede Trust 2008.

Nepalis in the United Kingdom: An Overview, Centre for Nepal Studies UK, pp132-138.

Office for National Statistics 2001.

"Realising the Diversity Dividend: Population Diversity and Urban Economic Development", *Environment and Planning,* 43 (2). pp. 487-504, 2011, Middlesex University, UK.

'*Migration and Development Brief*', World Bank 2012.

Nepal Standard of Living Survey 21011 , CNSUK England.

Jha, A. (2010): *Gurkha Health Camp Report*, Himalayan Development International and Nepalese Doctors' Association UK.

Casey, M (2010): *Health Needs Assessment of the Nepalese Community in Rushmoor*, NHS Hampshire 2010.

'Face-to-face with Nepalese Entrepreneur Pashupati Bhandari', *NepalisSamajUK,* 9 October 2012.

Chapter 5 The Durability of Pakistani Industries

"There are the young men and women tuned in to the accelerating pace of change in the Business and Public Sector landscape" – **British Pakistani Trust.**

Introduction

This chapter looks at the exemplary model of entrepreneurship among British Pakistanis. In spite of labour discrimination and other challenges, sections of this community represent leading minority enterprises in the country. In effect, they have a very influential place in British society. On completion of this chapter therefore readers should be able to:

- Understand the migration journey of Pakistanis to Britain;
- Learn about their successes in business and the professions;
- Understand their cultural and social values systems;
- Recognise the British Pakistani enterprise contribution; and
- Gain insights into the challenges and prospects of this group in the 21st century.

Origins

Today's Pakistani Muslims (prior to partition were of Indian Muslim heritage) including those from Kashmir and Sindh, arrived in Britain in the mid-17th century as *lascars* and sailors in city ports. Earlier arrivals married British wives because they were few South Asian women in the country at the time. Others came to the UK as scholars, and by 1945 there were 832,500 Muslim Indian soldiers most of whom were recruited from what is now Pakistan.

Pakistanis worked in Birmingham munition factories and after the Second World War, most remained, taking up job offers while others who arrived in the 1950s-1960s as Commonwealth citizens, secured employment in textiles, manufacturing, car production and food processing industries. Many were qualified teachers, doctors and engineers.

When the UK experienced a decline in manufacturing in the 1970s, Pakistanis were among many who became unemployed. Those with little education particularly in the Midlands and North of England, resorted to self-employment in the transport logistics sector (becoming taxi or cab drivers).

The last census figures showed that 1,125,000 residents were ethnically Pakistanis, making up 1.27% of the total UK population (**ONS, 2011**), with numbers increasing since the 1960s. (**Table 5.1**) The largest concentration of Pakistanis is in the:

- West Midlands (232,650);
- Yorkshire and the Humber (220,275);
- London (223,797);
- South-East (88,087); and
- East of England (58, 3875).

The remaining English Counties, Wales, Scotland and Northern Island make up 125,325 or 11.4% of total Pakistanis combined.

Table 5.1 Growth in the number of Pakistanis in the UK
(Source: ONS England 2011)

Year	Population	+% (average)
1961	25,000	-
1971	119,000	+29%
1981	296,000	+40%
1991	477,00	+62%
2001	747,00	+63%
2011	1,125,000	+66%

Notes: the figures and percentages have been rounded for uniformity

Socio-economic Indicators

Pakistani pupils have varied attainment levels compared to other UK learners. Girls have a GCSE pass rate of 86% compared to boys' 81% according to 2013 estimates in **Table 5.2**. Unemployment (12.8% to 20.5%) and 'inactivity rates' (21.3% to 63.6%) for Pakistani males and females vary, with half of all working-age women experiencing chronic joblessness **(2001)**. An estimated 60% of Pakistanis live within the 'low income household' thus making them part of the 'material deprivation' index in the UK.

British Pakistanis have an estimated 73% home ownership as well as 16% for both 'social' and 'private' renting accordingly (2011).

Table 5.2 Attainment of 5 or more A*-C GCSE Grades by key minorities
(Source: Department for Education, June 2015)

Pupils by ethnicity (Boys)	2008	2009	2010	2011	2012	2013
White (including British)	58.5%	64.7%	71.2%	76.85%	78.25%	78.55%
Indian	74.3%	78.8%	85.0%	87.6%	89.3%	88.6%
Pakistani	**52.7%**	**61.2%**	**69.8%**	**77.4%**	**79.9%**	**81.0%**
Bangladeshi	56.0%	65.5%	72.0%	79.4%	82.9%	81.5%
African	53.5%	65.7%	71.6%	79.1%	80.5%	81.3%

Caribbean	46.9%	56.4%	64.2%	72.2%	75.3%	76.3%
Chinese	80.9%	84.1%	87.6%	90.6%	91.9%	90.9%
Other Ethnic Groups	49.8%	60.%	65.9%	73.9%	76.6%	79.3%
ALL BOYS	59.1%	65.8%	71.9%	77.0%	79.8%	79.6%
Pupils by ethnicity (Girls)	**2008**	**2009**	**2010**	**2011**	**2012**	**2013**
White (including British)	66.65%	72.1%	78.2%	82.55%	85.05%	84.85%
Indian	82.7%	85.8%	89.7%	92.8%	93.1%	93.6%
Pakistani	**64.0%**	**72.0%**	**78.4%**	**84.1%**	**85.6%**	**86.4%**
Bangladeshi	68.9%	73.8%	79.9%	86.2%	87.6%	88.4%
African	87.6%	91.2%	92.3%	95.0%	94.2%	95.2%
Caribbean	60.8%	69.9%	76.2%	82.6%	83.9%	84.5%
Chinese	87.6%	91.2%	92.3%	95.0%	94.2%	95.2%
Other Ethnic Groups	62.5%	68.4%	77.3%	84.1%	82.8%	85.6%
ALL GIRLS	68.2%	73.9%	79.5%	84.0%	86.3%	86%

The above figures show the steady progress of young Pakistanis over the past five years. Despite multiple advantage, female Pakistani learners are competing favourably in the education attainment rankings when compared to both white and other minority ethnic learners.

Enterprising British Pakistanis

British Pakistanis are engaged in multiple industry sectors - food and hospitality, creative industries, business and professions, health and social care, personal care, manufacturing (including fashion textiles), technology futures, transport logistics and social enterprise.

Their participation in local politics and faith matters also has implications for other minorities. According to a leading foundation, Pakistanis are highly altruistic and make a significant impact on the UK and overseas.

"Pakistanis are one of the most philanthropic communities in the world; they contribute approximately £45 billion to the UK economy and they send approximately £500 million to their home country per annum. We have the resource, the human capital, the skills and the will to build. Without our efforts, we will be unable to tackle issues such as education, health and lack of civic engagement" **(Source: http://britishpakistanfoundation.com/).**

Through their diverse businesses, many have responded to consumers' changing self-identities as trends in market practices have shown since the 1970s. According to one analyst,

"I investigate the marketing practices followed by Chinese, Pakistani and Bangladeshi retail enterprises in Cardiff and London. I found that a major focus of their marketing practices was the reinforcement of culture of origin and the perpetuation and defence of

ethnicity among their co-ethnics. These business owners (author's emphasis) facilitated building and the negotiation of self-identities by consumers on the basis of contrasting elements taken from diverse cultural representations" (2006).

Having learnt from elders' experiences, second and third generation British-Pakistanis are excelling academically and professionally. This has boosted their chances of success in business and industry as well as the professions (**Fig 5.1**).

Figure 5.1 Pakistani students in Higher Education
(Source: Higher Education Statistics Agency Ltd, 2015)

- 2007- 9,283 (2.6%)
- 2008 – 5,311 (1.4%)
- 2009- 11,033 (2.7%)
- 2010 – 11,908 (2.9%)
- 2011 – 12,710 (3.1%)
- 2012 – 13,274 (3.3%)

Notes: approximately 65,513 Pakistanis were accepted as applicants for higher education during 2017-2012.

Even though they are disproportionately represented in the total student population averaging 2.3%, Pakistanis are the third leading minority group in higher education. Many attend Brunel, De Montfort, Kingston, Birmingham, East London, Greenwich and Westminster Universities, along with University College London, to name a few.

Education priorities aside, the interplay of other 'push' and 'pull' factors, is equally relevant for Pakistanis' performance in the British labour market (self-employment inclusive). These factors include: -

- Perceived Opportunities (40%);
- Perceived business capabilities (43%);
- Fear of Failure or risk taking (31%);
- Business as a 'status symbol (71%); and
- Entrepreneurship as a good career choice (74%).

(Global Entrepreneurship Monitor 2011 & Gallup Business Journal, 1 August 2012)

Self-employment

Much research has been done to measure UK self-employment by ethnicity. Over two million minorities (**2011estimates**) represent 'employees' and 'self-employment' categories respectively. From an ethnic minority standpoint, approximately 310,034 business owners were listed in the 'self-employed' category or 6.4% are involved in entrepreneurial activities with 13.9% participating in self-employment by ethnicity (**Table 5.3**).

Table 5.3 Employees/Self-employment by key UK Ethnic Minorities
(Source: Urwin, Peter: Self-employment, Small Firms and Enterprise, The Institute of Economic Affairs, Britain 2011)

Ethnicity	Employee	Self employed	% Self employed
African	285,654	18,416	9.6%
Bangladeshi	107,264	17,205	13.8%
Caribbean	232,271	18,416	7.4%
Chinese	98,964	22,448	18.5%
Indian	569,363	76,980	11.9%
Pakistan	**211,553**	**79,214**	**27.2%**
Nepali	50,000	271	2.6%
Other Asian *	220,356	26,523	10.7%
Other	362,109	50,832	12.3%
Grand Total	**2,087,534**	**310,034**	**6.4%**

*Notes: In this instance * 'Other Asian' refers to Afghanis and Sri Lankans among others.*

Statistics for the Pakistani group indicate that despite labour market discrimination, members are able to compete in niche markets. **Table 5.3** identifies this ethnic group with the highest (27.2%) business ownership rate for all South Asians and minority ethnic groups altogether.

Yet, similar to other South Asians, Pakistanis have identical cuisines though varied in distinctive flavours, tastes and styles. Such differences can of course help to illustrate the unique selling point (USP) of eating houses (**Fig 5.2**).

Figure 5.2 Mini-cases of British Pakistani Cuisine

The history of Pakistani food in Britain is legendary as most others particularly Indian and Bengali cuisine which is nearly 400 years old. After Indian-born Deen Mahomet founded the first curry house – **Hindostanee Coffee House -** in London in 1809, others grew rapidly thereafter across the British Isles.

The 1911-founded **The Shafi** owned by Mohammed Wayseem and Mohammed Rahim was taken over by Dharam Lal Bodua and run by an English manager with employees such as Israil Miah and Gofur Miah who later started businesses. Abdul Aziz opened a café shop selling curry and rice in Birmingham 1945. Rashid Ali moved from a café shop in London to Cardiff to open his own establishment.

Rana Riaz-ul-hassan Sabir founded **Mirch Masala** in 1995. The restaurant's specialities are karahi and barbecue dishes. The former teacher left Pakistan in search of a better future and after working for 12 years in restaurants, he started his own. The business attracts celebrities such as cricketers - Imran Khan, Rameez Raja and Courtney Walsh. In 2003, the business was voted one of the top '*100 restaurants of the UK*' by the *Evening Standard*. What is the key to Sabir's success?

"*We ensure that the quality of food and the services we render remain supreme, and the departing smile of every customer is our success certificate. I consider problems in the business as a challenge which can be solved by hard work, persistence, devotion and pursuing a logical path*" (**2010**). His plans are to consolidate operations by ensuring adequate professional staff, quality food, efficient customer services and intelligent marketing strategies to sustain the business overall.

It is estimated that 2,500 to 3,000 Pakistani food houses exist. Pakistani cuisine is similar to North Indian type(s). It is also an exotic blend of Arabic, Afghan, Central Asian, Persian and Turkish flavours. The popular Balti dish has roots in Birmingham where it was reportedly created by a Pakistani (Kashmiri) in 1977. Pakistani restaurants are located across Britain.

Remittances

The UK is a major 'beneficiary-exporter' of remittances which have a twin economic and social benefit for Pakistan. Pakistan received $13 billion in 2012 as inward remittances, benefitting from large numbers of unskilled migrants in oil-rich Gulf Cooperation Council (GCC) countries (**World Bank, 2012**).

South Asian remittances rose from 17% in 2005 to 27% in 2012 to boost weak exports. These represent income for Nepal (22%), Bangladesh (11%), Sri Lanka (7.9%), India (13.9) and **Pakistan** (5.7%) - **Table 5.4**.

Table 5.4 Migrant Remittances inflows to Pakistan 2007-2012

Year	Remittances (US$ billion)	% of the GDP
2007	6.0	4.2
2008	7.0	4.3
2009	8.7	5.4
2010	9.7	5.5
2011	12.3	5.8
2012	13.9	6.0
Total	**US$67 billion**	**4.89**

(Source: Migration and Development brief, World Bank, 2012)

Creative Industries

Pakistanis have a growing market share in the creative industries sector, combining media**, music, film, and publishing and allied literary production**. As of 2013, they owned an estimated 22 media companies including television channels. Programmes features are current affairs-news, general entertainment, Islamic lifestyle and other issues.

Bollywood dominates much of South Asia's cinematography but efforts are being made to promote 'Lollywood', the Pakistani film industry by encouraging young UK-based

Pakistani filmmakers to advance the industry beyond the so-called 'traditional pale'. **(Fig 5.3)**

Figure 5.3. A Snapshot of British Pakistani Audio-Visual Segments

The Pakistani film industry is known as **'Lollywood'**, a term first used by columnist Saleem Nasir in 1989. Pakistani film releases in the UK have grossed millions, a fact that is relatively unknown to the public in general. The South Asian Cinema Foundation (SACF) has been successfully '*promoting a positive film culture*' (**http://sacf.co.uk/about-sacf**).

Among some of the leading Pakistani artistic entrepreneurs honoured are; filmmaker, lyricist, screen writer and poet Sampooran Singh Kalra, popularly by his pen name, Gulzar. A festival of Gulzar Films was commissioned in 2010 while a similar fest was held in honour of filmmaker Saeed Akhtar in 2008. [*Note: Gulzar was born in pre-partition India*]

In 2010 three filmmakers – Atif Ahmad Quershi, M Umar Saeed and Kiran Mustaq, produced '*I Am Agha*'. This film is part of **Pakistan Calling**, a new initiative aiming to promote Pakistan and increase awareness of social and cultural issues affecting the country. Anwar Akhtar founder of the website, **The Samsoa**, said this about the initiative,

"*Everyone has an interest in Pakistan but the films reflect that the country is not a failed state. There are some extraordinary welfare organisations doing a lot of good work there –such as the Edhi Foundation and The Citizens Foundation and by showing the work they do, we can engage British Pakistanis to be a force for good in terms of development in Pakistan*" (**http://www.thenational, Huma Quershi, June 4, 2013**).

British Pakistanis also operate other media such as **Ary Digital, Geo News, PTV Global, DM, Islam Channel, AAP TV, DM Digital**. They are complemented by radio stations - **Asian Sound** (Manchester), **Sunrise** and **Kismat Radios** (London), **Radio XL** (Birmingham) and other digital communications. They also feature in popular sitcoms such as *Eastenders, Coronation* Street and *Emmerdale*.

Mishal Husain is a newsreader and presenter for the BBC (and at the time of writing), Radio 4. Saira Khan hosts the BBC children's programme, *Beat the Boss*. In 2006 she established **Miamoo**, specialising in natural skincare products sold in Boots stores nationwide (*Source http://www.sairakhan.co.uk/businesswoman-saira-khan.html*). Anita Anand is a Hindu Pakistani who is also a BBC presenter and journalist. Martin Bashir is a Christian Pakistani who previously worked for ITV before leaving to work for the American Broadcasting Company (ABC).

Adil Ray of **Citizen Khan** fame has helped boost public interest in Pakistanis traditions in Britain. As a practising mass media specialist, he started his career in 1994 after which time he worked for the BBC, Choice FM and other broadcasting media. The character of Mr Khan proved so popular that the BBC commissioned a series of episodes beginning August 2012.

Music

Indians and Pakistanis have a shared Punjabi culture but it is the latter's music which differs in certain genres; namely movie songs, pop, rock and Sufi songs. Pakistani music is influenced by the poetic influence of the Urdu language which is noticeable in (Pakistani) Punjabi songs. Such artistry represents a fusion of Central Asian folk, Persian, Turkish, Arabic and more recently, American music respectively.

In the 1960s, **Madam Noor Jahan** one of the most prominent female South Asian singers, introduced the trend where the melody of the flute and the vocal lead the music (**Salient Features of Pakistani Punjabi Music, http://sngspk.wordpress.com/**).

Nusrat Fateh Ali Khan was described as the influential figure for 'the survival of' Pakistani music (though not exclusive to Pakistan per se). He was the first singer of such ethnicity to globalise Pakistani music and later followed by pop singers - Junaid Jamshed and Ali Azmat. In the first half of the 21st century, Shahid Nazir Ahmad, caused a media sensation with his "***One Pound Fish***" video after its popularity with British music fans (**Fig 5.4**).

Figure 5.4 Case Study **Pakistani 'singing sensation'**

Shahid Nazir Ahmad became an internet sensation (with 2 million hits) for his viral video "One Pound Fish". Later, his appearance on *The X Factor* led to a Warner Music record deal. The Lahore- born grew up in the early 1980s listening to Bollywood and Punjabi music, and would sing religious songs during school assembly. Prior to emigrating to the UK Ahmad worked for the family-owned transport company.

Following a brief stint with a Pound shop, he began working at an East End fish stall where his employer instructed him to use a trader's call to attract customers. Ahmad soon composed the song "One Pound Fish" with the lyrics:

Come on ladies, come on ladies
One pound fish
Have-a, have-a look
One pound fish
Very, very good, very, very cheap
One pound fish
Six for five pound one pound each

Since his *X Factor* appearance, Ahmad's song has been promoted by celebrities - Alesha Dixon, Timbaland (real name Timothy Zachery Mosley) and Mindless Behavior, an American boy band. In November 2012, Warner Music signed the Pakistani as a recording artist, and released a dance version of his market sales pitch. A video was also filmed featuring Bollywood-style dancers and an appearance from former weatherman, Michael Fish. Ahmad's success is certainly influencing a new generation of Pakistani [Britons] to set new trends in music.

Other musicians contributing to British entertainment culture are **Metz n Trix**, two brothers who are Bhangra rappers and music producers; Zayn Malik of the British boy band, **One Direction** and Pervez Bilgrami, lead singer of the 1980s **Alien Kulture** band.

According to one observer,
*"Pakistani pop songs have exploded onto the world scene and have become much more popular than English songs in some movies. One example of Bollywood songs making into the western film audience is the song by **Najane Kyun** ("I don't know why?"), the*

featured single on the soundtrack for 'Spiderman 2'. This album made Indian pop songs successful throughout the world and won three awards. It is artists and music like this that is bringing India pop songs to the attention of people throughout the world who never used to focus on Pakistani music before" (**2010**).

In terms of technology literacy, British Pakistanis are engaged at varying levels of multi-media such as digital, telecasting, internet access and personal/mobile phones. The following indices illustrate the affect members of this ethnic group have on the British media:

- Multiple platform ownership – 65%;
- Digital TV ownership – 89%;
- Mobile phone take-up – 91%; and
- Internet take-up – 72% (**Ofcom, 2007-2008**).

In supporting the use of digital technology (in art forms), a panel of curators selected photographer **Mahtab Hussain** for documenting the evolving identity of British Pakistanis via the *'Culture Cloud'* digital project (2012). Hussain explained that;

"I have spent three years photographing the Pakistani community whilst living in Birmingham, exploring the important relationship between identify and masculinity. My portraits reveal men who consider and present themselves as both Pakistani men, but whose lives have existed wholly in the UK. These images are an insight into a shifting section within a minority group which has a profound collective identity and belief system of its own, yet exists within the framework of the West" (**2012**).

Theatre

In the last 30 years British South Asians have also developed a vibrant theatre by blending tradition with modernity. They have fashioned unique forms of adaption within the wider performing arts, as a new generation of playwrights emerged to ply their creative trade for wider audiences. Instead of alienating audiences, British Asian theatre remains 'urgent and topical' (**Bicknell, 2013**).

Most plays explore topical issues on multiculturalism, identity, religion, culture, politics, racism, economics, education and gender. Playwrights are mostly in their late teens or early 20s, while others are matured women from a working class background. *(Ibid)*

There were a dozen theatre companies and one leading arts group across England (**2012 estimates**). However, two firms that have modernised South Asian performing arts since the late 1980, are **Tamasha Theatre Company** and **Khayaal Theatre Company (5.5)**. Both companies benefit hugely from the services of professional artists and volunteer performers from different backgrounds.

Artists and cultural producers in particular, are exposed to different innovation (stimuli). They are part of broad creative themes – ranging from culture, education and economic to social trends of the wider South Asian as well as other ethnic communities.

Table 5.5 Sample of major British South Asian/Pakistani theatre companies

Name of Company	Activities
Tamasha Theatre Company was founded in 1989 by Director Kristine Landon-Smith and actor/playwright Sudhar Bhuchar.	Played a key role in driving the crossover of South Asian culture into British mainstream. Successes include *East is East, Strictly Dandia* and the *Trouble with Asian Men*, have won acclaim from critics and audiences alike.
Khayaal Theatre Company is an award-winning production enterprise founded in 1997.	Dedicated to the production of original dramatic interpretation of classic Muslim world literature and the experience of Muslims in the modern world for the stage, radio and screen. The company has created a formula combining wisdom with humour to 'sell' their creative 'wears'. Performances include *Sun & Wind, The Mullah's Physician, Souk Stories* and *Spray from the Ocean of Attar and Rumi*.

(Source: http://www.desiblitz.com/)

Taxi driver-turned playwright, Ishy Din, is author of '***Snookered***' the popular play and in 2012, was playwright in residence at the Manchester Royal Exchange and was developing a radio play and starting a project working with young people in Tees Valley on identity issues. In praising the work of Tamasha Theatre Company, Din remarked,

"I am a writer and without Tamsaha, I'd still be a taxi driver. My voice as a northern Asian would be muted and my attempts to open a window on a largely unexplored world would be firmly shut. I have been a cabbie a long time. I sat and worked out one night that I had 160,000 conversations with people. The minute they stepped out of my cab I picked up my notepad and started scribbling things down" (**Din, 2012**).

Publishing

English language poetry holds a special place in South Asian literature (Pakistani fiction inclusive), which gained recognition in the latter part of the 20th century (**Hashmi, 1993**). The earlier success of prose originated from **Ahmed Ali, Zulfikar Ghose, Bapsi Sidhwa**, the Parsi author of *The Crow Eaters, Cracking India* (1988) and others.

British Pakistanis **Hanif Kureshi** began a prolific career with his novel, *The Buddha of Suburbia* (1990), which won the Whitbread Award. **Tariq Ali** also showed his prowess with novels, plays and TV scripts. **Aamer Hussein** compiled popular short stories and **Sara Suleri** published her literary memoir, *Meatless Days* (1989). Other short story collections and play scripts were commended by diverse readers.

Pakistani novelists writing in English have either won or been shortlisted for international awards. **Moshin Hamid** published his first novel *Moth Smoke* (2000), which won the Betty Trask Award and was a finalist for the PEN/Hemingway Award. He has since published his second novel, *The Reluctant Fundamentalist* (2007), which was shortlisted for the Man Booker Prize. Female writer, **Kamila Shamshie** who won a literary award for her first novel, was shortlisted for the John Llewelyn Rhys award for her third novel, *Kartography* (2002). She has since published her fourth novel, *Broken Verses*. **Uzma Aslam Khan** was shortlisted for the Commonwealth Writers Prize (Eurasia region) for her second novel, *Trespassing* (2003).

Members of second and third generation Pakistanis are maximising the arts to publicise issues ranging from cultural, economic, education, faith and identity to social. In pushing boundaries of style, genres and language including English and other dialectic formats, Pakistanis are reflecting that as British South Asians, they do represent a 'community within communities' (**2004**). This trend is demonstrable of the increasingly young talent emerging from this ethnic group and their parents' countries of origin (**2011**).

The last official count on the British Council's website highlighted foremost Pakistani writers, literature partners and their different genres. Examples include **Imtiaz Dharker** (poetry/film), **Nadeem Aslam** (fiction), **Mohshin Hamid** (fiction), **Safraz Mansoor** (Non-fiction), **Jack Mapanje** (poetry) and **Qaisahra Shahraz** (drama, fiction and short stories).

Newspapers

British Pakistanis also publish newspapers, periodicals and related print media to fill the void in national and international markets. Since the 1980s these publications have developed readership audiences across London and the Home Counties (**Fig 5.5**). Advertising revenue from mainstream corporations and ethnic firms is used to help underwrite production costs of a range of printed materials.

The British Pakistani press is constantly evolving with publishers moving towards 'mainstreaming' content, style and presentation to reflect new models in journalism and professional writing. These publications were founded either in the first part of the 20th century and in the mid-21st century.

Most are tabloid-sized newspapers, glitzy magazines and a wide array of periodicals dealing with concerns affecting Pakistanis and other ethnic communities in Britain and elsewhere.

The ***Tarjumaan*** is described by Chief Editor Zulfikar Ali Bhutto, as '*The Voice of the Asian Community in Europe*' (2012/2013). It promotes individuals and businesses worldwide, covering food, hospitality, the trades, professional services, politics, community affairs, travel, education and training.

However, the drawback of this glitzy magazine was its lack of gender-balanced reporting, with the coverage of business owners being predominantly male. Although women were pictured in sections of the more than 150-page 'Special Issue' of the *Tarjumaan International* (March 2010), only a few females including an educationist and fashion designer, were featured.

Publications are produced in English, Urdu and other South Asian dialects. The history of publishers is also interesting; for example, the *Asian Times* newspaper which was first published by Hansib Publications (1983) -owned by Guyanese Arif Ali.

Nonetheless in other sections of the British Pakistani media, publishers are adapting towards a more gender-focus reportage, while targeting at the same time, both the minority ethnic and mainstream mass market audiences.

Figure 5.5 Mini-cases of British-based Pakistani/South Asian Newspapers

- *Ausaf* (2002), an international Urdu daily newspaper distributed in Pakistan, Germany and London (launched 2002). Its chief editor is Mehtab Khan. Managed by the Ausaf Group of Newspapers, the paper has a global circulation of 138,000 copies.
- The ***Daily Jang*** (1939), an Urdu newspaper that was founded in India. Chief Executive & Editor-in-Chief is Mir Shakil-ur- Rahman. The paper is published in the West Midlands with a circulation of 800,000 copies daily.
- *Sisters* (2007), is the UK's first Muslim women's magazine, edited by Na'ima B. Robert. Management is committed to publishing uplifting, inspiring and enlightening material on personalities, family, community, world, tastes and other gender issues. The magazine has a circulation of tens of thousands - online and in print.
- *Asian Times* (1983), was first published by Hansib Publishing Limited, aimed at providing a platform for Asians in general, to access news, features and other information on issues affecting their communities in Britain and home countries. The Ethnic Media Group now publishes this paper with a circulation of 7,000 copies.
- *Eastern Eye* (1989), printed by *The Guardian*. It then changed hands several times until January 2009 when the Trinity Mirror Group took it over, before a management buyout that created the Ethnic Media Group (EMG). Eastern Eye is regarded as the authentic voice of British Asians in the UK, with a circulation of 25,000. (**www.magazinesabout.co.uk/Eastern+Eye**).
- *Asian Lite* (2007), founded by Anasudhin Azeez and dedicated to 'bringing back the missionary values of journalism'. It has a monthly circulation of 100,000. (**www.ethnicnow.com**)
- *Asian Trader* (1985), established as a bi-weekly publication covering news, features

and other information for convenience stores, grocers, newsagents and off-licenses. With a circulation of 40,312 copies every fortnight, this publication is also produced in Urdu & Gujarati, two community languages not found in other such magazines (**https://uk.pinterest.com/pin/292874781998266351/**).
Other publications featuring Pakistanis are *Urdu Times, Passion Islam, Emel, Muslim News, Muslim Post and Muslim Weekly* (**2012**). Pakistanis also produce and contribute to scores of online print, broadcast and media-related materials. British newspaper vendors and news agencies are also operated by South Asians including Indians and Pakistanis (**Publisher's Note: circulation figures for the above publications are based on 2013-2015 estimates**).

Overall attitudes

Over the past 10 years, the Arts Council of England has been analysing English audiences' 'attendance at specific artistic and cultural events' for strategic planning in the arts. Pakistanis had the highest access rates (**2003 estimates**) for audio-visual media (72%) which included TV, video and DVD.

They also showed a propensity for film (56%) as highlighted in previous sections of this book. Their attendance at festivals and other creative arts activities highlighted typical cultural tastes. For example, Pakistani audiences had a 54% performance rating for 'South Asian classical music' altogether (**Figure 5.6**)

Figure 5.6 Arts and Cultural Diversity Representation among Pakistanis
(Source: Focus on cultural diversity: Arts Council of England, December 2003)

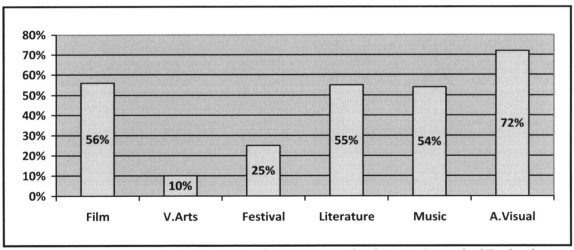

Note: The 2003 survey was by far the most diverse activity by the Arts Council of England. Despite its extensive publicity, the 2012 London Cultural Olympiad Festival was unable to provide an accurate picture of the number of minorities including South Asians, who participated. Although evaluations were done of the event, the figure of 11% for minorities attending festivities was quoted with no proper analysis done on each ethnic group's involvement.

Business Promotion

Recent media titles offer scope and opportunity for non-South Asian readers to learn about the invaluable work of Pakistanis in the field of business, industry and the professions. Two notable publications; *'Power 100: The Future Leaders'* **(2012)** and *'Women Power 100'* **(2012***)***, featured the creative industries, food, construction, healthcare, education, fashion and textiles, real estate and property, business professional services, manufacturing, information technology and social enterprise sectors accordingly.

Second and third generation British Pakistanis are making important strides into academia and the professions as sources of enrichment and leverage for competitive advantage. Quite often statistics don't reflect the true nature of British South Asians' contribution to the British economy. The 'positives' are 'drowned out' by media-driven issues; namely immigration, discrimination and prejudice, language and security matters.

Against this challenging backdrop, over a quarter or 25% of all Pakistani business owners –male and females combined – are qualified at degree levels and beyond, fusing commercial with social enterprise and/or philanthropic interests. Implicitly, the Pakistan *Power 100 Future Leaders* publication represents,

"part of a growing network of professionals determined to bring about positive change within the regions in which they live and work. They are the young men and women tuned in to the accelerating pace of change in the Business and Public Sector landscape – the trend spotters and entrepreneurs who stand to reap the biggest rewards over the next decade" **(2012). See also Table 5.6**

Table 5.6 Distinctive Competencies of Pakistanis Business Performance
(Source: Analysis of 'Power 100': The British Pakistani Trust, 2012)

Business Sector	Unique Selling Point
• **Accountancy**	Support for small businesses and high-net worth clients.
• **Architecture**	Empowering communities through a self-help sustaining process.
• **Education/Training**	Leadership and management in societal matters.
• **Fashion Textiles**	Offering bespoke designs and exclusive fabrics for global clients.
• **Financial Services**	Brand management, financial products for cross-selling markets.
• **Healthcare**	Medicare services combined with finance and education.
• **Legal Services**	Courage and fortitude to fight for the rights of the defenceless.
• **Media**	Helping to change stereotypes of South Asians in the media.
• **Real Estate**	Investments specialising in 'Shariah' compliant real estate law.
• **Social Enterprise**	Over 90% of Pakistanis believe in corporate social responsibility.

Table 5.6 highlights the diversity and versatility of British Pakistanis involvement in commerce across industry classification and owners' individual competencies. It illustrates the nature and type of economic activities owners are engaged in over a considerable period. Indeed, the cross comparisons and analysis of firm dynamics are often difficult to undertake because of the uniqueness of each firm. Yet these approaches can enable readers to access vital information on resource efficiency and the impact on levels of production and productivity, according to industry sectors.

Additionally, information in **Table 5.6** signifies the necessity for interrogating micro data to evidence broader themes and features on ethnic entrepreneurship in modern times. These themes reflect the unique selling point (USP) of firms overall, an approach or model that is seldom used by mainstream analysts when accounting for the differences in the efficiency or inefficiency of ethnic firms (**2004**).

Medicare Sciences

The state of medical education and practice in the UK is at an interesting phase. For the first time, the state examined in relative depth, the diversification and changes with respect to the composition of medicare and health practitioners. The latest figures (**2015**) showed that Pakistani GPs represented 2.2% of all UK registered doctors. There were 11,294 Pakistani doctors on the UK medical register (**GMC, 2015**) -**Fig 5.7**.

There are active UK-based Pakistani organisations such as **British Pakistani Doctors Forum (BPDF)**, **All Pakistani Physicians and Surgeons UK** along with **Pakistani Medical Association**. They provide support to doctors by helping them to find jobs and adjust to new surroundings. Dr Akmal Makdhum of the BPDF commented on the trend of Pakistani doctors coming to the UK to improve their profession –internationally:

"This is a happy augury for us in the UK and yet it has a sad tinge because Pakistan is not offering opportunities for so many young, qualified people. Our members are working on some initiatives to develop training over there and some have succeeded in doing just that. We are here to advice and support our young doctors, to flourish their careers and support them if they find any obstacles" (**2012**).

Figure 5.7 Number of South Asian doctors
(Source: General Medical Council, UK 2015)

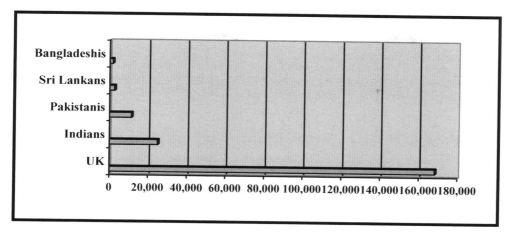

Nevertheless, career choices for medical students are hinged on individual preferences. An estimated 10,360 or 9.5% of all British Pakistani students pursued various specialities in medicine to include electives; namely *medicine and dentistry, subjects allied to medicine and biological sciences* (**Fig 5.9**).

Figure 5.8 British Pakistanis undergraduate students by subject area 2010/11
(Source: Higher Education Statistics Agency Limited, England 2012)

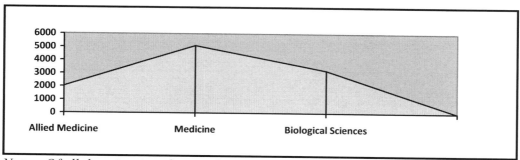

Notes: Of all the minority ethnic undergraduate students, British Pakistanis have the second highest percentage in enrolment rates for the above subjects: 5.0% in medicine and dentistry, 2.3% in subjects allied to medicine and 2.2% in biological sciences respectively.

Care Sector

Demographic changes including a growing and aging population have created enterprise opportunities for minority ethnic groups in the care sector. Busy lifestyles mean that many South Asians are unable to take care of their elderly as they would like to.

Recent trends suggest that with an ageing population such as those within minority ethnic communities, Pakistani-owned care firms are segmented according to multi-layered structures - private, local authority-sponsored and community/voluntary -type [composition]. These enterprises are registered as '*old age and nursing homes*', places for '*dementia, old age and physical disabilities*' and '*other specialist care services*' (**2011**).

To meet statutory requirements, offer value for money, satisfy customer demands and sustain operations, care operators have developed a range of healthcare sector models. Some have ventured into small respite care units while others have opted for medium-based care facilities for multiple service-users. Operators have also integrated property portfolios to complement care homes thereby increasing their asset base and competitive advantage in healthcare (**Case Study 5.9**).

Case Study 5.9 Profile of major British Pakistani Healthcare Firms

Khawar Mann is a Partner and co-head of **Apax Partners**, the healthcare team. He has led deals including General Healthcare Group Ltd, Capio, Unilabs, Apollo Hospitals and Marken. Mann was head of the Weston Medical Group plc. He is qualified in both medical sciences and law at Master's level, and is involved in charities such as the Graham Layton Trust that provides free eye care in Pakistan.

Mustafa Mohammed founded **Genix Healthcare** in 2005 to provide better access to NHS dental facilities for patients. The firm has grown rapidly with over 20 NHS Dental Practices, bringing innovation to the industry with a strong focus on staff development. Mohammed is aware of the acute shortage in the dental profession, and in 2011, he became an ambassador to the National Apprentice Programme, announcing plans to recruit 100 plus apprentices. Genix was the first to launch a programme with a commitment to increasing the workforce by a third. According to Mohammed, this significant investment will be a viable blueprint for national dental apprenticeship schemes.

Aashna House is a purpose-built care home set in a London residential area. The fully-furnished facility is equipped with television and other facilities. The spacious lounge areas provide a relaxing setting for residents from India, **Pakistan** and other South Asian backgrounds. One writer noted that Aashna *"is an unusual place that caters for exceptional cases. Residents were pioneers of the first wave of post-war Commonwealth immigration and now they are pioneers again; it seems inevitable that in future more and more elderly Asians will find themselves encouraged to go into care homes"* (**The Guardian**, **2011**).

The emergence of young minority ethnic professionals in the burgeoning UK healthcare sector, exemplifies the continuation of the indisputable contribution of first generation pioneers during the formative years of the NHS. The only difference however, is that today's British Pakistanis and other South Asian specialists, are sustaining this fine tradition of public service via the corporate route.

Successful Pakistani healthcare firms have benefitted from strategic models such as:-
- Consistent quality service;
- Alliances with public and private sector institutions;
- Investment in technical equipment and material resources;
- Recruitment of talented, experienced and corporate-driven staff;

- Efficient operational governance systems and procedures;
- Integration of care services, education, training, advocacy and promotion;
- Excellent management teams and investors; and
- International market leveraging to increase asset portfolio.

Business and the Professions

Historically, entrepreneurial activities within the South Asian community have been restricted to 'low profits; for instance, low growth industries in retail and clothing' (**2001**).

Over the passage of time, there has been a sea-change with more Pakistanis pursuing higher education and professional training (**See also Figure 5.2**). This has boosted their chances in business and enterprise careers in popular industry segments; namely accountancy and finance, travel and logistics coupled with property development and allied services.

The Pakistani *Power 100* (**2012 edition**) publication gave a 'snapshot' of nascent entrepreneurs, but it also highlighted industry trading sectors and segments. The estimated age categories of founder-owners and directors ranged from 25 to 60 plus, although there were other age categories offering innovative products and services (**Figure 5.10**).

Figure 5.10 Age group segments of Pakistani business owners
(Source: Textual analysis of The Pakistani Power 100 (2012 edition)

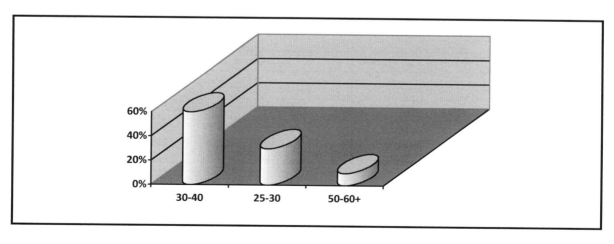

Notes: The percentage of founder/directors by age-group categories was as follows: 60% aged 30-40; 30% aged 25-30 and 10% 50-60 plus. Other British Pakistanis displayed enterprise propensity at a much younger age than those in the figure above because their families were in business and industry. Young

*professionals introduced new product and service lines to satisfy niche market demands locally, nationally and internationally (see also **Chapter** 7).*

The major of industry-business segments that British Pakistanis are engaged include:-
- Business Professional Services (*business management, events management, legal services, marketing*);
- Construction (*real estate, property development* etc.);
- Creative Industries *(media, public relations, film*);
- Education and Training;
- Personal Care (*fashion and textiles*);
- Food and Hospitality (*restaurants, take-away, retailing, hotels*);
- Health and Social Care (*care homes, medicare services etc.*);
- Information Technology (*sciences, teaching, consultancy etc.*);
- Manufacturing (*textiles, food and drink production etc.*); and
- Social Enterprise (all types of non-governmental organisations -NGOs).

The sector-segments in **Figure 5.10** illustrate the power and vitality of the modern British Pakistani enterprise culture in the 21st century. The collaboration across inter and co-ethnic markets acts as channels for the introduction of goods and services to mass markets. The industries represented also translate into significant features underpinning the organisation and performance of firms in the following manner:-
- Over 80% of enterprises were founded in the early 21st century;
- 25% were women straddling between public, private and social enterprise;
- Around 30% of owners were committed to a growth acquisition strategy;
- Diversification was used as a strategy for new product-services and locations;
- Proactive access to global markets - across continental-regions;
- Workforce diversity remained integral to securing market advantage;
- Viable alliances with sector distribution and supply chains; and
- Organisation structures were adapted for relevant sector/business operations.

Retailing

British-based South Asians are active retailers and most notably, **The Bestway Wholesale Group** is a leading UK corporate entity in this important sector of commercial and industry since the last century (**Fig 5.11**)

Figure 5.11 Case Study of The Bestway Wholesale Group

The Bestway Wholesale Group is reputed to be the largest independent food wholesale group in the UK. Sir Anwar Pervez arrived in the UK in the 1950s aged 21 to further his education and after working as a bus conductor, he founded the business in 1963 by establishing his first convenience store **Kashmiri** in West London. He went on to build the UK's 7 largest family business. Bestway contributes to the viability of over 100,000 businesses in the independent retail sector and the foodservice industry.

The business model is built on *'the concept of lower operating margin'* to maintain reasonable profits. The company also helped independent retailers to narrow the gap between prices at local stores and large supermarkets (**2012**).

When banks refused Bestway financial capital, Pervez and his associates mortgaged their properties to invest in the growth of the firm. The business employs thousands of employees in the UK and globally and have an estimated 18% market share of the wholesale cash and carry UK trade. Bestway has an annual turnover in excess of £2.2 billion (**2012 estimates**). Alongside its ensuring diversity, value and quality of multiple brands, the company has built its operations on these strategic pillars: -

- Low operating margins to compete on sale prices;
- Utilise personal capital to finance growth and expansion;
- Creation of retailing member networks to sustain customer loyalty;
- Wholesale exporting of grocery products;
- Compete on quality pricing for goods and services; and
- Support the continued growth and development of independent food retailers.

In 1987, the **Bestway Foundation** was established, to focus on health and education. The Queen conferred a Knighthood (2002) on Pervez and Bradford University granted him an honorary Doctorate of Laws degree (2002) for commitment to business and philanthropy.

The company's future plans include maximizing profit margins by 'analysing inventory data whilst retaining tight control over which products go where and in what quantity. Also display products properly and give prominence to brands that customers know. Reduce operational costs and improve compliance too, by producing simple merchandising instructions including layout, pricing and promotion in stores" (**The Bestway Group, 2012**).

Legal Services

This segment of the PBS sector is also popular with British Pakistanis especially for the young and highly talented who have developed into litigation advocate-specialists.

Out of a total of 15,581 persons, only 158 Pakistanis had qualified for the bar according to the 'gender and ethnicity matrix' (**2012 estimates**).

Men made up 107 and women 51 emphasising that female participation in the legal profession is evolving slowly within the broader South Asian community (**The Bar, 2012**) – Table 5.7.

Table 5.7 Sample of Self-employed barristers by gender and major ethnicity matrix
(Source: The General Council of the Bar of England and Wales, November 2012)

Ethnicity	Women	%	Men	%	Total	%
White (4 UK Regions)	2,970	74.87%	7,039	82.16	10,009	78.50%
Indian	120	2.92%	168	1.96%	288	2.27%
Pakistan	**51**	**1.24%**	**107**	**1.25%**	**158**	**1.25%**
Bangladeshi	16	0.39%	32	0.37%	48	0.38%
Chinese	23	0.56%	11	0.13%	34	0.27%
Other Asian	64	1.56%	91	1.06%	155	1.31%

The Anatomy of British South Asian Enterprise

African	68	1.66%	94	0.98%	180	1.32%
Caribbean	80	1.93%	70	0.81%	150	1.37%
Other ethnic group	16	1.18%	10	0.65%	26	0.89%
Total	**3,408**	**86.31%**	**7,622**	**89.37%**	**11,030**	**87.56%**

Fashion and Textiles

Similar to other British-located South Asian communities, Pakistanis have developed, fusing design with innovation, style and elegance to compete in the fashion and textiles trade. The majority of firms are owned by second and third generation British Pakistanis; that is, those born during the 1960s -1980s.

Despite challenges –personal, group and societal - they have shown commitment and purpose. The shared interest by men and women to create products and services to match generational tastes is also an interesting feature.

This strategy has helped bridge the generation gap which is often influenced by faith beliefs, cultural norms and related 'honour' codes (**Case Study 5.12**).

The adherence to customs and traditions and their blend with modern 'British (South) Asian' styles   appear to be the rule rather than the exception for today's entrepreneurs who excel in design, flair and adaptation.

The unique selling point (USP) of the British Pakistani fashion industry illustrates these features:

- Commitment to style, quality and variety;
- Integrating customer segmentation and social profiling into product range;
- Fusing traditional cultures with modern (accepted) western norms;
- Adapting to changing trends in the global fashion market;
- Operating in areas where low-cost retail customers are available;
- Managing lean bureaucratic organisations; and
- Creating innovative product and service lines for young fashion connoisseurs

Case Study 5.12 Sample of British Pakistani fashion designing firms

Nabila Fayyaz, a native of Lahore, began trading in 'Asian textiles from a home garage over 17 years ago, and her company **Seasons Asian Design Wear Limited**, is recognised as the UK's leading designer of 'Asian' bridal and fashion wear. When she arrived in the UK, the 1960s-born had a dream of opening a fashion house. Her success was built on working with mainstream, creating product ranges such as stand-out outfits, evening 'inspiration' wears, party and mehndi, versatile attire and wedding and ballroom fabric designs (**2010**).

Sameer Raza Latif established **Fabeha Fashions Limited** in 2008. Latif praised his mother and his Pakistani Kashmiri origins for enterprise success. The firm retails clothing in specialised stores with intricate fashion designs and innovation using a culturally sensitive approach. Latif is convinced that the sector will continue to reflect both 'Asian' customs and modern English/British trendy wear. *"The Islamic touch has given our outfits the reason for the business to flourish". Hard work and the introduction of new varieties of designs for customers provide us with further opportunities to serve people"* (**Ibid**).

Omar Mansoor is a London-based fashion designer of Pakistani origin, became popular for showcasing his work at *London Fashion Week* (**2008**). He is also renowned for his couture occasion wear with clients including British actresses, international royalty and members of the European aristocracy. Widely credited for reintroducing the fusion of clothing into modern fashion, Mansoor appeared at Royal Ascot and *Bahrain Fashion Week* and Top Model UK. Indeed, the adherence to customs and traditions and their blend with modern British South Asian styles, appear to be the rule than the exception for today's entrepreneurs who are excelling in design, flair and creative adaptation.

Transport and Logistics

British Pakistanis have a 25% market share in the *taxi operation* segment which was worth a market value of £9 billion (**2013 estimates**); that is, they contribute approximately £2.25 billion per annum to the British economy. There is fierce competition between taxis and hire cars for passengers even though they're integral to this burgeoning sector.

Transport statistics recorded 299,200 taxi drivers in Britain, with the total number of Muslim taxi drivers estimated at 85,485 –and one in seven being of Pakistani ethnicity (**ONS, 2011**).

One of the major reasons for Pakistani men pursuing self-employment in the transport sector resulted from a decline in manufacturing during the 1980s and 1990s recession. Thousands of minorities –men and women - lost jobs primarily in production, textiles and other industrial sectors.

For most Pakistani men especially in the Midland Counties and Central England, taxi or 'cabbing' became a viable employment alternative than being jobless.

With only factory-based skills plus little else going for them, these citizens returned to the job market, some learnt Standard English, pursued vocational training and developed new careers in the transport sector.

Perhaps the greatest concern for the average unemployed Pakistani at the time, was taking care of family; that is, trying to upkeep this noble and historic 'family honour tradition' despite economic circumstances (**Fig 5.13**).

Figure 5.13 Mini-cases on British Pakistani Taxi Drivers
(Source: 'You let a stranger in your life' *The Guardian, 7 March 2009)*

- **Taxi Driver A, 50 years old from Birmingham**: "I was born in Kashmir, and came to Birmingham as a child to join my family. I used to work as a machine operator at Cadbury's. I've been a cab driver for 10 years. It isn't my dream job. I make a decent living. My daughter is married and my only son works for TNT while the other works for a mobile phone company. I've got another son who's just left school. We're all worried about what's going to happen to us in the credit crunch; there are fewer customers for taxis than there used to be".
- **Taxi Driver B, aged 39 from Banbury**: "I was born in Pakistan and came to live in Leeds when I was five. After leaving school, my dream was to start a property business, but I ended up driving a taxi. It began as a part-time job. I've been doing it for 19 years. I've got four kids, a wife and a mortgage. We give the company a radio rent and they provide us with jobs. They're nice people around here - 99% are good customers."
- **Taxi Driver C, aged 30 South Wales**: "My parents are from Lahore, but I was born in Newport and have lived here all my life. I went to school and college here, and was studying IT, but my parents didn't have much money and I was in debt, so I gave up at 19 - I wanted things too quickly. Now I wish I'd stayed on. I had friends who drove taxis, and my elder brother does, too. There are a lot of 'Asian drivers' here; it's better than washing dishes in a restaurant all day - that's the way people look at it. When I started 11 years ago, I was making about £500 a week. I was living with my parents, so I could save, and started investing in property. With my brother, I now co-own two houses, a flat and a commercial property. Taxi driving was my way of raising money to do other things, but the industry is in a bad way. People are not spending; they're taking the bus instead".

The above examples highlight the effects of recession including the challenges posed during the transition from manufacturing to service-based employment. Although for most of the taxi operators it was not that difficult, for others with English as a second or third language, the situation was somewhat daunting. Yet, being able to work more flexible hours was a better option for Pakistani taxi [or cab] self-styled entrepreneurs than unemployment.

The Gender Equation

Stereotyping issues such as immigration (negativity), race, discrimination, prejudice and faith-based practices are central to the public discourse regarding British minorities. These 'talking points' have not prevented South Asian women from breaking through the proverbial 'glass ceiling' to succeed in business and the professions.

One typical example, is an education powerhouse, Nasreen Mahmud Kasuri, founder and chairperson of the 1975-established **Beacon Schools** located in over 31 Pakistani cities and eight in other countries including the UK, Malaysia, Thailand, Oman, the UAE,

Bangladesh, Indonesia the Philippines. An estimated 62% of its employees are women, with a high percentage occupying top management positions. Beacon's professional teacher-training is the hallmark of the enterprise.

Mrs Kasuri has empowered women in various disciplines and in September 2012 was a recipient of the *Women Power 100* award in London for her contribution to global education.

Besides Kasuri, other Pakistani women are operating businesses and managing professional entities whilst delivering high quality services to multiple customer segments. Recently, their works have been recognised with awards and other kudos from various sections of the British community and elsewhere (**Fig 5.14**).

Figure 5.14 Mini-cases of leading British-based Pakistani women entrepreneurs
(Source: 'Women Power 100', *The British Pakistan Trust, September 2012)*

- *Legal Services*: Ayesha Vardag founded **Vardag Solicitors** in 2005. Qualified as both a barrister and solicitor, she represents high profile divorce cases for royalty, tycoons, celebrities and other influential persons the world over. Vardag received the Times '*Lawyer of the Week*' award and is sought by media and public institutions to share her expertise on family law. She is considerered one of her proudest moments as, "*changing hundreds of years of law, to make prenuptial agreements work in England; a fundamental victory for the autonomy of the individual and the rights of couples*" **(2014)**.
- *Consultancy*: Farrah Quershi MBE is owner-managing director of **Global Diversity Practice Limited** and has pioneered global diversity consultancy. Her expertise comprises innovative learning and consultancy products for CEOs, Boards and management teams. Her work has impacted on clients in over 90 countries. She has received awards such as *The Aviva Toolkit* that won the UN Diversity Award in 2008 for innovation. The Royal Bank of Scotland included her in the *Asian Power 100* (2009) commendation and she was recognised as one of the '*Top Twenty Leaders too look out for*' (2010).
- *Food Sector*: Dr Nighat Awan OBE is an entrepreneur and philanthropist, known for her enterprising leadership of **The Shere Khan Group**. As a teenager, Awan was involved in her parents' garment business and after operating a chain of boutiques and a floristry business; she established the Shere Khan restaurants and curry sauces among other condiments - sold. Accolades include the Manchester's Food and Drink Festival Award (2004), business awards (2002, 2005) and an honorary doctorate from Manchester Metropolitan University (2006). "*Business is a rough and tumble game and you have to prepare to work hard if you want to succeed; for me being an entrepreneur is not a job, it is a hobby,*" said Awan.
- *Healthcare*: Doctors Kaukab Rajput , Sophia Khalique and Surraiya Zia are among three of the most distinguished medical specialists in Britain. Dr Rajput is a consultant audiological physician specialising in **Cochlear Implant at Great Ormond Street Hospital** in London. She has led modern research in the prevention of deafness as well

as unusual types of deafness especially for children. In 2008 she set up the UK Association of Medical Aid to Pakistan to help disadvantaged Pakistani children to combat disease as a result of the 2005 earthquake.

Dr Khalique is a director of **The Medical Practice** (established 1985). She is an award-winning anaesthetist whose work is considered to be 'extraordinary'. She is committed to relieve suffering and is keen on charitable causes. The British Pakistani has raised thousands of pounds for Leukaemia research.

Dr Zia is a director of **Sas Medical Limited** (incorporated 2011). She has a special interest in gynaecology, serving thousands of patients. She feels that community base teaching is vital for medical students since they can learn about daily health problems which they may not always witness on hospital wards. Dr Zia has helped many people affected by natural disasters in Pakistan, Bangladesh, Indonesia and Haiti, 2005 -2010.

Sector Attributes

From the foregoing, British Pakistani women are applying academic and professional training to introduce consumer-led products and services to culturally diverse markets. In the process, they are also building on the essential values associated with British female entrepreneurship. The achievements of female business leaders within the British Pakistani community could thus be summed up by the following excellence model principles:-

- *Education* –encouraging and promoting the vitality of global citizenship.
- *Business Professional Services* – legislative changes for rights-entitlement.
- *Consultancy* –building on innovation through corporate diversity, globally.
- *Food*- introducing new product lines to suit culturally ethnic markets.
- *Healthcare* –revolutionising treatment in key healthcare for all; and
- *Social Enterprise* – blending commercial and social investment interests.

In reviewing the contribution of Pakistani women to enterprise development, there are unique features in which few studies have examined in any great depth. For instance, the majority who are active in business and the professions, straddle public and private sector ownership as their experience showed (**Fig 5.15**). They further maximise opportunities by converting prospects evident in certain professions and in the process, gaining enterprise success with the setting up of corporate firms.

Figure 5.16 British Pakistani females active years in business and the professions
(Source: Textual analysis of 'Women Power 100', British Pakistani Trust, September 2012)

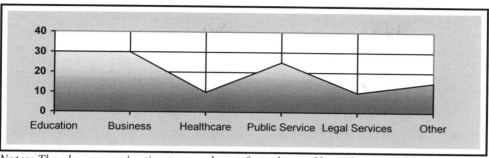

Notes: The above years' estimates are drawn from the profile evaluations of 100 leading British Pakistani women featured in 'Women Power 100' (2012). Their experience within business and the professions is as follows: Education 30 years, Business 30 years, Healthcare including medical research 10 years plus, Public Service 25 years, Legal Services 10 years and 'Other' refers to related enterprise activity – accounting for 15 plus years. The age category suggests that the majority of entrepreneurs are aged 30 to 55 plus, emphasising that these female business leaders are amongst second and third generation British Pakistanis.

Social Enterprise Sector

The South Asian population in the UK is very diverse – according to faith, class, country of origin, sub-ethnicity, language, gender, social, economic and cultural among other characteristics. Since this book is examining the Afghani, Bangladeshi, India, Nepali, **Pakistani** and Sri Lankan communities respectively, their collective richness impacts also on levels of social entrepreneurship (dynamics).

British Pakistanis are also known for philanthropy or what is often described today as *corporate social responsibility* (CSR). Their strong networks help drive the enterprise agenda particularly in the form of protected markets where firms are trading in goods and services. A notable example, is the provision of textiles and food products aimed at Buddhist, Hindu, Muslim, Sikh and/or other faiths.

In a survey of 100 Pakistanis (**2012**), we found that the majority were involved in CSR activity; donating capital and time for good causes such as supporting survivors of the 2010 earthquake in Pakistan. Though faith is a constant element in the engagement process including commercial activities, CSR is still relatively new to British South Asian firms.

Nevertheless, there are individuals who're making an indelible mark on this fast-growing sector; **Faraz Khan** and **Saeeda Ahmed** and the **British Pakistanis Foundation** are instinctively, 'corporate social leaders' in modern Britain (**Fig 5.16**).

Figure 5.17 Mini-cases of British Pakistanis promoting CSR

- **Faraz Khan** is a social entrepreneur, investor and author whose forward-thinking business model is remarkable. For the past 10 years, he has been an inspiration to young people especially. His mentorship has helped transform them into change agents. Besides his directorship of **SEED Ventures, Urbanics** and other public and private enterprises, the MBA graduate is a member of Catalyst UKTI, the All Party Parliamentary Group on Entrepreneurship. Khan is a recipient of honours and awards including 'Asia Society Young Leader' (2011) and 'Future Power 100 Leader' (2012). Among his achievements, is publication, the *Pukh Theory* described as 'Pakistan's first business parable that explores indigenous and unique solutions to a global challenge'.
- **Saeeda Begum Ahmed** holds directorships of companies such as **Trescom Research & Consultancy Limited**. Trescom was set up in 2001 to help and support disadvantaged communities that faced social exclusion. The enterprise achieves its social objectives through innovative training, community engagement projects, social enterprise support, policy work and research activities. Ahmed said that social business owners should be careful not *"to grow their firms too fast; they need to know what format the business should take and who is there to support"* (**YouTube interview 2010/2011**).
- **The British Pakistanis Foundation (BPF)** was set up in 2010 to counter negative images of British Pakistanis and to put forward positive aspects of the community. Its mission statement is *"To enhance the reputation and impact of the British Pakistani community, and through positive and proactive engagements and activities, improve their quality of life, equipping them with knowledge, skills, experience and opportunities, so that they may play a more active role with the wider community in the United Kingdom and be a positive bridge to Pakistan."* Priority areas are:
a) Research and policy development;
b) Trade investment links with Pakistan and economic development;
c) Training, job creation and business start-up training support in the UK;
d) Media and public relations;
e) Youth and community development;
f) Arts and culture, women's participation, sports, prisoners' rehabilitation; and
g) Other areas such as disabled and carer provision.

Overall, the Pakistani community maintains vibrancy in the cultural, political and social enterprise arena. They combine faith-based regional or ethnic alignments and organisations with a political orientation. Minority ethnics constantly apply cultural and faith experiences to manage stressful situations and adjustments to new or alien environments.

Much of these are evidenced by the increasing number of mosques, community centres and other faith groups to further the causes of this particular group. These trends are also indicative of Pakistanis' determination to remain engaged with civil society in every possible way and means.

'Public Enterprise'

Pakistanis' entry into British [mainstream] politics is fairly recent considering that members of this community have been involved in grassroots activism for decades. At the time of writing, there were Pakistanis elected along political party lines (Conservative, Labour, Liberal Democrats and Independent), serving as either MPs, members of the House of Lords and/or Local Government Councillors in England, Wales and Scotland.

Notable exceptions are solicitor, **Baroness Sayeeda Warsi** who became the first Muslim woman to Chair the Conservative Party, the third minister of her ethnicity and first of her kind to serve as a minister in the UK. **Shabana Mahmood**, a much younger British Pakistani barrister who became the first Muslim woman to win a Labour seat in Ladywood, Birmingham.

Former banker, **Sajid Javid** is reputed to be the 'first Muslim MP' to represent the Conservative Party. Apart from other ministerial roles, positions, he was appointed Secretary of State for Business, Innovation and Skills (July 2016).

Other distinguished members of the legislature include: former Labour cabinet ministers – **Sadiq Khan** and **Shahid Mailk**. Khan was elected the first Muslim/ethnic Mayor of London (**June 2016**). Those enjoying peerage are **Barons Nazir Ahmed** and **Tariq Ahmad**, with **Humza Yousaf** serving as a Scottish Minister and **Sajjad Karim**, as a Member of the European Parliament for North West England.

Following the 2015 General Election, there are about 41 'non-white MPs' elected to the House of Commons, 6.3% of all 650 members of the legislature (**2016**).

Tables 5.8 and **5.9** highlight the number of MPs and Peers in the British Legislature. Analysing minority ethnic representation in politics is problematic because ethnicity is both sensitive and difficult to define according to the House of Commons.

Table 5. 8 A sample of Minority Ethnic MPs in the House of Commons
(Source: Minority Ethnic Members of Parliament, June 2015)

Ethnic Group	Male	Female	Total
African	7	1	8 (19%)
Bangladeshi	1	2	3 (7%)
Caribbean	2	2	4 (9%)
Chinese	1	-	1 (2%)
Indian *	4	3	7 (17%)
Pakistani	**8**	**2**	**10 (24%)**
Sri Lankan	1	-	1 (2%)

Notes: the % total has been calculated using the 41 ethnic MPs as a baseline figure.

Table 5.9 A selection of Minority Ethnic Peers, House of Lords
(Source: House of Commons Library Briefing Paper, 4 March 2016)

Ethnic Group	Male	Female	Total
African	3	1	4 (7%)
Bangladeshi	1	1	2 (3%)
Caribbean	3	2	5 (9%)
Chinese	-	i	1 (1%)
Indian *	16	4	20 (39%)
Pakistani	**3**	**4**	**7 (13%)**

Notes: the % total has been calculated using the 51 ethnic Peers as a baseline figure.

Political Views

A study of ethnic voters showed divergent views on (im)migration, democracy, trust, the economy, opportunities, personal experience of discrimination and other issues (**2012**). Since minorities make up around 8% of the electorate, it was important that their views were given traction on sensitive issues affecting them and the rest of British society (**Table 5.10**).

Table 5.10 Attitudes of Minority Ethnic Groups on key British issues
(Source: Runnymede Trust, February 2012)

Ethnicity	Spend rather than cut taxes	Don't send asylum seekers home	Improve opportunities for minorities	Non-whites are held back by prejudice	Give priority to minorities	Very or fairly dissatisfied with democracy

British (white)	49%	39%	19%	-	1%	37%
African	43%	74%	75%	53%	36%	24%
Bangladesh	32%	43%	70%	41%	37%	20%
Caribbean	42%	59%	74%	58%	20%	49%
Chinese	-	-	-	-	-	-
Indian	33%	34%	65%	40%	26%	25%
Pakistani	**33%**	**41%**	**71%**	**38%**	**28%**	**23%**
Mixed	-	-	62%	54%	25%	52%
All MEGs*	+12%	-11%	70%	47%	28%	30%

*Notes: MEGs * mean minority ethnic groups. The percentages above are limited to selected themes and issues from the Runnymede Trust study of 2012. The issues are included in this book to reflect the representation of minorities as well as their distinct views on broad-based mainstream political issues.*

The table above highlights divergent views of the minority section of the British population. The responses to the following issues are important to both the apolitical and politically-minded. Legislation can impact on decisions that business owners and directors have to make on managing businesses including professional enterprises.

For instance,
- 12% of minorities considered '*spending rather than cutting taxes*';
- 70% said there was need to '*improve opportunities for minorities*';
- 47% stated that '*non-whites are held back by prejudice*';
- 28% agreed that '*priorities should be given to minorities*'; and
- 30% of respondents were either '*very or fairly dissatisfied with democracy*' in Britain.

Consequently, intense lobbying is required to increase the appointment of minorities (South Asians inclusive) to public bodies. This action should involve young people also who tend to be hesitant or cynical about getting involved in the process of development and change.

Such a campaign is imperative for these statistical reasons:-

- Only 0.9% of minority ethnic women are local authority councillors.
- 5.7% of minority ethnic women represent public appointments.
- 3.5% are Non-executives of National Health related bodies.
- 3.1% are Chairs of Local NHS Boards (**2010**).

Business Location

Having a proper business location is of strategic importance to firms irrespective of their composition and type. Consideration of this must be foremost in the minds of owners of commercial, industrial and social sector companies.

Location can also determine a firm's performance, under-performance and generally, its competitive advantage irrespective of particular industry sector or segment. Access to modes of transport -public and private – is necessary too.

For example, operating an engineering company in a 'run-down' area where customers are unable to access the business can pose a threat to sales even if it depends on the quality of buyers attracted to the firm.

No doubt, the quality of products and services on offer, is also a decisive factor in relation to customer loyalty and possible buyer retention, so business location is premium in the marketing mix of any company's operations.

As evidence suggests throughout this chapter, choice of location is indeed pivotal to the overall success of British Pakistani business owners. The various locations also indicate the geographic spread of firms across many UK Regions. Some owners tend to choose areas where there is a high concentration of ethnic communities. Others may opt for locations where low-income families reside and can ill-afford [to purchase] luxurious consumer items.

Principally, members of the British Pakistani business enterprise group feature mainly in 11 industry sectors. These cover a wider spectrum of business and industry as well as the professions. The use of industrial, office and other kind of premises is also important from the perspective of the nature of business segments that are being operated. **(5.11)**

For instance, a business owner who is operating a light manufacturing firm may also be running a small social enterprise trading in education and training services.

It means that he or she might decide to maximise space in the same locality to obtain maximum return on investment (ROI).

It might also be the case where owners are keen to ensure that employees recognise (through direct example) the meaning of corporate social responsibility at work.

Table 5. 11 British Pakistani Business Ownership by Location
(Source: textual analysis of firms by geographical dispersion, 2013)

Major Location	Principal Industry Sector
London	Food, retail, IT, transport and logistics, creative industries, social enterprise, health and social care, manufacturing, engineering, construction, business and the professions and the media.
South East	Retail food, creative industries, social enterprise, social enterprise, business and the professions as well as media.
East of England	Food, retail, education, social enterprise, business and the professions.
West Midlands	Education, retail, social enterprise, business and the professions.
East Midlands	Food and hospitality, transport and logistics, business and the professions, social enterprise, training, health and social care.
North West	Media, the creative industries, social enterprises, food and hospitality.
Scotland	Food and hospitality, social enterprises, business-professions, education and training.
Wales	Food and hospitality, retail, transport and logistics, manufacturing, training and social care.
Northern Island	Healthcare, education, training and food retail.

Challenges and Opportunities

In this section, we focused on the sector performance of British Pakistani business owners. Matters pertaining to their organisation, composition and integration into the British society were also examined in some detail.

Like other sections of this book that have profiled five other British South Asian business groups; notably Afghans, Bangladeshis, Indians, Nepalese and Sri Lankans. This chapter summarises key challenges affecting **British Pakistani** business and industry on a sector by sector basis. It offers useful suggestions for further growth prospects in emerging markets.

It is hoped that these pointers will help business owners to be better equipped to assess firm performance by linking growth patterns to UK and overseas markets. **Table 5.12** thus identifies sector challenges and demonstrates how these can be overcome by relevant market prospecting and focus.

Table 5.12 Challenges and Opportunities for key British Pakistani firms

Sector Challenges	Prospects and Opportunities
Education/Training: Male students are underperforming by 10% compared with females in GCSEs and 1% overall, enrolled for business and law degrees.	National and local minority company executives should endeavour to support career advancement initiatives for young, gifted and talented Pakistanis.
Self-Employment: Pakistanis have the highest rate of self-employment 27.2% than other minorities. This talent remains untapped.	This rate of entrepreneurship can increase since 70% of Pakistanis see entrepreneurship as an excellent, alternative 'career choice'.
Creative Industries: Pakistanis' are influenced by British traditions versus modern values.	Arts-cultural producers can introduce products and services to capture the 50% plus British Pakistanis interested in different art forms viz., film-literature.
Medicare Sciences: Practitioners represent 2.2% of the total UK medical profession.	Medical specialists should underwrite mentoring programs for the 10% of Pakistani students who're keen on professional medicine and allied health management sciences.
Social Care: The market share of firms in this sector is quite low compared to the need for domiciliary/respite care.	Businesses can optimise care markets with learning and physical disability segments and optimise the demands of users requiring 'assisted living' support.
Professional Services: Approximately 1.25% of Pakistanis are self-employed barristers (legal services).	Experienced ethnic barristers and solicitors can support the creation of more law firms amongst potential advocates. Help expand opportunities in other global regulatory markets.
Transport and Logistics: Pakistanis have a 25% market share in the taxi trade but little else by way of travel agencies and tourism services.	Current operators can expand their markets to include festival, cultural and adventure tourism to complement yearly Eid and Mela celebrations. Other events such as annual cricket tournaments could be integral to overall tourism services.

(Source: textual analysis of issues affecting British Pakistani firms, 2013-2015)

Conclusion

In this chapter, it emerged that despite perceived disadvantage of one sort or another, British Pakistanis have excelled and continue to do so, in various industry sectors including the professions.

Similar to other South Asians, Pakistani business owners have applied their culture, faith and social traditions to establish firms throughout Britain. By maximising informal network relationships, male, female (including young entrepreneurs) have set new standards, in their meteoric rise as the leading minority ethnic business group, nationally.

As part of a broader corporate (main) sector, many owners are operating within a legally defined environment with more than70% of companies formally registered and 5% plus being large companies with subsidiaries or branches both nationally and internationally.

Traditionally, ethnic business owners have direct contact or have strong ties to their ancestral homes (through birth or heritage background). This allows them to trade in dual or multiple consumer markets thereby spreading 'the risk' associated with having low-income markets.

Of particular interest, was the need to be more socially responsible in business deals/dealings. There was much evidence showing Pakistanis employing cultural networks to imbed business and social enterprise practices. Two notable examples of these were the veteran Nasreen Mahmud Kasuri, founder of the **Beacon Schools** group and the younger Faraz Khan whose entrepreneurial feat included **SEED Ventures, Urbanics** amongst others.

The optimum use of intellectual capital was also a central feature of enterprise development strategy with 50% of all Pakistani business owner-directors qualified in natural and social sciences respectively, apart from abundant knowledge and experience in industry and the professions. In many ways, intellectual capital in the business trade can make a real difference between great dividends and/or diminished returns **(2010)**.

Another major focus in this chapter, were owners desire to create vertical and horizontal integration or linkages with distribution and supply chains, using ethnic, inter-ethnic and mainstream sources. These alliances helped firms to develop informal market intelligence systems which further guided business decisions on customer segmentation, product type, pricing and volume.

Generally, whilst Pakistanis operate mostly within ethnic communities in Britain, judging by growth spurts in food, retail, manufacturing, healthcare, business and the professions, second and third generation (and probably fourth) entrepreneurs seem to favour expansion into co-ethnic as well as mainstream consumer markets.

Consequently, not only will this strategy aid in repositioning the Pakistanis business community, but it will further redefine cultural and ethnic diversity within the broader realm of entrepreneurship. In the next chapter, we will examine the '**Phenomenal Rise of Sri Lankan Commerce**' in Britain.

Notes

Ethnic Cuisine
Most restaurants in London and other inner-cities with South Asian migrants, catered for workers in the transport logistics and manufacturing sectors respectively. In Birmingham, Pakistanis and Indians worked on buses and in Bradford, they worked in textile mills. Men who operated café-style firms were originally factory workers who went into business for themselves whilst providing a service for fellow arrivals (George, Tyndale, "Urdu Brightens Up Yorkshire Streets," *Yorkshire Post*, Leeds January 22, 1976).

Barometer
During the 1960s and 1970s food, dress and mannerism became the 'cultural barometer' that defined the attitudes of English people towards Commonwealth immigrants. It was said that [South] Asian language signs on shops and what these establishments sold – either 'joined or replaced the old' ("Here You Can Enjoy Curry at Its Best," *Telegraph and Argus, Bradford*, January 23, 1967.

Highest
Pakistanis have the highest participation rate(s) in self-employment activity amongst minority ethnic groups in Britain. About 80,000 or 27.2% of members of this community are operating combined business and professional firms since the 1930s.

Souk Stories
Offer dramatic interludes of fun and entertainment to visitors of all ages. First staged as part of a year-long Shakespeare and Islam season at Shakespeare's Globe Exhibition in November 2004 receiving popular acclaim and capacity audiences.

Healthcare
There are over 11,000 Pakistani GPs on the UK medical register (2015). Numerous specialists and practitioners own healthcare firms whilst others are executives of various medicare and healthcare-type enterprise associations.

Segmentation
Like other ethnic groups, Pakistanis own or manage diverse business segments within a broader industry spectrum or spectra. These are evident within key sectors such as business and the professions, construction, creative industries, food and hospitality, information technology, manufacturing as well as social enterprise.

Family Law
Easy Living Magazine (March 2012) featured Ayesha Vardag of Ayesha Vardag Solicitors as 'The Diva of Divorce'. Her meteoric rise to fame stemmed from the

landmark Supreme Court case involving Katrin Radmacher. The ruling in that particular case changed the law on prenuptial agreements.

Web Links

http://britishpakistanfoundation.com/

http://sacf.co.uk/about-sacf

http://www.thenational, Huma Quershi, June 4, 2013

http://www.sairakhan.co.uk/businesswoman-saira-khan.html

Salient Features of Pakistani Punjabi Music, October 2010, www.sngspk.wordpress.com/

www.magazinesabout.co.uk/Eastern+Eye

https://uk.pinterest.com/pin/292874781998266351/

YouTube interview 2010/2011)

Selected References

George, Tyndale, "Urdu Brightens Up Yorkshire Streets," *Yorkshire Post*, Leeds January 22, 1976.

Labour Force Survey 2001, UK.

"Here You Can Enjoy Curry at Its Best," *Telegraph and Argus, Bradford*, January 23, 1967.

Easy Living Magazine, March 2012.

Werbner, Pnina: *Pakistani Migration and Diaspora Religious Politics in a Global Age*". Keele University. pp. 476–478. Retrieved 20 February 2011)

Ahmad Jamal, '*Cultural diversity and its impact on businesses*', Arts Council of England, 2006.

Global Entrepreneurship Monitor 2011.

Gallup Business Journal, 1 August 2012.

Tarjumaan International Edition, February/March 2010.

Migration and Development Brief, World Bank, 2012.

Media Literacy Audit: Media literacy of UK adults from ethnic minority groups, Ofcom, 2007-2008.

New Art Exchange 21 September 2012, England.

Bicknell, Sophie, 'The Rise of British Asian Theatre' *DesiBlitz*, 6 June 2013 UK.

Din, Ishy, Traverse Theatre, Edinburgh, Scotland February 2012.

Hashmi, Alagmir: *Pakistani Literature, Islamabad*, 2:1, 1993.

Richardson, Robin and Wood, Angela: *The Achievement of British Pakistani Learners,* Yorkshire Forward, 2004.

Focus on cultural diversity: Arts Council of England, December 2003.

'Power 100': The British Pakistani Trust, 2012.

Bartelsman, Eric J (2004. *The analysis of microdata from an international perspective,* OECD Statistics Directorate, 12, Paris: Organisation for Economic Co-operation and Development.

General Medical Council 2015.

Shah, Murtaz Ali: *The News*, 8 August 2012, Pakistan.

Manzoor, Safraz: 'Asian parents in care homes', *The Guardian,* 26 Saturday 2011.

The Bestway's Story, Autumn 2012, London

Store Development Planograms, The Bestway Group, 2012.

The General Council of the Bar of England and Wales, November 2012)

Designing with innovation and style, *Tarjumaan International*, February/March 2010.

National Taxi and Private Hire Statistics and ONS 2011.

'You let a stranger in your life' *The Guardian*, 7 March 2009.

'Women Power 100', *The British Pakistan Trust, September 2012.*

The Law Society Gazette, England 24 March 2014).

Hormiga, Esther; Batista-Canino. Rosa M & Sanchez-Medina, Augustin (2010*): `The role of intellectual capital in the success of new ventures', *Springer Science Business Media*, Las Palmas, Spain.

Chapter 6 Phenomenal Rise of Sri Lankan Commerce

"Being the brand of choice for one billion people by 2020" – **Lebara.**

Introduction

This chapter assesses the performance of Sri Lankan business owners in the British economy as mainstream research on the economic contribution of South Asians, has 'neglected the case of Sri Lankans' (**1999**). Among factors cited, are the use of terms such as 'problematisation', 'otherness' and 'Other Asian' to describe Sri Lankans. Critical issues affecting sections of this ethnic community comprise economic deprivation, structural poverty, social inequality, poor access to services, cultural and English language skill problems. Using existing studies, online directories, media stories, 'dedicated' websites and anecdotal evidence, this chapter will demonstrate the versatility of Sri Lankan entrepreneurs in Britain. Upon completion of this chapter, readers should be able to;

- Learn about the migration journey of Sri Lankans from 'home' to Britain.
- Appreciate their levels of enterprise start-ups over the past 20 years.
- Glean from Sri Lankans' overall enterprise [survival] strategies.
- Understand the challenges and prospects for British Sri Lankan firms.

Migration Settlement

Sri Lankans pattern of migration represents over 50 years of a phased critical movement from their homeland to the UK and elsewhere. A significant number of Tamils for example, came as labour migrants in the 1950s and were later joined by students moving for education purposes. In the 1960s Sri Lankan doctors and consultants were recruited to work for an understaffed National Health Service (NHS). Others found employment in the professional services sector.

During the 1970s and 1990s, a wave of Sri Lankan refugees who fled civil war, entered the UK. Most of them were young men who were less educated than previous others, and affected badly by the conflict back home.

Nevertheless, since the last century, second and third generation Sri Lankans have evolved into more highly professionals and are interested in either working for public institutions or becoming self-employed. The 2011 population census cited just over 60,000 Sri Lankans – divided into Sinhalese and Tamils - comprising 2%

of the UK population. However, the Sri Lankan High Commission considers the real figure as 500,000 since many of its citizens cannot be (properly) accounted for. This is primarily due to the level of spatial distribution or geographical dispersion of these and other South Asian groups across the UK including London and the Southeast, the Midland Counties, other Northern cities, Wales and Scotland.

This is evident throughout the history of migrant communities. Apart from Bangladesh, India and Pakistan, Sri Lanka is among the top 10 countries that have foreign citizens in the UK. This represents also a 'share of migrants in the population region' (**2013 estimates**) - [**See Fig 6.1 and Table 6.1**].

Figure 6.1 Percentage of selected South Asian 'sender countries' by migrants

(Source: The Migration Observatory, University of Oxford, England 2014)
Notes: India and Pakistan are among the top countries for foreign-born nationals, accounting for Bangladesh (2.3%) and Sri Lanka (2.1%) accordingly. London has Indian communities 8.6%, Pakistani 4.3% and Sri Lankan 3.7%, representing most South Asians in the capital.

Table 6.1 Growth in the Sri Lankans population 1991-2001 by region

National/Regional	1991	2001	+% (average)
Whole of Britain	39,402	67,832	72.15
London	25,382	49,925	93.27
South East	4,546	6,082	33.79
East of England	2,775	3,268	31.69
South West	1,178	1,433	21.65
North West	998	1,297	29.96
West Midlands	920	1,366	48.48

East Midlands	776	1,228	58.25
Yorkshire & Humber	773	863	11.64
Scotland	682	946	38.71
Wales	567	571	0.71
North East	375	493	31.47

(Source: BBC News, Born Abroad, Sri Lanka, 2005)

European student exchange programmes impacted on a trebling of 'Lankans' coming to Britain in the 1980s through to the early part of 2000. Changes in the law also meant the possibility of overseas students remaining in the UK after studying (**2008***)*.

This period witnessed a rise in male students (33%) as against 8% females who did so in 2008, coming to the UK (**Fig 6.2**).

Five years on (2013), student numbers from the Indian subcontinent like America, lessened. Enrolment went down for Bangladesh (6%), Pakistan (13.4%) and **Sri Lanka** (14%).

During 2010-11 saw 39,090 Indian students enrolled in UK universities; by the next two years there was a reduction - 29, 900 or 23.5% compared to the previous year.

Figure 6.2: Sri Lankan Student Migration to the UK 2000-2008

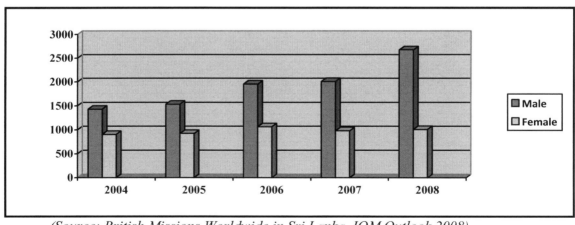

(Source: British Missions Worldwide in Sri Lanka, IOM Outlook 2008)

Attainment Levels

Educationally, British Sri Lankans learning attainment varies with girls having a pass rate of 51% and 60% plus whilst boys 38.9% - 58.7% respectively. On the one hand, inconsistent ethnic monitoring means that it is difficult for researchers to present or even reflect an accurate picture of minorities' performance in education and training.

On the other hand, the attainment figures for Sri Lankans during the periods 2007-2012, are indicative of continued progress by young learners from this community (**Table 6.2**).

More specifically, British Sri Lankan enterprise success is due to the growing realisation of the importance of academic and professional advancement. This can be seen by Sri Lankan students choice of disciplines; namely business finance, administration, mathematics, law, media, science and technology.

Evidence of this fact was made more pronounced in a report on science and engineering (**May 2014**) that highlighted critical gaps 'ethnicity and higher education' attainment.

Although British Sri Lankan students were not included in this cohort, it's worth capturing this data for readers information and guidance (**Fig 6.3**).

Table 6.2 Attainment of 5 or more A*-C GCSE Grades by key minorities
(Source: DCFS/DFE Publications, 2007-2012)

Pupils by ethnicity	Boys 07/08	Boys 11/12	Girls 07/08	Girls 11/12	All pupils
Chinese	80.9%	91.9%	87.6%	94.2%	88.6%
Indian	74.3%	89.3%	82.7%	93.9%	85.0%
Bangladeshi	56.6%	82.9%	68.9%	87.6%	73.8%
African	53.5%	80.5%	87.6%	94.2%	78.9%
Pakistani	52.7%	79.9%	64.0%	85.6%	70.5%
Other Ethnic Groups	49.8%	76.6%	62.5%	82.8%	67.9%
Caribbean	46.9%	75.3%	60.8%	83.9%	66.7%
Any other Asian *	46.4%	55.5%	59.5%	68.5%	57.4%
White (including British/Irish)	44.2%	54.2%	52.3%	63.6%	72.1%
Sri Lankan	**38.9%**	**58.7%**	**51.2%**	**65.6%**	**53.6%**

*(Notes: * This category includes Afghan, Nepalese and other South Asians not prominent in public statistics. Nepalese applying to study at British institutions such as London University, are*

expected to have 50%+ in the subject of their choice with the exception of English. Sri Lankans must demonstrate passes in 2 approved/ 3 further approved subjects in their country's Ordinary and Advanced Level exams accordingly). For the 2007-2012 period, the average gender ratio per pupil is based on the total number of boys and girls ÷ by 4.

Figure 6.3 Minorities achieving 3 A-levels in Biology, Chemistry and Maths
(Source: Improving Diversity in STEM, Campaign for Science and Engineering, May 2014)

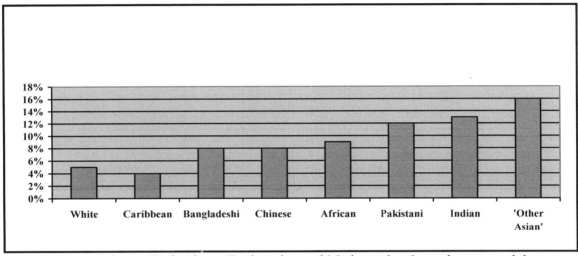

Notes: **STEM**- Science, Technology, Engineering and Mathematics. It can be assumed that *'Other Asian'* also includes Afghan, Nepalese and Sri Lankan candidates.

Commercial Inclinations

Despite attainment variables, **Figure 6. 3** illustrates the importance that minorities attach to higher education and training pursuits. Even with their disproportionate numbers, Sri Lankan 'young learners' showed a steady rise in academic performance which has a corresponding effect on further or higher education achievement. The latter is evidenced by the range of firms being established in business and the professions (**Tables 6.5 and 6.6**). Though further education remains a necessity, there are other substantive reasons for Sri Lankan enterprise and vocational successes;

- 71% of males and 67% females have entrepreneurial intentions.
- 55% of women are keen to earn income for families.
- 42% started businesses, independently.
- 60% received help from families.
- 65% felt a need for improved business development services.
- 15%- 20% of young graduates feared failure.

- 90% felt business gave them 'social acceptance and recognition'.

(Source: Antecedents of Entrepreneurial Intention, International Journal of Scientific and Research Publications, Volume 4, Issue 11, November 2014 1 ISSN, Uva Wellassa University of Sri Lanka &
Unlocking the potential of Sri Lanka's women entrepreneurs through better business development services, Institute of Policy Studies Sri Lanka and Oxfam International, Sri Lanka)

There are additional factors that contribute towards the movement, choice and eventual success of Sri Lankans in various commercial, industrial and social enterprises. These characteristics are seen as motivational-influences from cultural traditions to public attitude beliefs **(Table 6.3).**

Table 6.3 Factors behind Sri Lankan Entrepreneurial Success
(Source: International Conference on Sri Lanka Studies, November 2003)

Entrepreneurial Drivers	Impact
• **Cultural ethos**	• Sinhalese Buddhist civilisation.
• **Human nature**	• Collective values.
• **Code of ethics**	• Diligence and moral learning.
• **Education**	• Self-determination/discipline.
• **Public attitude**	• Social responsibility approach.

Notes: Social power, social relations and collective behaviour are the leading drivers for entrepreneurial motivation amongst Sri Lankans.

Ethnic Employment

Over the past years, much research has been done to determine self-employment rates by ethnicity amongst UK residents. In more recent times (**2009 estimates**), evidence has emerged that more than two million minority ethnic individuals represent categories of 'employees' and 'self-employment' segments combined. These rates were identified to demonstrate the comparison between 'disadvantaged' groups versus mainstream.

From an ethnic standpoint, approximately 310,034 business owners were listed in the 'self-employed' category; that is, 6.4% of entrepreneurial activities and/or 13.9% of overall ethnic self-employment. The 'Other Asian' description was a puzzle since it denoted either Afghanis and Nepalese and/or other South Asian businesses unaccounted for, by mainstream authorities. However, we managed to access vital information on **Sri Lankan** employment rates, thanks to the presence of online business directories (**Table 6.4**).

Table 6.4: Employees/Self-employment by key UK Ethnic Groups
(Source: Urwin, Peter: Self-employment, Small Firms and Enterprise, The Institute of Economic Affairs, Britain 2011& TamilNet 2016)

Ethnicity	Employee	Self employed	% Self employed
• Indian	569,363	76,980	11.9%
• Other	362,109	50,832	12.3%
• African	285,654	18,416	9.6%
• Caribbean	232,271	18,416	7.4%
• Other Asian	220,356	26,523	10.7%
• Pakistan	211,553	79,214	27.2%
• **Sri Lankan**	**150,000**	**7,000**	**5% (average)**
• Chinese	98,964	22,448	18.5%
• Nepali	50,000	271	2.6%
Grand Total	**2,180,270**	**300,100**	**7.2%**

Notes: figures for Sri Lankans are based on information from the British Tamil Chamber of Commerce. Online sources suggest an estimated 7,000-9,000 Sri Lankan firms are operating in Britain (Sinhalese and Tamils inclusive).

Stories of British South Asian entrepreneurial success are seldom reported in the public media. Policy think-tanks usually refer to Sri Lankans as 'Other Asian', in analysing their presence in Britain. Over the past 20 years, minority ethnic communities have been researched with the majority of issues featuring immigration/migration, ethnicity or race, faith and social deprivation.

However, Sri Lankans' economic and social contribution to the British economy is yet to be included in public discourse, let alone business literature produced by statutory authorities.

Notwithstanding this 'incredible' policy research challenge, the presence of accessible, online Tamil and Sinhalese business directories signifies proof of the level of industry sector representation and engagement by 'Lankan' entrepreneurs.

Theirs reflect more so, self-determination coupled with a 'can do' attitude amongst British-born Sri Lankan second and third generations. Their diversity is noticeable in an array of industry sectors and business segments which in some instances, are almost similar to other ethnic firms (**Table 6.5**).

Table 6. 5 Industry Sector Representation of Sri Lankan Entrepreneurs
(Source: Sri Lanka Business Directory UK –July 2016 listings)

Sector	Segment
❖ Building and Construction	Architects, builders, electrical services, heating services, painters and decorators, plumbers, surveyors, tools and equipment hire, property management and maintenance, engineering, land sale, estate agency.
❖ Business and the Professions	Estate agents, currency remittance, import and exports distributors, financial and legal services.
❖ Creative Industries	Conference halls, music groups, photography, videography, event planners, advertising agencies, newspaper and magazines, book shops, digital and satellite TV, sports and leisure.
❖ Education and Training	Education consultants, day nurseries, school and staff uniforms, tutoring in various subject-areas, job training etc.
❖ Information Technology	Graphic designing, internet café, network security, software development, web design, repairs and servicing, telecommunication services.
❖ Food & Hospitality	Bakers, caters, restaurateurs, supermarkets and off-licenses, cash and carry wholesalers, food manufacturers and suppliers, floristry, embroidery, weddings, banqueting halls, marquee and tent hire.
❖ Health & Social Care	Alternative medicine, clinics, dental surgeons, meditation centres, nannies and au pairs.
❖ Manufacturing	Food and sweets manufacturers.
❖ Personal Care	Barbers, cosmetics and toiletries, hairdressers, personal trainers, clothing and textiles, fashions, beauty salons.
❖ Social Enterprise	Faith groups, charities, associations, sports organisations, voluntary groups and other such non-governmental organisations (NGOs).
❖ Transport & Logistics	Removal and storage, vehicle repairs and sales, driving schools, taxi and cab services, vehicle import and exports, car rentals and allied trades.

Business Profiling

Ethnic communities use technology in the form of modern gadgetry, to facilitate easier access to information and data to publicise their respective message(s). Individuals and entities maximise *Facebook, LinkedIn* and other online platforms to promote commodities and services.

Indeed public spending restrictions and other statutory reductions in expenditure, haven't prevented minority entrepreneurs from marketing directly, goods and services.

When the publishers of Sri *Lankan -SL Pages UK*, launched their publication a few years ago, the reasons given were:

"For British Sri Lankans who visit the island (Sri Lanka) and looking for quality referrals in services. SL Pages UK want to cover this gap and advertise Sri Lankan business and people who are interested in penetrating the UK market. We have a circulation with a potential 85% market reach. Businesses interested in turnarounds, use the digital space to increase awareness of their presence. [The directory] is a tool for Sri Lanka to emerge in the UK business environment. Our target audience includes third- party entrepreneurs who like doing business within our community. The directory will provide an opportunity to voice skills and interests of British Sri Lankans, [while giving them the recognition] in society" (**SL Pages, 2015**).

By viewing online directories and snippets of published material (off-line), we were able to sample diverse British Sri Lankan industry sectors and business segments combined (**Table 6.6**).

This approach allowed for the validation of the organisation and performance of minority firms from an industry sector axis. It represented an effective qualitative method used in business research and related types organisational analysis (**2016**).

The application of innovative research methods to access material, also gives credibility to the necessity for publicising the value-add of Britain's minority [economic] or the 'diversity dividend' (**2015**).

Table 6.6: Sri Lankans' estimated market share according to industry sector

Industry Sector	Estimated market share
Building and Construction	8%
Business and the Professions	7%
Creative Industries	21%
Education and Training	3%
Food & Hospitality	12%
Health & Social Care	3%
Information Technology	7%
Manufacturing	3%
Personal Care	3%
Social Enterprise	6%
Transport & Logistics	6%
Total	**79%**

Notes: we sampled 200 firms in [industry sector] alphabetical order, using online business directories of Sinhalese and Tamil communities. Published information on firms was summarised for case study and narrative material; figures are rounded for uniformity.

Business and the Professions

Second and and third generation Sri Lankans have kept pace with changes in the British economy where the majority of firm owners trade in services. Owners have a relatively narrow but significant market share in business and the professions. Most enterprises are located in these industry segments; namely,

- Commercial cleaning;
- Currency exchange;
- Events planning;
- Marketing and advertising;
- Financial advice;
- Insurance brokerage;
- Import export distribution; and
- Legal provision (immigration advice – **Table 6.6**).

Gradient attainment levels in various disciplines, have given rise to the number of South Asians and other minorities who set up enterprises. These operations demand a high degree of knowledge, information, experience, flexibility or adjustment as well as people skills, all of which are essential for business success.

Legal Services

Over the past 10 years, the Bar Council has been monitoring the ethnic composition of barristers by gender in England and Wales. Yet, data cited under the rubric 'Other Asian', tend to exclude Sri Lankan para or quasi-legal enterprises, servicing clients especially those who can't afford to pay high legal fees.

The Law Society also assesses ethnic trends in the solicitor's profession. Official indices suggest that 11.4% of all 'solicitors on the Roll' are from minority ethnic groups.

Figures for the 'self-employed' at the Bar by 'gender and ethnicity mix', made interesting reading as **Table 6.7** illustrates. Males fared better than females although they both excelled in their respective law studies. As part of its monitoring evaluation, the Law Society trends reported on;

- The number of ethnic solicitor practices in the UK.
- The status of private practice solicitors by ethnicity.
- Ethnicity by size of solicitors firm.
- The ethnic gender of students enrolling with the Law Society.

However, poor ethnic monitoring in the 2009 trends pointed towards imprecise information on the number of industry sub-sectors owned or partnered by 'Asian' solicitors who comprised minority segments of the profession. Over half of all ethnic groups were solicitors (50.2%) who worked in firms with 4 or fewer partners, compared with 28.1% of their white European counterparts.

Table 6.7: Sample of Self-employed barristers by gender and major ethnicity matrix
(Source: The General Council of the Bar of England and Wales, November 2012)

Ethnicity	Women	%	Men	%	Total	%
• White	2,970	74.87%	7,039	82.16	10,009	78.50%
• Indian	120	2.92%	168	1.96%	288	2.27%
• Caribbean	80	1.93%	70	0.81%	150	1.37%
• African	68	1.66%	94	0.98%	180	1.32%
• **Other Asian ***	**64**	**1.56%**	**91**	**1.06%**	**155**	**1.31%**
• Pakistani	51	1.24%	107	1.25%	158	1.25%
• Chinese	23	0.56%	11	0.13%	34	0.27%
• Bangladeshi	16	0.39%	32	0.37%	48	0.38%
• Other Ethnic Groups	16	1.18%	10	0.65%	26	0.89%
Total	**3,408**	**86.31%**	**7,622**	**89.37%**	**11,030**	**87.56%**

Notes: the above estimates demonstrate the necessity for proper or precise ethnic monitoring.
* 'Other Asian' is reported as Afghanis, Nepalese and Sri Lankans.

Creative Industries

Accordingly, this section is multi-faceted with arts, cultural production and other creativity dominating. For the most part, Sri Lankans maximise cultural values to infuse enterprise success. Industry segments are performing arts, music, publishing, television and multimedia technology among others (**Fig 6.4**)

Figure 6.4 Mini-cases of audio and print media

Television: In 2006, Dr Sampath Wickremaratna, a professional banker and football enthusiast, launched **'Kesara TV'**, a channel catering for Sinhala-speaking people in the UK. He said that many had forgotten 'their roots when they live here" (Britain) and it was important to correct the situation. The channel features news in Sinhalese, Tamil and English, with an internet telecast facility for audiences.

Publications: Feature news, information, cultural, faith and other social issues about Sri Lanka, nationals and other members of this diasporic community. The publishers of *NewsLanka* and *Lankan Times* also cover news, features, tips and human interest stories from the UK, Europe and Sri Lanka. Readers are offered advertising space to promote goods and services. Described as 'UK Sri Lanka News Portal', *Lakeresa.net* is another resource for news and information in the UK and abroad. *SL Pages UK*, a business directory aimed at reaching businesses, charities and other interested parties. The publishers are keen to expand into European and other global markets. In 1997, veteran journalist, renowned poet and scriptwriter, Dava Ananda Ranasinghe, founded the *Lanka Viththi* to cover issues affecting the Sinhalese community. As one of the oldest directories, *Tamil Pages*, celebrated 23 years (April 2013). The entrepreneurial duo - T. Srikantha Rajah and A. Gnanendran - are largely responsible for sustaining this publication. According to them, the directory is an invaluable "resource for the Tamil business community to enhance their overall aim of making the UK the best place in the world to start and grow a business."

Mobile Communications

In 2012, an online news journal published a news story, headlined '**Finger on the pulse**', a direct reference to the telecoms giant, Ratheesan Yoganathan, founder of owner of **Lebara**. The company's revenue was reported to be €648m or £504m (**2011 estimates –Fig 6.5**).

Sri-Lankan-born Yoganathan emigrated to London aged 15 with his father. He studied aeronautical engineering at Kingston University, but couldn't afford to finance his Master's Degree. Knowing that his parents couldn't support his studies, he worked as a part-time salesman, trading in international calling cards. This gave him first-hand experience of the mobile telecommunications [business] segment.

Figure 6. 5 Case Study of the Lebara firm
(Source: LondonlovesBusiness.com, 25 July 2012)

In 2001, Yoganathan and two friends Leon Ranjith and Baskaran Kandiah visited Europe and were impressed by the success of the Norwegian mobile operator, Telenor Norway. Later, they compiled a business plan with these engraved letters [of the company's name] - Le from Leon, Ba from Baskaran and Ra from Ratheesan , **Lebara**. The firm's mission statement is: *"Being the brand of choice for one billion people by 2020"*.

Yoganathan used his brother's credit card to establish the company's London office base. At the start, the firm sold international credit cards to migrant customers. The owners utilised other telecom companies to bulk-purchase credit cards. This enabled them to sell at premium rates to accrue cashflow.

Ranjith and Kandiah then became Directors and Yoganathan Chief Executive Officer (CEO). His responsibility was to craft a business model including a company strategy, for attracting diverse markets. With a customer base exceeding four million across continents, the wireless network firm collaborates with Vodafone to provide network on its pay-as-you-go sim cards. Among Yoganathan's accolades are: being a finalist for the *Ernst & Young UK Entrepreneur of the Year* and the *Sunday Times Rich List*. Lebra's success is pivoted around these corporate gems (although not exclusive):

a) Investment into Remote Goat, a social-network for designers.
b) Investment into the Indo-western luxury brand, The Infusion Store.
c) Sealed a deal with Taj Hotels, the largest Indian hotel chains.
d) Ownership of new luxury hotel chains in Chennai (2012).
e) Frequent assessment of brand pricing and brand competitiveness.
f) Building a global brand to offer financial services in banking and insurance.
g) Optimising the worldwide web to service customers including migrant communities.

The mobile telecoms mogul intends to sustain the business while growing the **Lebara Foundation**, a charity that feeds tens of 'thousands of children daily in India'. He was inspired to kick-start this social enterprise after tsunami affected the lives of Indian and Sri Lankan communities in 2004.

Allied Creativity

Sri Lankans in Britain are also involved in other forms of creativity, as they seek to infuse aspects of culture and other traditional values of their 'new homeland'. Examples of such creativity are demonstrated in annual festivities, dance shows, film festivals, fashion shows and other types of artistic-performances. Other events include the following:-

- **The World Tamil organisation (UK)** celebrated its 10th anniversary of 'Chitrai Thriuvizha' (18th April 2015) in the Southeast. Cultural groups in Greater London and the UK as a whole, participated in classical dances and songs, with performances conducted in both traditional and English languages.
- **Wales Tamil Sangam (WTS)** promotes a 'tried and tested' style of teaching classical Bharatnatayam. Students have 'great fun' and feel a 'real sense of achievement'. It is a vital platform for professionals, entrepreneurs and academics to 'harmonise and transcend' individual potential skills. The WTS focuses on ratios provision, by offering 90% teamwork, 87% engagement, 70% tradition, 80% authenticity, 76% commitment, 65% well-being and 85% support to individuals and organisations.
- **Filming:** The remastered **'NAYAKAN' (1987)** was dubbed as 'Europe's Largest Indian Film Festival'. It reflected the cinematic and linguistic diversity of UK's South Asian communities in 15 major languages, including films from Bangladesh, Pakistan, Nepal and Sri Lanka. All films were English subtitled.
- Other UK releases include the Tamil thriller, **'Mariyaan' (July 2013)**, featuring a story of human survival adapted from a newspaper article of a real-life crisis event, when three oil workers from India were kidnapped and taken hostage in Sudan by mercenaries.
- **'Paradesi' (March 2013)** was a hit movie as well; it depicted a couple's trials and tribulations while working on a tea estate and raising their son. The film attracted audiences across London, the Home Counties, Scotland and enthusiastic viewers from other parts of the UK.

The owners of film distributors, **B4U Pictures**, have developed a brand image that caters for Tamil [and other] audiences, by promoting and distributing box office hits across the UK.

Education and Training

The Higher Education Academy conducted a study **(2012)** on the 'degree retention and attainment' levels of minority ethnic students. The findings covered areas such as academic expectations and preparedness; learning, teaching and assessment practices and developing a sense of belonging. Although many learners spoke about the challenges and lessons learnt from their respective studies, some had high praise for their tutors:

"Even if you email them there is an instant reply. They don't delay unless they are in a lecture. And they're really active, I mean they don't sit when they teach which I really like" **(Ibid)**.

Using their cultural, faith and social networks, Sri Lankans feature in scores of education and training segments. They range from day care nurseries, education consultancy to several personal development tutorials and school/staff uniform production.

The emphasis on the ratio of education to skills is very pertinent since it illustrates the regard many ethnic entrepreneurs have for formal learning vis-à-vis wealth creation activities.

Sri Lankans have an estimated three per cent market share in 'private sector' education-training services. Yet, they're amongst prominent figures in academia and other [sector] disciplines **(Table 6.8)**.

However in light of such disproportionality, the information below reflects the quality of achievement by this British South Asian community segment, in the 21st century.

Table 6. 8 Samples of eminent Sri Lankans in public 'enterprise' disciplines

Name	Discipline	Gender
Dr. Shailini Wickremesooriya	Consultant Speech & Language Therapist and Counselling Psychologist	Female
Professor Visakan Kadirkamanathan	Control and Systems Engineering	Male
Dr. Rajith W.D. Lakshman	Financial Economist (stock market)	Male
Dr. Vishvarani Wanigasekera	Neurophysiologist	Female
Dr. Vasanthy Ravichandran	General Medical Practitioner	Female
Dr. Roshan Jayalath	Consultant Dermatologist	Male

Dr Melanie Weerasuriya	General Practitioner	Female
Professor Abhaya Induruwa	IT Security and Forensic Investigator	Male
Professor Sunitha Wickramsinghe	Academic & Haematologist	Male
Nalin Chandra Wickramsinghe	Mathematician, Astronomer/Astrobiologist	Male
Dr Shanty Parameswaran	Child & Adolescent Psychiatrist	Female
Professor Dilanthi Amaratunga	Disaster Resilience & Built Environment	Female

Source: Independent research, cited from sampled education staffers, hospital trusts, and other public authorities employing relatively disproportionate numbers of South Asian and other ethnic professionals.

Food and Hospitality

This is perhaps one of the most buoyant sectors, operated by Sri Lankan and other South Asian business people in Britain today. Thousands of 'eating houses' and hospitality entities exist in almost every English Region and other parts of the UK.

This sector is a test to the commitment, determination and 'intelligence' marketing skills of this South Asian community.

Their firms' popularity is evidenced by the increasing 'rave' reviews – both in print and electronic – by customers and supporters alike (**Fig 6.6**).

Owners have diversified across the food and hospitality sector while lobbying authorities to offer greater recognition to ethnic cuisine, nationally.

Figure 6.6 Samples of the top 10 UK-based Sri Lankan Restaurants
(Source: http://thelankatimes.com/sri-lankan-restaurants-uk/)

- **Elephant Walk** -   has won several awards and acclaimed by well-known food critics as well as by discerning customers.
- **Sambal Express** – one stop Sri Lankan fast food outlets and owned by the Ruby's group, a UK catering company. Products include package meals, chilled food, frozen food, savouries, snacks, sweets and ready-made meals.
- **The Dorking-based Ceylon Tavern's** vision is to offer customers exceptional Sri Lankan dishes and share the 'welcoming culture'. Diners who sample dishes and experience friendly customer service, are likely to return.
- The Essex-located **Hopperbox** is a brand new concept specialising in exotic Sri Lankan cuisine. The food and décor is casual, relaxed and friendly. Customers can sample delicious and healthy seafood grills, exotically spicy or popular Chicken Manchurian and String Hopper.
- The **Ceylon Cinnamon Restaurant**, in Cambridge, is vibrant and modern, serving tasty Sri Lankan cuisine. Meals are served along with palate-licking cocktails. The décor is quite impressive.

- The Edinburgh-headquartered **Britannia Spice** specialises in Indian, Nepalese, Sri Lankan and Thai cuisine. It is a convenient location for diners who want to have a good night out sampling delicious multi-purpose menus.
- The Sheffield-located **Sai Nivas South Indian Sri Lankan Restaurant** – offers fresh and affordable meals from the best ingredients available. The diner's uniqueness is its South Indian food which is a brilliant blend of flavours, colours, seasoning, nutritional balance, taste and visual appeal.

Health and Social Care

Doctors and other medicare specialists have made vital contributions to the National Health Service (NHS) since the first half of the 20th century. Sri Lankans are among resident-South Asian practitioners who have enriched the health and social care sector even though their achievements are largely unknown to the general British public.

A rare university study (**The Open University, 2009**), revealed that South Asians who worked in the health service had mixed fortunes in career opportunities. And while 'geriatric medicine' offered chances for vocational progression, minority doctors faced discrimination through the 'hierarchical system of the medical profession'. In the study featuring 60 interviewees, South Asian medicare professionals spoke of their varied experiences such as unfairness in promotional opportunities and lack of recognition for their work.

"When I first came (to the UK), I sent lots of job applications with copies of my glowing reference from my consultant in Sri Lanka, but they didn't help at all (**p21, born in Sri Lanka 1944, arrived in UK 1973**).

Over the years, Sri Lankans have helped to redefine the health and social care sector in modern Britain. They represent a small but growing contingent of specialists dedicated to healthcare advancement. Estimates suggest that around 150 countries are represented on the UK medical register with 867 or 0.3% of **Sri Lankans** registered as doctors whilst 1,378 or 0.5% operate at clinician Level 2 (**Fig 6.7**).

Figure 6.7: List of Registered South Asian Medical Practitioners
(Source: The General Medical Council, updated 14 July 2015)

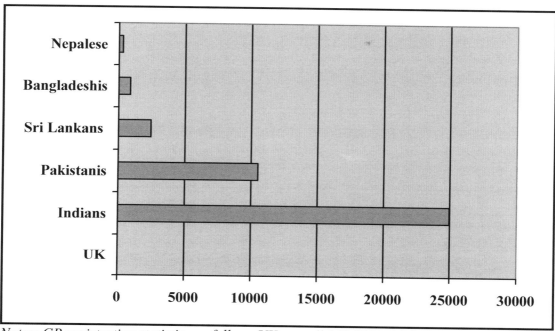

Notes: *GP registration statistics as follows UK overall 168,334, with Indians representing 24,960; Pakistanis 9,998; Sri Lankans 2,451; Bangladeshis 867 and Nepalese 300 estimate of GPs.*
Estimates suggest that Indians make up 9.3% of all UK doctors; Pakistanis 3.7%, Sri Lankans 0.9%, Bangladeshis 0.3% and Nepalese 0.1%. Afghanis make up 18% of all 'refugee' doctors in Britain BBC 2002).

Remittances

The UK is a major receiver and sender of remittances which have twin benefits (economic and social) for Sri Lankans, contributing to 33% of the total foreign exchange revenue. Expatriate workers to Sri Lanka are a valuable export for the country. Nationals' money transfers have been growing over the past few years. In 2009 Sri Lankans sent home US$3.3 billion a US$400 million increase from the year before. It was expected that 2010 would exceed US$4 billion. In mid-2010 there were more than 1.8 million Sri Lankan expatriate workers.

Figures for the period July 2015- April 2016, showed a decrease to US$578m in April from US$697.10m in March 2016 (**Fig 6.8**). Yet, this much-needed financial support has brought 'welcome' economic relief and social benefits for communities 'back home' struggling to eke out a living.

According to the High Commission of Sri Lankan to Great Britain and Northern Island, " *Remittance of management fees, royalties and licensing fees are also permitted for companies with majority foreign investment approved under Section 17 of the Board of Investment (BOI) Act-2016"* (**http://www.srilankahighcommission.co.uk/**).

Figure 6.8 Remittances inflows to Sri Lanka from overseas nationals

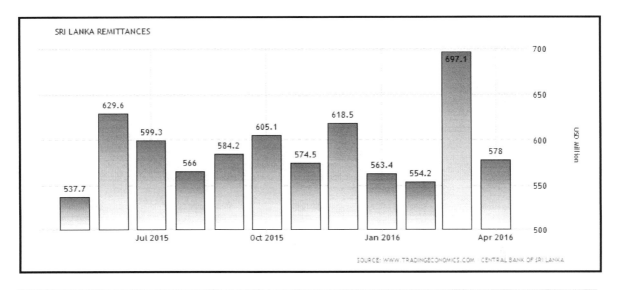

Retail Sector

Recent estimates (**2015**) suggested that South Asians have a market value of nearly half of all retail outlets which also represent leading food and hospitality segments. The majority of firms are 'linked' to the £37.7 billion sales-value convenience stores trade in Britain. The significance of this particular area of enterprise trade, illustrates that Sri Lankans are amongst market leaders in the wholesale and retail industry across England, Scotland and Wales.

They own and operate numerous shops, petrol stations, supermarkets or mini-marts, newsagents, cash and carry wholesale firms, bakeries and confectionaries, to name but a few segments. From young entrepreneurs to matured or older Sri Lankan traders, both male and female (including families), work arduously - 16-40 hours weekly - to keep businesses ticking over.

In a sense while on the one hand, the 'corner shop 'tradition is waning among some of the earlier South Asian 'settlers', one the other hand, retail commerce is very much alive within British inner-cities. This trend is very noticeable in areas where members of this British ethnic community live and work.

As a percentage of total shops in London, South Asians including 'Lankans' operate over eighty percent of all 'convenience stores' in the capital. They also have an ownership rate exceeding 50% in the West Midlands, Eastern England and the North East accordingly. They own or manage between a third and nearly fifty per cent of all local shops in East Midlands, North West, South West and Yorkshire and Humber. In Scotland and Wales, Tamils especially, have a market share of 43% and 21% in retail entrepreneurship (**Table 6.9**).

Table 6.9 Profile of South Asian (SA) Shop Owners in Britain

Region	Total shops	% SA ownership	Estimated SA ownership
London	51,842	83%	43,028
South East	50,798	48%	24,383
Eastern England	34,527	59%	20,370
West Midlands	38,175	60%	22,905
East Midlands	30,657	31%	9,503
North West	44,997	48%	21,598
North East	17,924	52%	9,320
South West	38,587	12%	4,630
Yorkshire & Humber	30,839	42%	12,952
England in Total	**338,346**	**48% average**	**168,689**
Scotland	44,332	43%	19,062
Wales	25,063	21%	5,263

(Source: The Local Shop Report 2015, Association of Convenience Stores p15)

Public 'Enterprises'

Like other areas of British society, Sri Lankans are under-represented in the national legislature. As of June 2015, only two such representatives were either elected to serve in the House of Commons and or appointed as Peers in the Lords. However, there are approximately 13 elected local councillors serving London and Greater London Boroughs. They service constituents in East London (Newham and Redbridge) and West London (Brent and Harrow) as well as the South East (Croydon) (**Tamil Pages, 2016**).

Those elected were males, as the equalities issue competed with traditional beliefs and modernity. For Sri Lankan and other ethnic communities, gender parity is being strenuously fought to reverse the outdated tradition of female subservience. Through partnership-working in welfare activities, men and women are finding a 'common purpose' [of expression] to achieve results that are mutually beneficial to local communities and the wider British society. In helping to set up multiple social enterprise-type organisations, second and third (Sri Lankan) generations particularly, are influencing a shift in the status quo by encouraging increased gender inclusivity.

Social Enterprise Sector

In scoping numerous local and national agencies and groups associated with the Sri Lankan community in Britain, we found a range of social enterprises representing key issues around children and young people, culture, education, the environment, legal matters and general welfare.

They were established between the latter part of the 20th century and earlier in this century, resident in the UK and overseas (**Fig 6.9**).

Figure 6.9 Mini-cases of reputable Sri Lankan Social Enterprises

Sri Lankan Medical and Dental Association (SLDMA) UK founded 1982, to 'support and foster' undergraduate/postgraduate medical-dental education in Sri Lanka. A membership of over 450 practitioners and spouses. An active Youth Forum supports young medical and dental intern-students.

The Meththa Foundation UK, inaugurated in Birmingham 1995, by Sri Lankans in the UK. Aim to serve disabled people in Sri Lanka. A sister organisation, Meththa Rehabilitation Foundation in Sri Lanka, facilitates the work of the charity at a local level.

The UK-Sri Lanka Trauma Group (1996). As the civil war affected lives, expatriate Sri Lankan and British mental health professionals coalesced to find practical solutions to help-support victims traumatised by the Sri Lanka conflict. Supported by South London and Maudsley NHS Foundation Trust (other NHS Trusts) and the Institute of Psychiatry. Links also with the University of East London.

The Rahula Trust was established in 1998. It solicits funds to sponsor education programmes for the world's poorest children. Donations come from private and public donors including British corporate firms.

Sri Lankan Psychiatrist Association UK was formed in July 2001 as a forum for professionals of Sri Lankan origin, practising in the UK. The organisation collaborates with the Royal College of Psychiatrists.

The Association of Sri Lankan Lawyers in the UK, formed in May 2003 by lawyers of Sri Lankan background (Sri Lankan and British born). To provide a forum where barristers, solicitors, academics and students in the legal field along with others associated in the legal field, can interact and exchange ideas. Collaboration with the Bar Council, the Law Society and related bodies.

The Senahasa Trust, was founded in 2005, following the December 2004 tsunami which wreaked havoc in Sri Lanka and its environs. The charity is involved in a range of development activities including providing homes, education, job opportunities, healthcare facilities and improved access to water. The trust complements the work of the UK-Sri Lanka Trauma Group.

Child Lanka Organisation, set up 2007 to provide secondary education for under-privileged children. Although its work is focused on young people abroad, education and social welfare services are delivered for young people and communities in London.

The British Tamil Chamber of Commerce was set up in the UK, January 2010 with an aim to invest in the socio-economic advancement of the Tamil business community in the UK and worldwide. In 2011, the organisation referred to the presence of 5,000 Tamil-owned firms in Britain with a combined turnover of £1billion and 150,000 employees. The chamber offers training development for young entrepreneurs, including support for new start-ups. Service 'offerings' include financial, legal and tax advice.

Source: an estimated 100 organisations representing Sri Lankan communities sampled under the headings of 'temples and centres', 'professional associations', 'charity, welfare and other organisations in the UK' and 'associations in the UK' (Sri Lankan UK Business Directory; UK Sri Lanka Contact Centre, Sri Lankan High Commission London, TamilNet, 2012-2016)

Transport and Logistics

Since the mid to late 20th century, minorities have founded companies in this sector. With their enterprise flair, Sri Lankans have a slender market share of less than 10 per cent (or 6%) and growing, in transport and logistics. Owners are keen to satisfy market demands especially those travelling to and from South Asia and other popular destinations, globally.

This author undertook independent research (**July, 2016**) involving 90 firms. This investigation revealed that firms traded along the lines of 'hotel booking agents', 'tours', 'hotels' 'tourist 'attractions', 'travel agents' and 'travel and tour air ticketing'.

Over 15% of all services were operating in business segments ranging from adventure and leisure tourism to paradise-type (sunset beach) locations. The inclusion of hotel accommodation with a choice of restaurant as a 'holiday package', was also a unique selling point for an estimated 10% of operators in the tourist trade-segment.

The choice of either business name or services provision by industry segments, also illustrated owners and operators general understanding of key competitive advantage. For them, this strategy is vital in a highly-driven customer market. This fact is best illustrated by the following brand-name choices;

- *Chamathka Holidays*
- *C.K. Exotic Travels*
- *Lion Soul Travelling*
- *Lanka Travel & Tours*
- *Flyplaces Travel & Tours*
- *Sunset Beach Residence Panadura*
- *Sri Lankan Nature Tours*
- *Time Travel.*

As is customary with South Asian market geographic patterns, transport and logistic firms operate in London, the Southeast and (English) Home Counties. They collaborate with a host of large, reputable companies including ticket agencies, to ensure that customers have access to affordable fares and reasonably priced accommodation.

Overall, the key to the success of Sri Lankan firms in the transport and logistics trade, are owners knowledge, experience and the understanding of the (constantly) changing customer-travel market.

Faith 'Economics'

Faith is a spur to economic and social development within diverse communities particularly for groups who're considered 'new arrivals' in Britain. As a value asset, it has reinvigorated sections of the minority population affected by persistent [economic] deprivation and [social] exclusion. Despite integration challenges facing Sri Lankans, faith has influenced their desire, hope and confidence in the creation of start-ups across the British Isles.

Drawing from a sample of over 70 faith organisations, the evidence showed the impact of faith as a predicator in planning and developing ideas on different types of industries and business segments. Yet research on the utility of faith as an instrument to facilitate business development amongst British minorities, remains a work in progress.

The multiplicity of faiths within the Sri Lankan community, is quite extraordinary too. Aside places of worship, faith organisations are described as 'cultural' and 'meditation centres' where other communities participate in religious and non-religious observances. 'Lankans' have established numerous social enterprises, the majority of which are driven by a plurality of faith-based practices, as illustrated in **Table 6.10.**

Table 6.10 Sri Lankan faith-based practices in Britain

Type of Faith (%)	Regional Areas
✓ **Buddhism (45%)** ✓ **Christianity (39%)** ✓ **Islam (8%)** ✓ **Hinduism (7%)**	Scotland (Glasgow), East of England (Hertfordshire), London (North, West, East and South), South East (Oxford, Billericay and Surrey), West Midlands (Birmingham), East Midlands (Leicester and Kirby), North West (Manchester, Warrington), North East (Liverpool), Wales (Cardiff), Yorkshire & Humber (Yorkshire).

Notes: we sampled 72 faith organisations from the Sri Lankan UK Business Directory along with anecdotal evidence from owners; that is, commercial and social entrepreneurs.

The Gender Equation

For decades, there have been a plethora of newspapers, magazines, journals, research papers and other literature rehearsing themes around *immigration, race, gender, discrimination, prejudice and faith* among other issues involving ethnic groups in Britain and Europe.

In some respects, these themes preoccupy the minds of sections of society who are trying to decipher the economic contribution of migrants compared to the welfare dependency of 'others'. This situation can sometimes distort the increasing visibility of minority females in British entrepreneurship.

Even when progress is made within ethnic communities, reactions to this is either muted, ignored or discounted as 'token gestures'. The 'gender divide' has implications for the social interaction dynamics of society overall. It is in this vein, that educated Sri Lankans are working more strategically with like-minded partners in leading the way towards gradually creating greater male-female parity.

Public knowledge of Sri Lankan businesswomen in the UK is virtually unknown. Evidence suggests that the success of micro, small and medium sized enterprises (MSMEs) within South Asian communities, has a lot to do with support from spouses or partners.

The Local Shop Report (**2015**) cited over 30% of female participation rates within [the ownership of] South Asian convenience stores'. Based on these firms' market share of £37.7 billion per annum, it can be reasonably assumed that South Asian women are contributing billions of pounds to the British retail trade overall.

If further proof from observation research is also a reliable yardstick, then participation rates for female owned and co-owned Sri Lankan businesses are commonplace within these industries:-
- Business and the Professions;
- Creative Industries;
- Education and Training;
- Information technology;
- Food and Hospitality;
- Health and Social Care;
- Personal Care; and
- Social Enterprise.

However, striving to actualise a 'gender-balance' in social enterprises can give the impression that [professional] Sri Lankan women are being challenged to maximise their true potential or talent in a commercial setting. And thus their interest in social entrepreneurship can be perceived as either a gateway or 'disguise 'opportunity to advancing their careers; academically and/or professionally.

Judging by the number of ethnic firms involved in charitable activities in the UK and overseas, it is not surprising that Sri Lankan women are staking a claim for their [overdue] 'enterprise credentials'.

Health and medicare associations are proud to showcase on web-based platforms, professional women who occupy leadership or management positions. **Dr. Melanie Weerasuriya** is a renowned General Practitioner and is an executive member of the SLMDA UK. She is also founder of **MRW Medical Services Ltd** (incorporated August 2011). Second generation Sri Lankan men and women are involved in directing the affairs of the **Association of Sri Lankan Lawyers in the UK**. Practising solicitor, Mrs Surya Samaraweera and counterpart Mrs Chrishanthi Vincent, had a pivotal role in the service administration of the organisation. The composition of male to female membership, is an estimated 55:45.

Within children and social welfare organisations, female ownership and co-ownership exceeds 50% in many instances. Notable examples are the **Senahasa**

Trust, The UK-Sri Lanka Trauma Group and Child Lanka Organisation (SLO). In explaining her reason for establishing the SLO in 2007, founder Padma Priya Siriwardene said;

"I was brought up to believe that compassion and humanity rewards the person, giving more than those who receive. If someone has the ability to give a light to create a better future for a deprived child, those merits will follow you immensely" **(www.childlanka.com/about/).**

The above samples of key industry segments, were chosen to explore the level of female participation in Sri Lankan entrepreneurship in Britain. Though small, the examples are indicative of a narrowing gender divide within ethnic firms throughout the country. Quite noticeably too, research points to the pillars of enterprise success for Sri Lankan women in key industry sectors (**Table 6.11**).

Table 6.11 Success pillars by Sri Lankan female according to industry sectors

Industry Sector	Segment	Success Pillars
Business & the Professions	Legal Services.	Advocacy, forum for legal practitioners/specialists to discuss and exchange best practice in the profession.
Education and Training	Primary education.	Purchase of education materials, training teaching staff. Providing help and support especially for under-privileged children.
Health and Social Care	General medicine, dentistry and allied health care.	Advocacy, research, training and delivery of primary healthcare services.
Personal Care	Textiles & jewellery.	Products and services to meet cultural, religious and social needs of Sri Lankans and other ethnic communities.
Social Enterprise	Associations, faith groups, welfare organisations and other voluntary bodies.	Helping to manage, raise finances, plan and deliver culturally sensitive services to members and service-users.

(Source: Textural analysis of selected profiles of Sri Lankan social enterprises, 2015/2016)

Business Location

In this chapter, we have learnt of Sri Lankans commercial and social enterprise endeavours. Their dispersion across Britain means that business activities are situated within cities, suburbs and other conurbations where diverse communities live and work.

Apart from other strategic and operational factors, the choice of locations can and do make a considerable difference between the performance and under-performance of firms. Also having quality premises to operate from along with competent staff and adequate materials and equipment, are absolutely vital to the productivity of all firms.

Therefore, Sri Lankans enterprise achievement can be attributed strategically, to focusing on areas where there is a high concentration of ethnic groups alongside the local populace. Principally, owners within this ethnic group operate within different industry sectors and business segments in London, the Home Counties, Wales and Scotland respectively.

Clearly, it is indicative of owners understanding of, and appreciation for suitable business locations in terms of convenience, product segmentation, quality service, customer care and various industry linkages associated with minority ethnic firms generally (**Table 6.12**).

Table 6.12 British Sri Lankan Business Ownership by Location

Major Location	Principal Industry Sector
London	Food, retail, IT, transport and logistics, creative industries, social enterprise, health and social care, manufacturing, engineering, construction, business-professions and media.
South East	Retail, food, creative industries, social enterprise, social enterprise, business and the professions as well as media.
East of England	Food, retail, education, social enterprise, business and the professions
West Midlands	Education, retail, social enterprise, business and the professions.
East Midlands	These include food and hospitality, transport and logistics, business and the professions, social enterprise, training, health and social care.
North West	Media, the creative industries, social enterprises, food and hospitality.
Yorkshire & Humber	Food, retail services, social enterprises.
Scotland	Food and hospitality, social enterprises, business and the professions, education and training.
Wales	Food and hospitality, retail, transport and logistics, manufacturing, training and social care.
Northern Island	Healthcare, education and training along with food retail.

Challenges and Opportunities

Throughout this chapter the focus has been on the sector performance of **British Sri Lankan** businesses. Like previous chapters that profiled other business groups – notably Afghans, Bangladeshis, Indians, Nepalese and Pakistanis - this section summarises key challenges affecting key enterprise areas.

It also offers recommendations for sector growth, development and prospects for emerging markets. It is hoped that business owners will be in a better position to evaluate their firm's performance by linking opportunities with those of growth patterns in the UK and overseas markets.

Table 6.13 thus identifies sector challenges and demonstrates how these can be overcome by relevant market prospecting and focus. With appropriate systems and procedures, business owners and management teams can optimise emerging market opportunities – nationally and internationally.

Table 6.13 Challenges and Opportunities for Sri Lankan Enterprises
(Source: textual analysis of each Sri Lankan industry sector 2015/2016)

Sector Challenges	Market Opportunities
Building Trades: competition by large firms; changes in building codes.	Build on market share [8%], maximise advantage by focusing on project management training/other skills.
Business and the Professions: under-achievement in management sciences and competition from consultancies.	Add to 7% market share by supporting youngsters interested in this sector. Offer alternative/affordable services for new clients and loyal customers.
Creative Industries: limited public knowledge of Sinhalese, Tamil and Sri Lankan traditions generally.	Fusion of 'Lankan' cultures with British creativity to bolster market share [21%]. Artistic and cultural events in schools and other public places.
Education/Training: English Language fluency and formal communication issues.	Increase attainment among young learners. Invest in vocational training to create employment opportunities including business start-ups.
Food & Hospitality: rivalry from well-known companies and popular consumer brands.	Improve customer relations, product guarantees, service warranties, affordable commodities; increase existing market share (40%+) in 'convenience stores'.
Health & Social Care: competition from local primary care and health trusts. Also from other reputable bodies.	Improve existing 3% market share via well-being programmes to help communities manage ill health conditions because of lifestyle behaviours.
Information Technology: industry competition, new app technologies, cash flow/operational start-up issues.	Build on the 7% market share by using modern technology to design toolkits for business performance and market intelligence training for young people.
Manufacturing: large-scale diversity, limited technical support production and gaps in manufacturing sub-sectors.	Increase existing market share (3%) by analysing manufacturing trends. Innovative goods and services to meet customer demands.
Personal Care: competition from large companies introducing alternative remedies for beauty care especially.	Gain market advantage by increasing the 3% share; maximise natural ingredients to produce a range of remedies for diverse community needs.
Transport & Logistics: competition from large travel and tour operators, shipping agents and one-stop transport companies.	Enhance market share of 6% by conducting periodic research to determine client needs. Expand services in the festival, cultural and adventure tourism markets – nationally and overseas.

Conclusion

This chapter showed that despite incidences of economic deprivation and social exclusion, British Sri Lankans are excelling in business and the professions. Often described as 'new arrivals', their contribution to economic and social advancement is largely unknown to the public, more so, acknowledged by public institutions.

Yet, like other South Asians, Sri Lankans are influenced and motivated by faith and other creeds to establish different enterprises in Britain. Through community activism, many have developed possibly, an 'unwritten' code of ethics, as they add value to Britain's corporate social responsibility (CSR) goal for commerce and industry.

As an integral part of the small and medium-sized enterprise part of the SME sector, an estimated 60% plus businesses are sole traders and the remainder, operate as limited companies including private limited companies (PLCs), charities and other formal trading structures. A fraction of enterprises operate overseas trading arms or social entities. These help in promoting commercial entrepreneurship and civic governance thereby creating wealth and building capacity in poor communities particularly.

Industry market share varied between 6% and 21% according to the type of sectors and segments gleaned from the enterprise organisations researched. In the absence of concrete studies on British-based Sri Lankan business formation rates, we used various methods to access information and data.

It was vital that creative and innovative approaches be utilised also, to at least, measure the [relative] organisation and performance of commercial firms and social enterprises. This chapter thus benefitted from these 'source-methods' (though not exclusive):-
- Selected databases and directories;
- Interviews with business owners;
- Discussions with sections of the Sri Lankan media;
- Reviewing the '*Lankan Times*' and '*Confluence*' among others;
- Observation research or 'mystery shopping' to glean customer habits; and
- Informal discussions with individual employees working in Sri Lankan firms.

As with most minority firms in Britain, issues are often considered to be either complex, complicated and/or beyond the understanding of sections of the public realm. It is hoped that this chapter, like previous sections, will offer readers a greater insight into the contribution of Sri Lankans, their South Asian 'cousins' and other minorities make to the British economy as a whole.

In the next chapter, we will focus on the enterprising talent of young South Asians – *'Third Age Entrepreneurs'*. Undoubtedly, their inclusion will add value and further credence to the significance of this book, at this juncture of our global economic history.

Notes

Migration
Sinhalese and Tamils comprise the majority of Sri Lankan migrant population in Britain. Despite years of civil unrest in Sri Lanka, these two nationalities have developed working partnerships to resolve differences. Evidence of this can be gleaned from the various commercial and social firms established to service fellow 'Lankans' and other local groups.

Education
Young Sri Lankan learners have the lowest attainment level for GCSE exams. Although up to 20% of graduates 'feared failure', over 60% of male and female Lankans have strong entrepreneurial intentions.

Success
Sri Lankans own thousands of business across the British Isles, with self-employment rates averaging 5% (British Tamil Chamber of Commerce, 2015). We sampled 200 firms to obtain material to profile the contribution of 'Lankans' to economic development in Britain.

Communications
To its credit, Lebra is a transformation-enabler of telephony products and services. Its mission '*Being the brand choice of one billion people by 2020*", is perhaps a strategic manifesto for contemporary mobile communications in this century and beyond.

Food
Thousands of Sri Lankan eateries exist across the UK, offering multi-cuisine for Indians, Nepalese, Thais and other ethnic diners. These food houses have maintained distinctive South Asian flavours blended with colours, spices, nutritional balance, taste and visual appeal.

Tourism
Firms sampled in the transport and logistics sector, highlighted various tourist/leisure packages for Sri Lankans and other travellers alike. Approximately 10% of tour operators were keen to ensure that holidaymakers had the opportunity to venture into eco-friendly destinations as part of the 'paradise-type attractions (July 2016).

Faith Economics

Used to describe the influence and application of faith beliefs as well as its impact on business-enterprise success. Faith communities such as Buddhist, Confucian, Christian, Jewish, Hindu, Muslim and Sikh are making distinctive contributions to the '*search for more fateful economics and finance*' ('Faiths and Finance: A Place for Faith-based Economics', *Manchester Centre for Public Theology*, November 6, 2002).

Web Links

Lakeresa.net

LondonlovesBusiness.com, 25 July 2012.

http://thelankatimes.com/sri-lankan-restaurants-uk/

http://www.srilankahighcommission.co.uk/

www.childlanka.com/about/

Selected References

'Faiths and Finance: A Place for Faith-based Economics', *Manchester Centre for Public Theology*, November 6, 2002.

Asian and Pacific Migration Journal, Vol 8, No. 4, 1999.

The Migration Observatory, University of Oxford, England 2014.

'Born Abroad', Sri Lanka, *BBC News* 2005.

British Missions Worldwide in Sri Lanka, *IOM Outlook* 2008.

DCFS/DFE Publications, 2007-2012.

Improving Diversity in STEM, Campaign for Science and Engineering, May 2014

'Antecedents of Entrepreneurial Intention', *International Journal of Scientific and Research Publications, Volume 4, Issue 11*, November 2014 1 ISSN, Uva Wellassa University of Sri Lanka & 'Unlocking the potential of Sri Lanka's women entrepreneurs through better business development services', *Institute of Policy Studies Sri Lanka and Oxfam International, Sri Lanka*).

International Conference on Sri Lanka Studies, November 2003.

Sri Lanka Business Directory UK –July 2016 listings.

Business News, SL Pages UK, 12 July 2015.

Eriksson , Päivi and Kovalainen, Anne: 'Qualitative Methods in Business Research', 2nd edition, *SAGE Publications Lt*d 2016.

Tamil Pages, April 2013.

Stevenson, Jacqueline: British Asian Sri Lankan, Female, 25, 1st generation, Chemistry: 'Black and minority ethnic student degree retention and attainment', *The Higher Education Academy*, October 2012.

'*Overseas-trained South Asian doctors and the development of geriatric medicine'*, The Open University, October 2009.

The Local Shop Report 2015, Association of Convenience Stores p15, England.

Tamil Pages, July 2016.

Sri Lankan UK Business Directory; UK Sri Lanka Contact Centre, Sri Lankan High Commission London, TamilNet, 2012-2016.

Chapter 7 – 'The Third Age' Entrepreneurs

"I particularly remember the '80s and early '90s when fashion and the textiles industry grew and prospered in Britain" – **DressMe.com.**

Introduction

Throughout this book we have examined the contribution of various South Asian groups to business and industry. Much of their input lies within key industry sectors of the British economy. In recent times however, discussion have centred on the impact of enterprise on young people although it has been viewed through the lens of traditional employment per se. On completing this chapter readers should be able to:-

- Recognise the importance of youth entrepreneurship.
- Appreciate the contribution of young South Asian entrepreneurs to Britain.
- Understand the attainment successes of Britain's young minorities.
- Learn about the challenges facing young entrepreneurs in business and the industry.

In this section, we will profile some of Britain's young South Asian entrepreneurs (the under-40s group or 'third age' entrepreneurs) who are making an unsung contribution to the economy. This will be linked to the increasing levels of graduate attainment across academic and professional disciplines.

Information and data on UK self-employment tend to vary between young and matured (older) persons. In 2012, only 5% of 16-24 year olds were working for themselves, compared to 37% of 65 plus (**ONS, 2013**). At 47 years, the average age of self-employed workers in the UK (2014) was higher than that of employees by seven years (**ONS, 2014**). About 43 per cent of self-employed workers in that same year, were aged 50 or over, compared to 27 per cent of employees (**ONS, 2014**).

By contrast, early-stage entrepreneurial activity (TEA) is highest among middle-aged groups in the UK. In 2013, 5.7% and 4.6% of 18-24 and 55-64 year olds respectively displayed early-stage entrepreneurial activity, compared to 9.2 per cent of 35-44 year olds (**2013**).

In its report, '*Generation Entrepreneur*', The Prince's Youth Business International (2011), stressed the importance of understanding entrepreneurial attitudes, aspirations and activities of young people. These factors are relevant to the way these talented wealth creators can and do influence the economic and social well-being of British society.

The Anatomy of British South Asian Enterprise

The report also detailed the influences and motivations of young business people from roughly 10 continental regions globally. The statistics below illustrate young people under-40 who're 'new' or 'nascent' businesses and/or 'reliant on personal/family or friends for funding to start a business':-

- European Union 9.2%;
- Non-European Union 8.5%
- Sub-Saharan Africa 77.7%;
- Latin America and the Caribbean approximately 75.7%;
- Asia Pacific and South Asia 73.2%;
- MENA Region between 18.6% -20.6%; and
- The USA 12.6% **(2011)**.

Education

The Higher Education Academy **(2014)** reported that minority ethnic students pursued several disciplines ranging from biological sciences, business and management sciences and economics to engineering, law, marketing, maths and statistics.

Young people from all ethnic groups showed a high propensity towards '*Business Management*' and '*Law*' programmes, which probably explains the conversion rate between academic-professional achievement and actual enterprise creation. After the white student community, Africans, Indians and Pakistanis are among the leading minorities who excel in the field of '*Finance/Accounting*' (**See Table 7.1**).

Table 7.1 Selected University subject attainment rates by major British ethnic students
(Source: Woodfield, Ruth (2014), Undergraduate retention and attainment across the disciplines, The Higher Education Academy, UK P28)

Discipline	African	Bangladeshi	Caribbean	Chinese	Indian	Pakistan	White
Art and Design	1,590	415	1,498	972	1,487	683	71,785
Biological Sciences	1,886	458	379	365	1,542	1,502	38,250
Business/Management	5,523	1,367	2,007	1,041	4,411	2,883	68,360
Computer Science	3,816	988	1,026	741	2,894	2,414	41,524
Engineering	3,940	579	757	1,000	2,775	1,858	64,097
Finance/Accounting	2,137	555	397	545	1,826	1,690	14,268
Health	4,538	775	993	741	5,685	3,849	51,828
Hospitality, Leisure etc.	1,481	155	1,098	246	843	397	47,954
Law	3,661	1,076	1,291	357	2,888	3,524	34,844
Marketing	629	79	310	111	501	257	8,172
Maths and Statistics	584	269	165	508	1,172	486	18,512

Notes: Overall, 85,592 students took part in 'Business Management' courses with 79% (68,360) coming from a white background; 20% (17,232) minority ethnic origin and 11% (10,028) specifically of South

Asian origin. If figures for both Nepalese and Sri Lankans were included the participation rates for business management courses might have been higher.

Categorisation

This deals with classifying different types of young entrepreneurs according to levels of enterprise activity. Country studies suggest that youth entrepreneurship varies according to broad categories (**Chigunta, 2002**). Chigunta proposed a phased, tri-transitional approach to youth entrepreneurship as follows:-

a) *Pre-entrepreneurs* age 15-19 years): This is the formative stage where there is a transition from home or education to the work place.

b) *Budding entrepreneurs* age 20-25 years, growth stage where young people are likely to have gained some experience, skills and capital to run enterprises. They also face hurdles such as jettisoned by marginal activities; going out of business; and/or running successful enterprises.

c) *Emergent entrepreneurs* age 26-29 years, a prime stage where they have valuable experiences in business and more matured than lower-aged groups.

However, although this type of categorization serves to identify broad distinctions of enterprise formation generally, this classification is applicable to South Asian and other minority ethnic young entrepreneurs. Actually, it also relates to the transitional process of youth enterprise development across key industry sectors.

Noteworthy, in spite of the growing number of youth enterprises in the UK, perceptions of enterprise among young people regarding the concept of business still exist. Perceptions vary from the 'fear' factor and impact of the media in general to the 'version' on apprenticeships versus traineeships – **Fig7.1**.

Figure 7.1 Perceptions on Youth Entrepreneurship in Britain

- A gap between the number of young people who want to start and the number who actually do.
- Fear plays a 'pressure' role especially in cases where parents encourage young people into 'safe' professions or employment.
- The 'media personality' approach to enterprise is unhelpful; the way business is presented in the media affects young people's decisions particularly language and terms associated with enterprises as a whole.
- Enterprise education is not a national brand compared to traineeships and apprenticeships.

(Source: Final Report: Commission into Young People and enterprise January 2015 England P9)

Changing Trends

In the mid-990s, there was considerable interest within academic, media and other circles regarding the reluctance of second and third generation South Asians' to sustain the 'corner shop' legacy of the 1950s-1980s, pioneered by the first generation (**McEvoy, 2002**).

Various studies showed that apart from the intensive labour and long hours involved, 21st century ethnic retailers are competing with the 'One Pound' evolution and other industry variables. This meant that young graduates sought self-employment into business and the industry as well as the professions that were once a male preserve of mainstream.

In particular, members of the under 40s generation (or 20s-30s group) are very active in the creative industries sector as they carve out media careers, for example. South Asian young people have chosen subjects like 'media and communications' along with 'music, dance and drama'.

With the impact of western culture (**Trivedi, 1984**), either in the form of, or lack of poor media images of their existence, young British-born South Asians' have developed varying descriptive identities. They include *'Indian', 'Muslim', ' Sikh', 'Punjabi', 'Bengali', 'Gujarati'* and other ethno-religico-identities (**2009**).

Young women have displayed artistic versatility in communications segments inter alia radio, television, print, web, live events, satellite, cable, advertising, marketing and music. While many South Asians attempt to maintain a single but integrated identity of either Britishness or Englishness, others are engaged in ['cultural splitting-hairs'] traversing the realms of British and 'Asian' culture respectively (**1996**).

Creative Industries

Further, the 2001 UK Census revealed that the media was fast attracting young South Asian graduates. In the category of culture, media and sports, the following ethnic-gender groups were featured:- **Fig 7.2**

Figure 7.2 South Asian gender participation in creativity

13,335 Indian men and 10,847 women;
4,546 Pakistani men and 1,045 women; and
1,045 Bangladeshi men and 602 women.

(*Source: Bachkaniwala, Darshan, Wright, Mike and Ram, Monder (2001) Succession in South Asian Family Businesses in the UK,* International Small Business Journal, *9 (4), pp.15-27*)

An exhibition of new Indian and Sri Lankan talent in fashion and design, showcased participants in the British Council's Young Creative Entrepreneur (YCE) programme.

The event recognised excellence in creative entrepreneurship, fostering dialogue between young entrepreneurs in the UK and overseas.

The work of South Asian designers reflected an interest in traditional techniques and crafts whilst projecting cutting-edge creativity using sustainable methods of production and materials.

Artistic designers included **Subhabrata Sadhu**, a textile designer who designed and developed collections of pure contemporary pashmina by working closely with traditional weavers in Kashmir.

The duo, **Sarthak Sengupta** and **Sahil Bagga** also produced design solutions and forms of innovation incorporating the belief that designing beautiful and functional products and spaces should be combined with efforts to preserve local traditions.

Kasuni Rathnasuriya, founded KUR, a Sri Lankan brand of contemporary sustainable womenswear. It features unique crafts such as traditional beeralu lace and new approaches such as recycling and redesigning **(2011)**.

Textiles
Over the past few years, the British Council has been organising its annual 'International Young Fashion Entrepreneurs' (IYFE) Award. In 2014, approximately 24 young people aged 25 to 35 years, were involved as they gave fresh impetus to the garment industry operated by both British-based South Asians and their counterparts from the Indian sub-continent.

An innovative project (**CEAL, 2014-2015**) promoting textiles heritage amongst South Asian women created much interest among under-30s. Many youngsters were unaware of the invaluable contribution made by elders – grandmothers *(nannies)* or aunts *(chachis or masis)* to the textiles industry in the early part of the 20th century.

"We didn't know very much about what our elders did in the textiles factories at that time. They would come home and say a little. I can remember seeing my grandmother and hearing about others bringing home work from the factory. They all sat quietly doing piece-work. It was as though they were doing one job twice. Through CEAL's heritage project, I learnt much about the fashions back then and the contribution textiles made to the economy. Now I understand a little better the role of my family in all of this" **(Interviews, October 2014)**.

Services Sector
The services sector plays a dominant role in business and industry in Britain and South Asian young entrepreneurs are influencing this trend too **(Dewitt, 2011)**. Her study

captured the driving forces and strategies such as financial input, support networks and market opportunities.

Under-40 entrepreneurs are operating multiple firms in the accounting, financial, marketing and other segments of the 'Business and Professional Services' (BPS) industry sector.

Their market entry is based on these drivers: social influence and support, sound education, inspiration from entrepreneurial family networks, the desire to achieve status and flexibility, support networks including the role of co-ethnic, community-based and business associations.

Demand-side opportunities also relate to the implementation of specific plans tailored for niche markets for goods and services.

According to Dewitt **(Ibid)**, a vital component is the way in which members of British South Asian third generation optimise their ethnicity and dual citizenship to access clients and widen service sector markets through innovation, style and responsiveness to new market trends - home and abroad.

Engineering

Young British South Asians are known for their passion in engineering sciences as reflected by choice of studies and overall success in recent years. This is translated into business flair and elective automobile brands as Murtaza Arif depicted in a rare feature on *British Asians and their Cars by, DESIblitz* **(2012)**.

DESIblitz undertook a study to find out which cars British Asians admire and operate. The study showed that many liked luxury cars, though the recession meant they opted for cheaper or more affordable vehicles.

Traditionally, wealthy South Asian buyers and tycoons will drive prestigious brands, especially if they have a resale value. According to Murtaza's depiction,

"British 'Asians' love their cars, and the youngsters of today prefer to buy cars, which have been appealing to generations for a long time. German cars are most popular amongst the South Asian Community with Mercedes leading the way. Some people have a strong preference for cars such as Ford, whilst others like sports and hyper exotic cars.

With increasing numbers of young British South Asians and other minority ethnic entrepreneurs and consumers opting for luxury goods and services, the automobile industry is underpinned by certain ethnic features - **Fig 7.3**.

Figure 7.3 Main features of the South Asian automobile industry

- Prestigious brand imagery;
- Demographics, location and social income;
- Types of garages and choice of vehicles;
- Special events such as weddings, anniversaries, birthdays etc.;
- Reliability factor in choosing particular brands;
- Maintenance and allied costs;
- Sports 'followers' buy Golf, Subaru, Impreza, Mitsubishi, and Evo brands.
- Speed, sound, hyper and exotic as well as other vehicular features.

(Source: DESIblitz, 2012)

Undoubtedly, young British South Asians combine purchasing power and entrepreneurial gravitas to command a multi-million currency value, market share in the automobile/engineering trade.

From current evidence, this trend in both a passion for owing luxurious vehicles and operating garages, looks set to continue for a very long time.

Entrepreneurship

Britain is cited as a 'top investment destination in the EU' (**2015**) for ethnic enterprise success. One newspaper report indicated that young Indian entrepreneurs are among top five nationalities whose citizens have set up companies and created jobs in Britain (**2014**).

The Centre for Entrepreneurs and the financial technology company, DueDil, stated that 32,593 Indians set up companies with turnovers between £1 million and £200 million pounds as of **September 2013**.

On average, migrant entrepreneurs were younger than their British counterparts and twice as entrepreneurial as Britain-born working age population. The top five nationalities were Irish, Indian, German, American and Chinese.

Migrant entrepreneurs represent one in seven of all companies operate in the UK. Nearly half a million people from 155 countries have settled in the UK and launched businesses, the report added. Migrant-led SMEs are creating 14% of all jobs.

Challenges such as access to finance and cultural and language barriers have not prevented migrant entrepreneurs from building companies.

The Anatomy of British South Asian Enterprise

London benefits disproportionately, with 20 times the number of migrant-led businesses based here (188,000) than Birmingham, the second most popular location with 19,000. Centre for Entrepreneurs chairman Luke Johnson said:

"The majority of the public appreciate the value of migrant entrepreneurs, yet our politicians and media send out negative signals that risk alienating this vital group of job creators. Given the huge contribution of migrant entrepreneurs, we are calling upon the media and politicians to join us in celebrating those who come to our country and launch businesses" **(2013)**.

Food and Hospitality

The growing influence of elders has had a profound effect on young minority ethnic communities across the British Isles. It has triggered creativity and innovation amongst South Asians of different faiths and social mores, ushering in the process, new types of ethnic entrepreneurship **(Fig 7.4)**.

Figure 7.4 Case Study of Ieat Foods
(Source: BBC News, 23 February 2014)

Shazia Saleem from Luton is the founder of a ready-meals business, **Ieat Foods** (as in "I eat"), which makes a range of traditional British and Italian dishes - such as shepherd's pie and lasagne according to Islamic dietary tradition. Ms Saleem's business idea was prompted while at Warwick University in 1987. *"Most of my friends at university were non-Muslims, and when we did a weekly food shop their trolleys were full of really tasty-looking ready meals, and all I could buy were things like cheese and onion pasties".*

After leaving university Ms Saleem first got a salaried job, working for UK entrepreneur Peter Jones, one of the "dragons" from the BBC TV show Dragons' Den. Getting a job in Mr Jones' investment and portfolio office was an "unbelievable opportunity", and a great way to learn about running a business.

Later, she resigned, and using her savings, left the UK and went to Cambodia. Despite no travel experience, Saleem bought 50% of a run-down holiday resort. After returning to the UK, she launched Ieat Foods after her father's death in 2013. *"One of the last things he said to me was, 'You must go and do it, and make it successful'.* Saleem conducted market research which proved thousands of second-generation UK Muslims wanting to buy halal ready-meal versions of British and Italian dishes composed of natural ingredients, and that tasted good.

With a small staff complement, Ms Saleem has big plans to expand Ieat Foods. *"I get my ambition from my parents, who came to this country from Sri Lanka with nothing and both worked in multiple jobs to make a good life for themselves and their family,"* she says. *"And my faith and my British identity is why I'm doing this particular business. I'm just mixing the two."*

In recent years, sections of online media have been publishing snippets of emerging British young entrepreneurs; that is, those with the potential to succeed as well as the many who've achieved enterprise stardom.

Below, are a selected number of industry segments/sectors founded by third generation British South Asian entrepreneurs (**Fig 7.5**).

Figure 7.5 Mini-Cases of Third Generation South Asian Entrepreneurs
(Source: www.yhponline.com)

Mobile Technology: **Ambarish Mitra** is the CEO of **Blippar**; he grew up in India and pursued higher studies in Britain. His likely entrepreneurial heroes were the likes of Bill Gates, Michael Dell, Steve Jobs, Steve Wozniak and Jeffery Bezos among others. Blippar is an image recognition app/platform allowing brands to cover all its press ads, product packaging, outdoor ads into wide range of digital content from communications, gaming, research/collaboration, promotions/incentives, entertainment, information and education, social engagement and many more.

The challenges were; namely, making the enterprise a scalable business and 'convincing world's biggest brands that this technology will revolutionise traditional advertising and help connect better with their customers'. Business growth is based on hiring quality staff, imbedding research and development and exploiting mass markets in the technology industry.

Education: Sabirul Islam got his first taste of business at 13, working for his cousin; he got fired within 2 weeks. He started his entrepreneurial career at 14, designing calendars for teachers in schools and became an investor at 16. Sold 42,500 copies of his book *"World at your feet"* in 9 months, speaking at numerous events and hundreds of secondary schools. He has spoken in several countries. In 2011, it was reported that he was preparing to launch his Teen-Trepreneur Board Game which will be sold globally. Islam's most memorable moment is being a recipient of the *Mosaic Entrepreneur of the Year* award by the Prince of Wales and Princess of Jordan 2008.

Fashion: Harpreet Gill is the CEO/Founder of **DressMe.com**, a fashion-focused web & mobile app that helps consumers locate fashion stores, brands and products. He grew up in the textiles industry through the extended family business. *"I particularly remember the 80's and early 90's when fashion and the textiles industry grew and prospered in Britain. One of my uncles from East London was inspirational; great at spotting trends and willing to venture outside his comfort zone"*. Obstacles included finding innovative brands, financing and building the technology to demonstrate concept surety. Growth is inspired by 'core focus of training online search into in-store footfall' and satisfying consumer demands for clothing and footwear in-store and offline.

Data Visualisation: Pallav Nadhani was born in Bhagalpur, India and founded **FusionCharts** (2001) aged 16-years after being dissatisfied with Microsoft Excel's charting capabilities. He subsequently authored an article on *'Macromedia Flash'* that earned him $1,500 and feedback from developers, which together acted as seed money and motivation for establishing the FusionCharts concept. In 2002 at 17, Nadhani founded Infosoft Global; he worked alone developing the product, website, documents, sales and marketing and customer support for the first three years. Since that time, he has expanded, servicing numerous customers –globally and attracting a range of business sectors.

The company received global kudos when it was selected in 2010 by US President Barack Obama to design digital dashboards for the US Federal Administration. The company also runs Seeders Inc., a venture capital fund enterprise. Growth strategy is premised on expanding its portfolio including products for PowerPoint and SharePoint along with making the company's site fully JavaScript compatible with all devices.

Retail: Sudip Gautam who was born in Nepal, moved to London with his mother in November 2002 and 9 years later, was 'announced as Britain's biggest seller on eBay'. Starting from humble beginnings as a 13 year old, he borrowed his mum's credit card to buy a domain for £10, an initial step towards building an online retail empire. He started his eBay shop in 2004 expanding its range to include consumer electronics and mobile goods, growing rapidly especially in 2009. He worked long hours, generating over £3million in yearly revenue, finally ascending to number one thereby becoming Britain's biggest seller on eBay with over 600,000 sales in the last 5 years. Still in his early 20s (2015), Gautam was trading in

---

> thousands of eBay items daily and has opened the London Magic Store which sells mobile accessories. With a small dedicated staff, this young entrepreneur is determined to ensure excellent customer service is maintained.

The success of third generation South Asians in various industry sectors has been discussed so far in this chapter. The enterprise formation rates of business owners in this ethnic group are based on essential features. These include skills acquisition, being able to manage institutional processes, ignore as much as they possibly can, labour market discrimination or ethnic typecasting. Other contributory factors comprise:

- Traineeships/internships that provide skills training in key professions.
- Unlike previous generations, young South Asians thrive on professionalism.
- Market disadvantage was not always a compelling reason for self-employment.
- Keen to maintain independence in business and the professions.
- Young women viewed deregulation as business opportunities.
- Young owners were interested less about institutional processes that are typecasting.

(Hutnyk, 2000)

Start-up Challenges

Like most enterprise start-ups, founders have to confront and overcome challenges, drawbacks and obstacles of one kind or another. These represent part of the ongoing experience in the day-to-day running of a firm and what is often described as a rather 'steep learning curve'.

However, it is the ability to be resilient and sustain business goals that is an object lesson for today's ambitious entrepreneurs of any age, ethnicity, gender and other socio-economic persuasions.

Mainstream literature is filled with examples and citations of issues affecting business people of the 'third generation age'. The cases involving South Asian entrepreneurs in this chapter have highlighted similarities in type and degree. The major challenges faced are:

- Access to quality technical assistance and enterprise support.
- Application of modern technology to revolutionise traditional advertising.
- Researching appropriate brands for new products and services.
- Having a 'disruptive model' that can induce consumer scepticism.
- Financing and building technology to demonstrate concept surety.
- Ensuring the right kind of investment for business strategy.
- Prioritising multiple role-functions without losing sight of initial objectives.
- Securing the trust of distributors, suppliers, staff and supporters.
- Focusing on consistency, reliability, affordability and warranty.

- Work-life balance whilst making initial personal sacrifices (**2015**).

There are of course, other remarkable examples of industry success amongst British South Asian under-40s. The majority of them are highly segmented spanning England and Wales. Their pace of success is also measured by levels of adaption to 'cultural' markets as well as types of goods and services which are also synonymous with commercial operations.

They have tended to move away from the old traditional way of doing business and instead, develop modern approaches to trading practices locally, nationally and internationally. In doing so, they are contributing to economic development in various UK Regions (**Fig 7.6**).

Figure 7.6 Mini-cases of other UK-based South Asian Young Entrepreneurs
(Source: www.asianenterprise.biz/fast_fortunes_young_asian_millionaires/full.html)

- Philanthropist Azeem Ibrahim, 31, set up an **IT consultancy company** (1997) which is estimated to be £60m. The Glasgow-born entrepreneur has also made his name in financial services – the **European Commerce and Mercantile Bank** specialise in accounts for corporations and wealthy individual clients involved in commodity trading.
- Shaf Rasul, 37, made his £82m fortune by creating Edinburgh-based **E-net Computers** and then investing in **property**, with his portfolio now extending to Dubai.
- Telecoms based fledgling giant, Yoganathan Ratheesan, 32, launched his own London-based telecoms company, **Lebara**, in 2001 and is now worth around £50m. The company started selling international telephone calling cards, helping immigrants to keep in touch with family with cheap call rates. The company has moved into the mobile phone market, going into partnership with Vodafone.
- Ajaz Ahmed, chairman of **AKQA Limited**, made his fortune from advertising and at 36 years old is worth around £45m. AKQA is a pioneering digital advertising firm set to expand worldwide and boasts premier league clients such as Nike, Unilever, Microsoft and Coca-Cola.
- Afzal Khan, 39 is worth at least £40m through his Bradford-based company **Khan Design**, which designs and styles cars for high profile clients such as footballers.
- Manchester-based developer Aneel Mussarat, 38, who tops the league with a whopping £145m accumulated through **property.**
- Walsall-based Raj Chatha ran his first retail shop at the age of 18. Now 38 years old, Chatha and family are worth £70m through the family's **European Food Brokers** group. The **Whittalls Wines** operation is part of this group.

  Ages of business owners are based 2016 figures

Awareness of Support

In January 2015, a commission report alluded to endeavours by the British Government to support youth enterprises; be they start-ups or existing firms. Much of the report centred on youth work, social capital and the means to which enterprise can add leverage to alternative forms of employment for the young unwaged, untrained, jobless, disengaged and not trustful of the system.

In reviewing the type of agencies facilitating youth entrepreneurship activities, the National Youth Agency (NYA) observed that with the exception of the **Prince's Trust** and to a lesser extent **Young Enterprise**, brand awareness 'is low for organisations working in the entire sector and there is not enough awareness of these organisations amongst young people' (**2015, p15**). **Fig 7.7 below**

All of the youth enterprises featured in this chapter, had one thing in common; technical proficiency, as a main driver towards ultimate success. Since creativity and ambition were construed as less of a problem for young people, the NYA emphasised that other skill sets –age, experience, leadership and decision-making – were also important to young people excelling in all aspects of entrepreneurial activity. The following 'soft skills' are also important to personal (inter-personal) development:

- Communication;
- Teamwork;
- Creativity;
- Determination;
- Ambition;
- Confidence;
- Decision Making;
- Problem Solving;
- Planning;
- Leadership;
- Resilience; and
- Risk-taking (the author's inclusion) – [**NYA, 2015**] **Fig 7.8.**

Figure 7.7 Percentage of respondents' knowledge of enterprise organisations

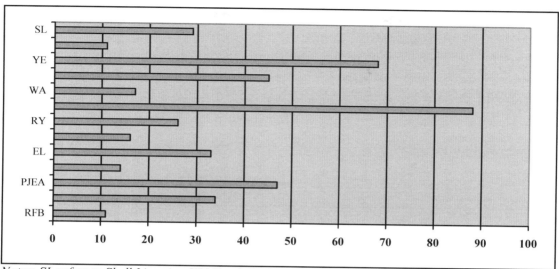

Notes: *SL refers to Shell Livewire, YBI Youth Business International, YE Young Enterprise, WA Wayra Academy, PT - Prince's Trust, RY - Rockstar Youth, NEW - New Entrepreneurs Foundation, EL - Enterprise Lab, SO - Striding Out, PJEP - Peter Jones Enterprise Academy, NEA – New Enterprise Allowance and RFB - Ready for Business. The National Youth Agency (NYA) received 93 responses.*

Enterprise Initiatives

There are a plethora of regional and national schemes aimed at mainstream and minority communities keen on enterprise start-ups. Among these are:

- *The 2008-founded Enterprise Finance Guarantee,* operated by the UK's Department for Business, Innovation and Skills' 'Business Bank'. It offers a loan guarantee scheme to viable SMEs which have been refused loans by the commercial market, due to inadequate security and/or the lack of a track record.

- The publicly-funded *Business Angel Co-Investment Fund* (2011) makes initial equity investments of £100,000 - £1 million into high growth-potential SMEs – with individual investments limited to 49 per cent of the value of a company's total investment round, and less than 30 per cent of a company's total equity at the close of an investment round. Follow-up investments can be made by the CoFund at a later date.

- *The 2012-developed Seed Enterprise Investment Scheme (SEIS)* provides 50 per cent capital gains tax relief to individuals wishing to invest in small companies of less than 25 employees

- *The Phoenix Development Fund* (2000-2006), a £198 million fund in England, sought to tackle social exclusion by promoting entrepreneurship in deprived areas and among under-represented groups. 20 projects funded under the scheme focused on minority ethnic firms. The aim was to involve locally, trusted intermediaries in the provision of business support. Other services included peer support (advice, micro lending), start-up training, mentoring, qualifications and networking within communities.

- *The SIED/REFLEX Programme* was first launched in Islington; it delivered community-based business support to groups perceived by mainstream agencies, as too difficult to reach or engage, most notably minority ethnic, faith and lone parent groups. Advisers within local communities were trained to provide information, advice and consultancy to new/established entrepreneurs.
A Kingston Small Business Research Centre survey revealed that over 1,000 entrepreneurs or businesses were advised during the funding period, 1,665 counselling sessions were held, 237 workshops delivered and 21 cases of assistance with funding applications offered (**Ibid, NYA, 2015**).

Figure 7.8 Mini-case of an Enterprise Innovator

Sumit Jain who was born in 1980, left India over a decade to reside in Britain. Since his arrival, he has been involved in several enterprise activities –ranging from education to the food and hospitality sectors respectively.

Jain is owner of the Midlands-based **Bright Learning Academy**, an education institute that provides a high calibre of training for individuals of all ages. The academy helps overseas learners to adjust to British life through citizenship programmes and other such courses.

He co-manages a franchise of the Indian burrito company, **Wrapchic** in Birmingham. His desire is to '*cater for the grab-and-go-market with an exciting Indian option, where customers can enjoy the taste of Indian food from breakfast time rather than the traditional setting*' (**2015**).

According to Jain, the business has employed many young people who have learnt not only about Indian/South Asian food, but other ethnic cuisine. His views about [calculated] risk-taking and resilience in business and industry are summed up this way, "*As a young man coming to Britain, my dream was to be a highly successful entrepreneur. The challenges were many –a different environment, the language, the culture and the people in general. They all had different ways of doing things, but I had to adjust. I was determined to face these obstacles. I used my culture to inform and guide my actions. I did make mistakes along the way but I learnt from them quickly. One thing I learnt also, was to develop good networks – people, organisations and institutions. These are influential and powerful and anyone who wants to succeed especially in Britain, must utilise this strategic approach*" (**Interview September 2014**).

Business Location

Similar to their 'elders', young people are keen on the types of locations including business premises, for the sake of commercial viability and enterprise sustenance. Their academic and professional training has enabled them to identify other market variables for choosing business locations. Their choice of location is also dependent on the presence of ethnic communities and available (consumer) opportunities amongst other competitive factors.

Table 7.2 highlights key industries and their complementary UK Regions British South Asians are operating. It should be borne in mind too, that some of the more successful firms have branches overseas – the Middle East, South Asia, Africa, Europe and the USA, to name but a few international locations.

Table 7.2 Selected Business Location Profiles
(Source: Textual analysis and public information –printed and electronic, January 2015)

Industry Sector	UK Regional Location
Creative Industries	London, South East, East of England, The Midlands, North West, Midlands, London, Yorkshire & Humber, Scotland and Wales.
Business and the Professions	London, West Midlands, North West, Yorkshire & Humber, Wales, Scotland.
Construction, Engineering and Real Estate	London, Midlands, Yorkshire & Humber, Scotland and Wales.
Education & Training	London, East of England, Midlands, Yorkshire & Humber and Scotland.
Food and Hospitality	London, South East, East of England, Midlands, North East, North West.
Health & Social Care	London, South East, East of England, Midlands, Yorkshire & Humber, Scotland and Wales.
Manufacturing (light and heavy)	London, South East, East of England, Midlands, Yorkshire & Humber, North West, Scotland and Wales.
Information Technology (IT)	London, West Midlands, North West, Yorkshire & Humber, Wales, Scotland.
Personal Care (fashion/textiles)	North East, Yorkshire & Humber, Wales.
Social Enterprises	Almost all English Regions plus Scotland, Wales and Northern Ireland.

Challenges and Opportunities

Throughout this chapter, we have witnessed significant trends in business and industry, which are indicative of the type of challenges young founder-owners confronted especially during the start-up phase.

However, these very obstacles gave rise to owners' determination to excel by optimising market advantage through customer segmentation and other strategic approaches.

Despite composition and size, South Asian youth firms have shown that they are prospects for overall success in different industry sectors as the evidence below illustrates (**Table 7.3**).

Table 7.3 Industry Sector Challenges and Opportunities
(Source: Textual Analysis from Chapter 7, December 2015)

Challenges	Opportunities
• *Creative Industries*: cultural differences, typecasting, trying to fit in; using ethnicity to create innovative products and services.	• This sector is worth £76.9 billion yearly with over 5% of growth per annum (**DMCS, January 2015**).
• *Professional Services*: low market entry, finances for start-up is a problem; still dominated by mainstream companies; new to respond to new markets at home and abroad.	• This industry has a market value of £6.02 billion- this market too is growing (**www.consultancy.uk, March 2015**).
• *Engineering:* Vacancies are difficult to fill in technical and management roles; start-ups can be quite a challenge due to high cost entry barriers; limited support exists.	• Engineering firms contribute about £27 billion and this is set to rise year on (**Engineering UK 2015**).
• *Food and Hospitality:* issues around quality, pricing, packaging and procedural regulations plus the influx of supermarket chains and the 'One Shop' business-consumer concept.	• This area contributed £57 billion (2014 estimates). Turnover in this trade is estimated also at £118 billion (**Oxford Economics, England September 2015**).
• *Mobile Technology*: make the business 'scalable', acquiring committed staff, developing the right business model.	• Advertising across digital platforms was estimated to reach £20 billion per year (*The Guardian*, **28 March 2014**).
• *Education*: start-up costs can be prohibitive, competition with mainstream, market intelligence including customer segmentation can prove difficult because of inexperience.	• This sector has exporting potential worth £17.5 billion to the British economy (**Department for Business, Innovation & Skills, July 2013**).
• *Fashion:* lack of innovation brands, financing, building technology to demonstrate concept surety, untrained and inexperienced staff.	• Direct value of the UK fashion industry to the economy is £26 billion (**British Council, autumn 2014**).

Conclusion

In this chapter, we examined the role and contribution of third generation South Asian entrepreneurs to the British economy. There was evidence to suggest that only in the last 10 years attempts have been made to publish information on youth entrepreneurship, though much of it tended to be around surveys or literature reviews.

Seminal reports such as those from the *National Youth Agency* (**January, 2015**), the *Institute of Employment Studies* (**March, 2015**) and the *International Labour Organisation* (**2015**), have merely discussed recurring cultural, economic and social concerns affecting the youth. These coupled with an overview of youth self-employment as well as barriers and incentives to enterprise start-up by young people. Issues such as ethnic profiling, spatial distribution, industry sector representation and gender diversity were excluded from these authoritative blueprints.

So that, much of the profiles featured in this chapter were sourced from online or press publications and face to face interviews, based on selected individuals or recommendations of young entrepreneurs. These played a pivotal role in the research process. It is hoped that these 'live cases' will help readers access and understand more about the true workings of youth entrepreneurship from a British South Asian dimension.

Since there was difficulty in obtaining information and data on the quantum of young enterprises in the UK by location and general demography, we identified existing firms in the public domain. By using a relative sample size approach, it gave us room to assess and evaluate start-up challenges, product and service lines, and demonstrate measured growth prospects, according to founder-owners' perspective. Through 'selected cases, too, other signifiers such as image, reputation and overall personality of founders, were evidenced.

One noticeable trend while researching this book, were the increasing numbers of South Asian students and their peers, pursuing multiple graduate studies in the professions and sciences. These disciplines consisted of management, computer science, engineering, financial and accounting, health and law especially. On average, 11% or 10,028 South Asian students demonstrated attainment rates over a dozen subject areas (**2014**).

The categorisation of young entrepreneurs was also instructive since it made a clear distinction between young entrepreneurs from different age groups. Although each had the age factor that limited his/her experience, factors such as creativity, motivation, technical skills and abilities, all played a part in start-up and eventual success rates.

Although there were limitations on the range of South Asians by sub-ethnicity, an appreciable number of case studies or mini-cases were compiled to showcase British South Asian youth enterprises in the 21st century. Among the sectors profiled were

creative industries, engineering, food and hospitality, technology, personal care, fashion and retail.

Several indicators emerged as 'contributory factors' that exemplified the unique success of South Asian third generation businesses, as contained in this chapter. These indices were:-

- 80% of all founders used *online technology* to introduce product and service lines.
- 40% had *co-ethnic/inter-ethnic partners* in their firms (mobile technology especially).
- 75% considered *family influence*, as a decisive factor (food and hospitality in particular).
- 80% conceived their business ideas at *school, college or university*.
- Ownership rates were *60% males and 40% females*.
- Gaps in mainstream literature on the enterprise performance of British youths overall.
- Minority ethnic agencies seldomly discuss the subject of British 'youth economics'.

As a compensatory measure, previous sections either profiled or alluded to the enterprise success rates of third generation South Asians. In an effort to give credence to the contribution of these wealth creators, the publishers took into consideration the limitations of poor media coverage on the overall success of British young entrepreneurs.

By profiling examples of business owners' sector-based achievements, it was felt that this approach would encourage and stimulate greater public discussion on an emerging, but highly intelligent and successful group of British enterprise 'standard bearers'. Interestingly, this represents too, concrete signs of a sea-change whereby more minority ethnic communities are using their integrative power-status to influence a new economic and social dynamic in Britain, for good.

Notes

Youth Entrepreneurship
The Prince's Youth Business International (YBI) in conjunction with Global Entrepreneurship Monitor (GEM) conducted a comprehensive study on '*The state of global youth entrepreneurship*'. The study covered the European Union, Non-European Union, Sub-Saharan Africa, Latin America and the Caribbean, Asia Pacific and South Asia, MENA Region and the USA (GEM Report, 2012; Tackling youth unemployment through Technical Vocational Education and Training –TVET - *UNESCO* 2013).

YBI

Youth Business International (YBI) is a global network of independent non-profit initiatives whose aim is to assist young people to start and grow businesses and create employment. Its members assist under-served young entrepreneurs with training, [financial] capital access and mentoring. This common approach is adapted to local environments via partnership-working with governments, businesses, multilateral institutions and civil [society] organisations (www.youthbusiness.org)

Migrant Entrepreneurs

The Centre for Entrepreneurs was set up in 2013 as an independent think-tank, to promote the role of entrepreneurs in creating economic growth and social well-being. It is home to the national enterprise campaign, *StartUp Britain*. Core activities include advocacy, research and campaigns, thought-leadership, and resources (http://centreforentrepreneurs.org/)

Web link

The online information source – www.yhponline.com – captured profiles of young entrepreneurs by age, gender, ethnicity and industry sector representation. It is one of few such web links that has attempted to focus on the diversity of youth enterprises across the British Isles.

Enterprise Agencies

Apart from selected organisations that focused on young enterprise start-ups, there were hundreds of other 'arms-length' bodies whose remit was to provide technical assistance and enterprise support ('*Smart Cities Briefing*', Centre for Cities, London 2014). The current patchwork quilt system is affecting the smooth delivery of services especially for fledging and/or young entrepreneurs operating within inner-city [disadvantaged] areas.

Web Links

http://centreforentrepreneurs.org

DressMe.com.

www.yhponline.com

www.asianenterprise.biz/fast_fortunes_young_asian_millionaires/full.htm

www.desiblitz.com, 26 December 2012.

Selected References

Levie, J., Hart, M. and Bonner, K. (2013). Global Entrepreneurship Monitor: *United Kingdom 2013 Monitoring Report*. Also ww.gemconsortium.org/docs/download/3371.

Tackling youth unemployment through Technical Vocational Education and Training – TVET - *UNESCO* 2013.

YBI 2011, *Global Entrepreneurship Monitor*, England p53-55.

Woodfield, Ruth (2014), *Undergraduate retention and attainment across the disciplines*, The Higher Education Academy, UK p28.

Chigunta, F. (2002): *Youth Entrepreneurship: Meeting the Key Policy Challenges*. Wolfson College, Oxford University, England.

Final Report: Commission into Young People and Enterprise January 2015, England p9.

'*Smart Cities Briefing*', Centre for Cities, London 2014.

Basu, Dipannita and Werbner, Pnina: 'Who Wants to be a Millionaire? Gendered Entrepreneurship and British South Asian Women in the Culture Industries', *Revue Européenne des Migrations Internationales*, 2009 (25) 3 pp. 53-77.

Sharma, Sanjay, Hutnyk, John and Sharma, Ash, eds. 1996, 'DIS-ORIENTING RHYTHMS: The Politics of the New Asian Dance Music', *Zed Books*, London & New Jersey.

Bachkaniwala, Darshan, Wright, Mike and Ram, Monder (2001) 'Succession in South Asian Family Businesses in the UK', *International Small Business Journal, 9 (4), pp.15-27.*

Young Creative Entrepreneurs, British Council, South Bank University, London April 2011.

Dewitt, Sunita (2011): *Second and third generation South Asian service sector entrepreneurship in Birmingham*, Ph.D. thesis, University of Birmingham, England.

Dhaliwal, S. (2001) '*Which Way Now? Second/Third Generation Asian Business Entrepreneurs*,' paper presented at the 24th ISBA National Small Firms Policy and Research Conference.

Jacoby T (2000) 'Second-Generation Question Mark' *American Enterprise, December 2000.*

Janjuha, S and Dickson, K (1998) *'Succession within South Asian Family Firms in Britain'* 21st National Small Firms Policy and Research Conference Proceedings pp311-323, Durham, 18-20 November 1998.

Dhaliwal, Spinder (2000) 'Asian Female Entrepreneurs and Women in Business – an Exploratory Study', *Enterprise and Innovation Management Studies, 1 (2), pp. 207-216.*

Dhaliwal, Spinder and Adcroft, Andy (2003) *Success 2003: The Young One*, London, Ethnic Media Group.

Levie, J., and Hart, M. (2011). 'The Contribution of Migrants and Ethnic Minorities to Entrepreneurship in the United Kingdom', In M. Minitti (ed.). The Dynamics of Entrepreneurial Activity. Oxford: *Oxford University Press.*

Edmunds, June and Turner Bryan (2002a) 'Generations, Culture and Society', Milton, Keynes, *Open University Press.*

"The South Asian Presence in Britain and its Transnational Connections" and Singh, H. and Vertovec, S. (Eds) Culture and Economy in the Indian Diaspora, London: *Routledge,* 2002.

Hindustan Times, London 5 March 2014.

BBC News, 23 February 2014.

Hutnyk, J. (2000) 'Critique of Exotica: Music, Politics and the Culture Industry', London: *Pluto Press.*

Business Start-ups & Youth Self-employment in the UK, Institute of Employment Studies UK, March 2015.

Chapter 8 Strategies for Business Enterprise Growth

"We have to continue promoting the work of our businesses so that succeeding generations will know and learn more about the contribution we are making to British society"- **Suman Marriage Bureau.**

Introduction

In the preceding chapters of this book, we examined in appreciable detail, the contribution of South Asian firms to the British economy. We have appropriated the 'organisation and performance' model to highlight key industry sectors that business owners compete in **(2015)**. On completing this chapters, readers would be able to: -

- Gain further insights into the migratory trajectories of South Asians.
- Appreciate the contribution of South Asian firms to the British economy.
- Learn more about industry sector dynamics from this ethnic group.
- Recognise the challenges faced, and the prospects for future growth.

The notion of profiling six leading Britain South Asian groups – **Afghanis Bangladeshis, Indians, Nepalese, Pakistanis and Sri Lankans** – is rare in the field of ethnic entrepreneurship more so, that of the small and medium-sized enterprise (SME) sector.

On the one hand, Bangladeshi, Indian and Pakistani firms are given degrees of national coverage and are the subjects of ongoing research. Perhaps the reason is that they have greater numerical strength and presence. It is also perceived that they're more integrated than the other three South Asian communities -Afghanis, Nepalese and Sri Lankans - because of their duration as settlers in Britain.

On the other hand, the labour market activities of Afghanis, Nepalese and Sri Lankans are reported for the most part, in either London or South East England. Noteworthy, South Asian entrepreneurs who operate in other parts of Britain, receive little coverage in the media **(2008)**.

Anecdotally, there are multiple 'informal' businesses and other entities owned by South Asian 'sub-ethnic' groups such as Gurkhas (Nepalese), Sinhalese (Sri Lankans) and Sikhs (Indians), to give but a few examples. This trend reflects the critical importance of capturing the performance of British South Asian firms – locally and nationally.

Studies on 'Asian' businesses remain inconclusive and few have attempted to go beyond investigating the conventional 'triple-group' (Bangladeshis, Indians and Pakistanis). Information on ethnic groups in Britain is often restricted to heritage, faith, immigration, culture and other issues rather than the actual contribution they make to society.

It is for this reason that the term '*Asian*' remains problematic when references are made to business owners who hail from either the Indian-subcontinent or belong to parents from the South Asian region per se (**2015**). Making a proper ethnic distinction [of all minorities] helps to reduce if not alleviate, recurring demographic or geographic anomalies that affect the nature and scope for researching minorities, according to their natural or birth-hood ethnicity.

From a legacy standpoint, chronicling minority entrepreneurs whose communities experience social exclusion and economic deprivation, must be underpinned by sound, tested and corroborative information; be it empirical or anecdotal.

Attempts at creating a 'diversity playing field' by showcasing the contribution of minority firms to the British economy, apart from improving race relations, could enhance Britain's moral standing in the world.

Challenges

Overall, researching, analysing and compiling the unsung contribution of British minority ethnic groups, remains a formidable challenge on the business literature front. Gathering information and data can be daunting if resources are either insufficient or there is a lack of data on ethnic firms particularly. This sub-section therefore focuses on the challenges faced in interpreting, defining and chronicling the contribution of British South Asian firms from the 1800s to present (**Table 8.1**).

Table 8.1 Lifespan of South Asian Businesses Sectors

Industry Sector	Age of Business Sector
• Business and the Professions	• 97 years (from 1919)
• Construction	• 39 years (from 1976)
• Creative Industries	• 44 years (1972)
• Education and Training	• 40 years (1976*
• Food & Hospitality	• 207 years (from 1809)
• Health and Social Care	• 60 years (from 1948)
• Information Technology	• 40 years (from 1976)
• Manufacturing	• 40 years (from 1976)
• Personal Care	• 10-15years (estimate)
• Social Enterprise	• 125 years (from 1891)
• Transport & Logistics	• 32 years (from 1984)

Notes: the above figures illustrate minority entrepreneurs' resilience against odds.

Definition

Profiling six major South Asian representative groups that have growing 'concentrates' of business and industry across British inner-cities, is a strategic challenge for policy makers. For professional and lay savants interested in economic and social justice, this type of work is even more imposing. The term 'Asian', used to define anything remotely on citizens of Indian-subcontinental ancestry, is confusing and distorts the authentic identity of citizens and their communities from a heritage perspective (**Table 8.2**).

Table 8.2 Major countries of origin for South Asians in Britain
(Source: Office for National Statistics, England 2011)

Group	Countries of Origin
Afghanis	North-West Frontier Province of Afghanistan.
Bangladeshis	Primarily from Sylhet, north east of Bangladesh.
Indians	Punjab, Gujarat, Malayal & East Africa (Kenya, Tanzania and Uganda).
Nepalese	Nepal (mostly Gurkhas).
Pakistanis	Mipur, Punjab regions, Sindh, Khyber Pakhtunkhwa and Balochistan.
Sri Lankans	Sri Lanka

Notes: the table gives readers a bird's eye view of the migration journey of South Asians.

If the phrase 'Asian' is adapted contextually, then there is a risk of conflating 'Indian-sub continentals' with Chinese, Japanese, Koreans, Vietnamese and other nationalities from the broader Asia peninsula (**2005**). Thus the term 'Asian' was used interchangeably where citations, quotations or other information sources were used to give credence to material included in this book.

Population

Statistics on British South Asian communities as per ethnicity and sub-grouping, vary due to layers of cultural, faith, social and other characteristics that underpin this diverse community. Publicly, the narrative of this ethnic group appears disjointed, piecemeal and stereotypical especially when issues on identity are discussed.

Sections of mainstream and the ethnic media are not absolved from this reality either, particularly when covering sensitive issues on one or more South Asian group
(**Tables 8.3 & 8.4**).

Sampling

On the issue of datasets, where representative samples are restricted or deemed too small, lumping Bangladeshis and Pakistanis as a single ethnic category can be misleading. This is prevalent in matters dealing with employment, welfare, education, culture, health and other demographic indices (**ONS, 2003**). **See Table 8.**5

In specific studies on minority ethnic groups, the rubric of either 'Asian' or 'Other Asian' is used as a standard classification to define or highlight issues impacting on the lives of the six South Asian business groups covered in this book.

This ploy is counterproductive as it impinges on efforts to examine objectively, the socio-economic dynamics of citizens from a South Asian heritage background.

Table 8.3 Spatial Distribution of South Asians in Britain
(Source: Office for National Statistics, England 2011)

Ethnic Population	Major UK Regions
Afghanis (56,000)	London, Midland Counties, North West, North and Manchester
Bangladeshis (451,529)	London, West Midlands, North East, Manchester, Yorkshire & Humber, Scotland.
Indians (1,451,862)	London, the Home Counties, Scotland and Northern Island.
Nepalese (50,881)	London, Southeast, East of England, Midland Counties, South West.
Pakistanis (1,174,983)	London, the Home Counties, Wales, Scotland and Northern Island.
Sri Lankans (200,000)	London, Southeast, Midland Counties, Scotland and Wales.

Notes: The nature of locational presence of South Asian firms according to spatial distribution.

Table 8.4 Linguistic Diversity and Faith-based Practices by British South Asians
(Source: Office for National Statistics, England 2011)

Group	Spoken Languages	Faith-based Practices
Afghanis	English, Dari, Hindi, Pashto, Punjabi, Russian and Urdu.	Islam, Zoroastrianism, Sikhism, Judaism, Hinduism, Baha'i
Bangladeshis	Sylheti, Bengali, English.	Islam, Christianity, Hinduism, Sikhism, Buddhism.
Indians	Malayalam, Hindi, Tamil, Punjabi, Gujarati, Urdu, English and other language 'families'.	Hinduism, Sikhism, Jainism, Buddhism, Baha'i, Christianity, Judaism, Zoroastrianism and Islam.
Nepalese	English, Nepali, Khambu, Gurung, Magar.	Hinduism, Buddhism, Kirant (Kirat) Mundhum and Christianity.
Pakistanis	English, Hindi, Urdu, Potohari, Mirpuri, Punjabi, Pashto, Sindhi, Balochi, others.	Islam, Christianity, Hinduism, Sikhism, Judaism, Buddhism.
Sri Lankans	English, Tamil, Sinhalese.	Buddhism, Hinduism, Islam, Christianity.

Notes: The table captured the linguistic dexterity and multiple faith based practices.

Contribution

British South Asian literature has a London and South-Eastern focus/foci contrary to the presence of millions of South Asian communities across the UK. Geographically, analysing the true nature of minority ethnic groups' contribution to British society, remains a 'work in progress' as attempts to unearth information and data for this book, proved.

At the beginning of this century, some UK Regions began showing a real interest in the contribution of minorities in their respective areas. Apart from previous studies by the London Development Agency in the last century, ongoing work on the participation of minority ethnic groups in the labour market in other UK Regions has been subject to much scrutiny.

The Welsh Assembly (**2015**); the Scottish Executive (**2005**) and the Northern Island Assembly (**2008**) have conducted a range of studies on minorities in each of the three UK areas. Officials within these devolved assemblies must be commended for 'invoking' the equalities principle to publicise the invaluable contribution of minority ethnic groups in Scotland, Wales and Northern Ireland.

Since ethnic groups are dispersed across inner-city and conurbation areas within the UK, these regional reports enabled us to obtain useful information and data for the purpose of firms-sampling and actual case studies for this book (**Table 8.6**).

Table 8.5 Case Study Samples of British South Asian firms
(Source: information and data from direct interviews, directories and projects, 2013/2016)

Group	Sampled Firms	Actual Case Studies
• Afghanis	150	54
• Bangladeshis	300	73
• Indians	350	109
• Nepalese	200	49
• Pakistanis	200	100
• Sri Lankans	200	86
• Youth Entrepreneurs	100	30
Total	**1,500**	**501**

Notes: The rate of return for sampled firms was 36%; mini-cases/case studies including firms and public agencies & institutions (between 9 and 38 such cases profiled for the latter).

However, the inclusion of South Asians in regional assembly strategies also poses another identify challenge. Sections of this community define themselves on the basis of faith rather than natural ethnicity or ancestral heritage.

For example, some describe themselves as: '*East African Sikhs*' '*Pakistani-Muslims*', '*Indian- Sikhs*' and '*Sri Lankan Christians*' among other prefix identities.

This trend in identity-affirmation or confirmation, requires further investigation by ethnographers particularly in light of the recent acceptance of another terminology, '*Asianess*' (**2013**.

Yet, it is these forms of identity 'labelling' that distort the meaning, significance and the authenticity of South Asians in terms of their impact on British society.

Table 8.6 South Asian Industry Sector by Location
(Source: Companies House and information from firms' websites, 2013/2016)

Industry Sector	Predominant Location
Business & the Professions	London, Southeast, Home Counties, Scotland, Wales and Northern Ireland.
Construction	London, Southeast, Midlands, North West.
Creative Industries	London, Southeast, Home Counties, Scotland, Wales and Northern Ireland.
Education and Training	London, Southeast, Home Counties, Scotland, Wales and Northern Ireland.
Food & Hospitality	London, Southeast, Home Counties, Scotland, Wales and Northern Ireland.
Health and Social Care	London, Southeast, Home Counties
Information Technology	London, Southeast, Home Counties, Scotland, Wales and Northern Ireland.
Manufacturing	London, Southeast, Midlands and other UK Regions.
Personal Care	London, Southeast, Home Counties, Scotland, Wales and Northern Ireland.
Social Enterprise	London, Southeast, Home Counties, Scotland, Wales and Northern Ireland.
Transport & Logistics	London, Southeast, Midlands.

Notes: Examples of the geographic span of entrepreneurship by firms.

Prospects

Like all challenges, there are opportunities to be had and this section will examine those that are available for South Asian firms and their ethnic 'cousins'. It was not surprising to discover the level of entrepreneurship that existed within the South Asian community in Britain. In key industry sectors –commercial, industrial and social - there was clear evidence of initiative- prowess by matured, young and fledging owners and directors of companies (**Table 8.7**).

The buoyancy of these trading markets highlighted the changing landscape of Britain's economic frontiers. Such trajectory lends itself towards rethinking appropriate strategies to sustain the development and growth of ethnic firms in Britain.

Whilst there were marked differences in various industries, there were also similarities in almost every aspect of the business chain. Much of this was evidenced by the level of progress from the start-up stage to the development and growth phase. This situation meant that there was little difference between mainstream and ethnic firms at least, in terms of the early stages of business formation.

Although difficult to quantify, South Asian communities showed variations in the level of culture, education, faith, health, social and other matters; be they local or national as highlighted in **Table 8.4**. Yet, each owner had a similar approach to business development – to ensure maximum profits for resources invested or a ('reasonable') return on investment (ROI).

Table 8.7 Industry Sector Performance of South Asian Firms
(Source: Analysis of sampled South Asian Enterprises, 2013-2016)

Industry Sector	Approximate Contribution	Estimated UK Value 2015
Business and the Professions	£2 billion	£6.02 billion
Construction	£2 billion	£103 billion
Creative Industries	£27 million	£76.9 billion
Education and Training	£100 million	£73 billion
Food & Hospitality	£2 billion	56.3 billion
Health and Social Care	£100 million	£7.8 billion
Information Technology	£250 million	£6.1 billion
Manufacturing	£2 billion	£140 billion
Personal Care	£200 million	£17 billion
Social Enterprise	£5 million (*)	£24 million
Transport & Logistics	£220 million	£55 billion

Notes: the table highlights the scale of performance outputs by South Asian firms in key sectors. (*) The social enterprise sector contribution was calculated on the basis of the 14% stated industry sources.

Sector Dynamics

In the food and hospitality, retailing, creative industries and the knowledge (IT) sectors of the South Asian business community, these demographic factors impacted on buyers and sellers alike:-

- *Social* – Affluent-led customers chose shops further from where they lived. This was evidenced by the increasing number of small franchises in high streets. Low-income consumers were dependent on the small shops nearby; 'corner shops' being a typical example.
- *Technology* – Self-service technology favoured large retailers due to economies of scale. Small retailers adapted basic technologies to counter the competition such as money machines and credit facilities.
- *Policy* – British authorities in charge of competition, should maximise competitive policy to defend the small shops and other retail owners similar to European countries (**2015**).

Organisation Performance

This is the first attempt at publishing British South Asian firms by industry sector. The intention was to evaluate their contribution to wealth creation in Britain. By examining six groups – **Afghanis, Bangladeshis, Indians, Nepalese, Pakistanis and Sri Lankans** - within this multi-layered ethnic classification, a more informed perspective was possible.

Each chapter was underpinned by migratory contexts such as epochal events that occurred at either the pre, post-partition and/or independence period. It was vital to highlight these trends among each ethnic group since these developments have influenced enterprise start-ups by South Asians across Britain.

The book is premised on the 'organisation and performance model', a similar device applied by this author in the award-winning *British Caribbean Enterprises* (**2008**) publication.

This tool was used to highlight the challenges confronting owners, the 'opportunity structures' and varied niche market 'openings' owners used to counter restrictive market practices by mainstream (**2015**).

Business Clusters

The effect these firms have on the British economy was also marked by their engagement in different industry sectors and business segments. Each chapter addressed issues pertaining to South Asian business performance, subsequent challenges and future business opportunities.

In addition, this section was complemented by the geographical location of firms according to industry sector-segments. The aim was to provide useful information on the importance and value of location to a firm's overall development and growth strategy (**Table 8.8**).

Table 8.8 Sample of South Asian business clusters by location
(Source: Analysis of sampled firms by UK regional locations, 2013.2015)

UK Region	Key Enterprise Clusters Location
London	Brick Lane (East London), Southall (West London).
Southeast	Basingstoke, Rushmoor.
West Midlands	Coventry, Soho Road and Lozells (Birmingham).
East Midlands	Derby, Narborough Road, Nottingham (Leicester).
Yorkshire & Humber	Bradford, Dewsbury, Leeds, Rotherham, Sheffield.
North West	Rushlome, Wilmslow Road (Manchester).
South West	Brighton, Taunton, Devon, Bristol, Bath and Shaftesbury.
Scotland	Edinburgh, Glasgow.
Ireland	Dublin.

Notes: Business clusters represented the level of diversity among ethnic firms in Britain.

Chapters 1 to 6 examined in some detail, the organisation and performance indices of the six South Asian groups; namely Afghanis, Bangladeshis, Indians, Nepalese/Nepalis, Pakistanis and Sri Lankans. Discussions also centred on factors that affected communities; as citizens and entrepreneurs accordingly.

Differences were noticeable in the levels of cultures, faith practices and the means by, and through which business transactions were done. As a heterogeneous group, South Asian business owners also reflected layers of sub-ethnicity, [average] age and other features all of which were analysed to demonstrate the rich diversity of this segment of British society (**Table 8.9**).

Table 8.9 Age factor of South Asian Business Owners
(Sources: Centre for Entrepreneurs and DueDil, 2014 &Companies House UK)

Group	Average Age
Afghani	33.7
Bangladeshi	35.3
Indian	37.1
Nepali	35
Pakistani	35.3
Sri Lankan	38

Notes: The table illustrated the importance of human talent as integral to firms.

The analysis of gender enterprise was seen through the lens of an industry sector approach featuring successful entrepreneurs who co-owned or partnered family businesses. Other profiles included high-achievers who managed independent commercial and social firms.

Evidence suggested that more women operated multiple industries in health and social care, personal care, creative industries as well as education and training sectors across the UK. South Asian women displayed a high level of confidence matched with 'a can do' attitude. This gender-based approach to business profiling, was deliberate to illustrate the significance of cultural sensitivity and heritage sensibility regarding modern trends amongst ethnic SMEs in Britain **(2013)** – **Fig 8.1**.

Figure 8.1 Essential factors contributing to South Asian Women Entrepreneurs
(Source: Independent evaluation of case studies of female business owners)

- Acquisitive: different ways of developing self and business ideas.
- Creativity: imaginative approaches or 'thinking outside the box'.
- Determined: persistence towards achieving aims, objectives and goals.
- Ethics: consideration of commercial imperative vs customer care.
- Faith: importance of a moral and spiritual compass.
- Focus: beyond the lure of the 'quick buck' or getting rich quickly.
- Intelligent: investment in academic & professional skills development.
- Tasking: striving to maintain a healthy work-life balance.
- Vision: incremental paths to business development and growth.

Female enterprises that reflected these characteristics included: -
The Saffron House Ltd (2004), Vardags Ltd (2010), 12 Perham Road Management Ltd (2002, Community Education Academy of Leadership (2002), Yllume Ltd (2009), Sampad (2011), Ruby Hammer Ltd (2011), Nameless Media Group (1999) and DealIndex (2009).

Youth Enterprises

Another notable exception in the realm of contemporary business literature, was evidenced in **Chapter 7** which focused on the increasing enterprise trends among young (under-40s) British South Asians. Numerous case studies demonstrated the heights these fledging business owners had ascended to, in economic terms. It was a perfect counter-weight to the recurring media imagery of young people (some of whom are) castigated for indolence, lack of industriousness and/or enterprise.

Other examples of youth entrepreneurship were founded on the determination, zealousness and ambition of this South Asian cohort who above all, maximised technology to create cost effective and efficient-run firms.

Most knew their customers, considering advertising and promotion as essential to marketing, more so, a major part of long-term strategy planning.

Their understanding of survival was based on a clear view of inevitable changes in cultural, social, faith and other areas of British society. They all seemed to have a tactful, but global view of business and the professions according to interviews and comments made by owners. Their intention was no doubt, to make a lasting contribution to the land of their birth or naturalisation (**Fig 8.2**).

Figure 8.2 Strategic Qualities of 'Third Age' Entrepreneurs
(Source: Textual analysis of sampled South Asian young entrepreneurs)

Type	Impact Features
• Cultural	Less rigid, flexible, more outward-looking, inquisitive mind.
• Education	Technically adroit, articulate, negotiation skills and resourceful.
• Ideas-driven	Confident, positive, driven by ideals, customs and traditions.
• Financial activities.	Short/medium-term goals, pursuance of multiple enterprise
• Leadership	Laissez faire and cultivated consultative-style approach.
• Management	Collaborative, delegative-type, partnership, clarity and purpose.
• Social	Traditional/modern, keen on business inter-ethnic relationships.
• Structuralism	Organisation structure less defined and reduced bureaucracy.
• Technological	Savvy, modern, adaptive, creative and innovative.

Above all, the presence of diverse South Asian groups in Britain, do represent a challenge and opportunity as they compete at times, for the same market as well as different 'niche trading' spaces. Factors such as culture, faith (or rituals), symbols and others, played a manifold role in the way firms were established, managed and visualised by owners (**Table 8.10**).

Sector Distribution

British South Asian business owners are engaged in various industry sectors according to the **Standard Industrial Classification (SIC, 2007)**. These make up different businesses, the professions and allied services. Public information on these however, were limited to Indians, Pakistanis and Bangladeshis with 'Other Asian' given token mentionable (**Table 8.11**).

Table 8.10 Trading features of South Asian Firms
(Source: Evaluation of profiled business-enterprises, 2015/2016)

Trading Feature	Measured Impact
Competition	60% felt competition from mainstream firms affected business growth.
Diversity	Afghans, Sri Lankans, Nepalese diversified into non-retailing sectors.
Entry Barriers	Owners sought entry into market sectors with the least entry barriers.
Internal Support	Extended family assistance to help cope with start-up challenges.
Heterogeneity	Ethnically diverse, linguistically versatile & faith plurality.
Legacy	60% of owners had parents who operated businesses before.
Livelihood	70% of owners started companies for economic/business reasons.
Succession Planning	Owners were keen for children to be involved in professions too.
Viability	80% of firms had sales turnover exceeding £50,000 per annum.

Notes: The table pointed to the changing dynamics and trends impacting on South Asian firms.

Table 8.11 Samples of ethnic self-employment by gender in Britain
(Office for National Statistics, 2011)

Males:

Nationality Type	A-E Sectors	F Sector	G-I Sectors	J-U Sectors
UK	11.1%	31.4%	20.6%	36.9%
Other Europeans	4.4%	25.3%	40.0%	30.3%
Africans	5.0%	13.6%	32.8%	48.6%
Bangladeshis	3.5%	3.6%	74.4%	18.5%
Caribbeans	3.1%	10.2%	7.1%	27%
Indians	6.4%	14.3%	39.0%	40.3%
Pakistanis	5.0%	6.3%	66.2%	22.6%
Other Asian	4.5%	9.0%	49.9%	36.5%
All Nationals	**10.0%**	**29.9%**	**23.2%**	**36.9%**

Females:

Nationality Type	A-F Sectors	G-I Sectors	N-Q Sectors	J-M, R-U Sectors
UK	10.2%	20.0%	33.0%	36.7%
Other Europeans	7.6%	18.1%	31.3%	43.1%
Africans	6.0%	23.7%	37.3%	33.1%
Bangladeshis	8.5%	36.2%	33.0%	22.3%
Caribbeans	2.3%	6.4%	16%	24%
Indians	5.2%	41.6%	30.2%	23.1%
Pakistanis	10.1%	39.9%	32.4%	17.6%
Other Asian	5.7%	35.7%	27.0%	31.7%
All Nationals	**9.6%**	**20.6%**	**33.9%**	**36.0%**

Notes: Sectors A-E primary & secondary industries; Sector F is Construction; Sectors G-I are Retail, Food/Restaurants & Transport. Women are involved in Sectors J-U Other Services. Females are engaged in A-F combined and Other services were split into two Sectors N-Q ; Health, Education, Administration and Public Services.

Competitive Advantage

As **Table 8.10** illustrated, the performance of ethnic firms in Britain is underpinned by a series of impact. In the case of South Asians businesses, there are certain distinctive values that more experienced owners exhibited.

For example, in confronting, personal, family, industry, structural and societal challenges, they followed basic principles and practices to maintain both market share and profitability of their respective companies (**Table 8.12**).

Table 8.12 Examples of South Asian Enterprise Unique Selling Points (USPs)
(Source: Analysis of selected reputable companies, 2015-2016)

Company	Institutional Values
East End Foods plc (1972) turnover exceeding £180m (2016).	Chair and founder, Tony Deep Wouhra and brothers - Paul, Monty, Jas, Don and Jason – promote a corporate ethos based on sourcing materials from cost-effective distribution supply chains. Boosting independent retailers, family owned stores and emerging Indian restaurants. A *'trusted supplier of the highest quality of product'*. Founding principle, that 'food should be as natural as possible' (**ChamberLink, 2013**).
Noon Products -Kerry Foods (1988) value £44.6m (2015).	The late founder Lord Gulam Noon, believed in altruism. Used his experience in US food processing to rebrand products. Used private equity to invest in business growth. *Author of Noon, With a View: Courage and Integrity* (2008).
Ram Gidoomal CBE over 30 years' experience as Company Director specialising in International Trade and Development.	Enterprise zeal matched by strong moral and spiritual values along with a corporate social responsibility outlook. An advocate of 'ethical business', Gidoomal has authored books on culture, fashion, food and business. Co-author of the book, *The British and How to Deal with Them: Doing Business with Britain's Ethnic Communities* (2001). Urged corporate Britain to value ethnic firms' contribution to the UK economy.
Vardags Limited net worth £22.2m (2016)	Founder/Director Ayesha Vardag built her company into a highly reputable family law firm, described by some commentators as the "magic circle". Vardag received the 2015 *Natwest Everywoman Award* in recognition of the landmark ruling that brought enforceable pre-nuptial agreements in the UK. Female employees have the opportunity to achieve their highest potential in what is still considered to be a male-

	dominated industry.
Lebara net worth £107m (2015)	Founder/Director Ratheesan Yoganathan, is dedicated to developing a mobile telecoms brand "*of choice for one billion people by 2020*". The firm's business model is based on a combination of investments in social networks, luxury brands, optimisation of worldwide web services for customer demands. The second generation business leader is also dedicated to social entrepreneurship.

Notes: 'Turnover', 'net worth' and other corporate valuations were obtained from public sources including Companies House and other [reputable] statutory authorities.

Reaching Outwards

While over 30% of South Asian firms are engaged in commercial and social enterprise activities, there are increasing opportunities elsewhere. The adage that '*don't put your eggs in one basket*' is so true for business owners who tend to concentrate on home-based ethnic markets for survival or viability.

Globalisation has pros and cons, but it presents existing and fledging-like companies, potential opportunities to market innovative products and services to mass [consumer] markets. Take for instance, the increasing Commonwealth trade where exports in goods and services has increased from $1.3 trillion to $3.4 trillion, accounting for 14.6 % of global exports in 2013 alone (**2013**). A strategy for targeting markets in regional trading bloc is also useful for ethnic firms including British South Asian businesses (**Table 8.13**).

Table 8.13 Profile of selected Regional Trade Blocs
(Source: Analysis of global trade blocs, WTO 2012)

Regional Trade Bloc	Total Imports ($US)	Total Exports ($US)
Asia (incl. SAARC)	5.86 trillion	5.77 trillion
North America	8.20 trillion	9.42 trillion
Europe	6.59 trillion	6.4 trillion
Commonwealth Independent States	575 billion	778 billion
South America	773 billion	737 billion
Africa	628 billion	599 billion
Middle East	770 billion	1.33 billion

Notes: Variations in regional trade blocs are indicative of global market dynamics.

The engagement of British South Asian firms in global markets outside of their cultural and ethnic sphere, will indeed be a strategic leverage test. Besides social capital, there are other structural issues that require consideration.

Each country or regional trading bloc, has different ways of running its respective economy/economies. Owners must think carefully about the demand and supply chain linkages. They should also pay attention to competitive factors impinging on import and export trade. These factors consist of the following:-

- Institutions;
- Infrastructure (physical and social);
- Macroeconomic Environment;
- Health and Primary Education;
- Higher Education and Training (all levels of orientation);
- Goods Market Efficiency;
- Labour Market Efficiency;
- Financial Market Development;
- Technological Readiness;
- Market Size;
- Business Sophistication;
- [Creativity and] Innovation (**Schwab, 2014**).

Other Diasporas

As part of their network, British South Asians can benefit from the network of fellow communities or potential trading partners across North America. These range of migrant communities are interconnected with entrenched histories plus disposable mass markets viz., consumer, financial, products and services.

Coupled with their diversity and equal homogeneity, these diasporic 'enclaves' are firmly imbedded, if not established in inner-cities and conurbations where affluence and poverty often collide. These communities have developed too, intra and extra-ethnic relations with other minority groups, businesses, non-government organisations (NGOs) and influential representatives (leaders and their constituent organisation).

Knowingly, South Asian North Americans are numerically stronger with increasing links 'back home' and elsewhere. Such advantage is ideal since these 'diasporic entities' can be trading partners and 'market conduits' for their British 'cousins'. The sheer numbers and span of influence over wide geographical areas, lend themselves as well, to mutual partnership arrangements along commercial, industrial and social entrepreneurial lines, as **Table 8.14** clearly shows.

Table 8.14: Profile of South Asian (SA) Groups in North America

SA Group	Canada	USA
Afghanis	80,000 (2011 estimates)	97,865 (2014 estimates)
Bangladeshis	100,000 -1.5m (2016 estimates)	500,000 (2014 estimates)
Indians	1,355,653 (2015 estimates)	3,443,063 (2014 Census)
Nepalese	9,780 (2011 Census)	500,490-1m (2016 estimates)
Pakistanis	155,310 (2011 Census)	363,699 (2010 Census)
Sri Lankans	139,415 (2011 Census)	45,159 (2010 Census)

Notes: Each South Asian group has claimed individual nationality/nationalities.
For example, 'Afghan Canadians', 'Nepalese or Nepali Americans', Indian Americans.
These reflect migrants' strong affinity with (their) 'naturalised' overseas settlement.

The Future

As British South Asian traders look externally to consolidate market status and build on wealth creation, they should be mindful of the South Asian Region. This area has potential for tremendous growth opportunities that should be maximised. For instance, market capitalisation in the region was evidenced by the estimated **$trillions** involving the Bombay and Karachi Stock Exchange accordingly.

The region is also home to two other countries –Bhutan and the Maldives. Commentators have surmised that **India, Pakistan** and **Sri Lanka** are among countries in the region that have increasing domestic revenue streams (**Table 8.15**). These can be of tremendous benefit to small and large-scale ventures operated by British-based South Asian firms.

Table 8.15: Potential trading opportunities in South Asia Region
(Source: The World Factbook: South Asia, March 2015)

Country	Population (million)	GDP (nominal
Afghanistan	32.007	$21.3bn
Bangladesh	159.857	$205.3bn
Bhutan	0.779	$2.2bn
India	**1,276.2**	**$2308.0bn**
Maldives	0.38	£3.0bn
Nepal	28.4	$21.6bn
Pakistan	**190.4**	**$250bn**
Sri Lanka	**21.7**	**$80.4bn**

Using intelligence data from these countries, British South Asians can tap into key commercial, industrial and social markets in each of the above countries in the region. In so doing, businesses can share best practice in technology, management, orientation, product development and customer service models.

In addition, this innovative arrangement can be mutually beneficial to both British and subcontinental partners. It can also be a real boost for existing and fledging companies that are striving to compete, build market share and generally, increase profitability. In the process, some business owners might be keen to renew their acquaintance with their *'ancestral-home'* markets.

Demand Side

The growth prospects for minority ethnics in Britain will impact on demand-side economics. With more consumers at their disposal, there is a likelihood that ethnic firms (as they have done historically) can introduce products and services to appeal to newly-emerging markets. The forecasts for minority growth between 2013 and 2056 for at least three South Asian groups, were as follows:-
- Indians from 3,172,000 (4.47%) to 5,318,000 (6.81%);
- Pakistanis from 2,074,000 (2.92%) to 3,386,000 (4.34%); and
- Bangladeshis from 813,000 (1.15 %) to 1,297,000 (1.66%).
(Coleman: Tran, 2010)

It also projected that there will be further increases in self-employment activity across the minority ethnic divide. South Asian enterprise activities will therefore feature mostly in the Home Counties as studies showed that *"SMEs tend to flourish in areas where there is a relatively high density of their co-ethnic groups"* **(Haq, 2015)**.

In this instance too, there are key growth sectors in the British economy that firms can maximise advantage (**Fig 8.3**).

Figure 8.3 Profile of key Industry Sectors in the UK
(Source: Adapted from House of Commons Briefing, December 2015)

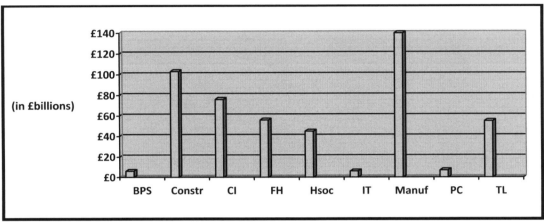

Notes: Figures rounded for uniformity. BPS – Business and the Professions, Constr – Construction, CI - Creative Industries, Hsoc –Health and Social Care, IT – Information Technology, Manuf –Manufacturing, PC – Personal Care and TL –Transport and Logistics. Data obtained from industry sources for each of the above sectors (2014/2015).

Research Methods

In trying to formulate a definitive structure for this book, it was necessary to access credible, reliable and verifiable information and data (as much as possible) to give credence to this first ever publication.

Initially, the author sourced information from annual '*Who's Who*' encyclopaedias particularly those of Bangladeshis and Pakistanis. Directories of Indians (Sikhs especially) and Nepalese communities were made available by publishers. This exercise was conducted between 2012 and 2014.

As the timetable for publication drew nearer, a small research team was formed in late 2015, to corroborate information obtained initially. A questionnaire was used to elicit basic information and data on the organisation and performance of firms. Routine visits were made to **Afghani, Sri Lankan, Indian** and **Nepali** businesses in *London, the Midlands, Scotland* and *Wales.*

Some of these visits entailed 'mystery shopping' techniques or participant observation (research) to identify customer care and leadership-management skills, product portfolio, services on offer, marketing techniques (including advertising and promotion), pricing tactics, customer buying decisions, and levels of competition across the South Asian and other ethnic minorities' divide.

Almost every method of research or investigation was supported by a range of privately and publicly-funded employability, enterprise and other developmental projects delivered to diverse communities during 2012 and 2016. Overall the following methods were used to obtain suitable material for this book:-

- Companies House searches that offered business names and locations.
- E-business directories/databases that provided briefs on firms.
- Informal interviews or media clippings of companies.
- Annual *Who's Who* publications of South Asian personalities.
- Presentations at conferences, symposia and workshops.
- Regional and national projects for minority ethnic groups.
- Project proposals for selected South Asian countries and states.
- High-level official discussions on development programs for South Asia.
- Analysis of information-data newspapers, journals, books, electronic media etc.
- Monthly articles written for the *Phoenix* newspaper by this author since 2015.
- Peer reviews of international development ventures.
- Evaluation of regional and international ventures funded by multilateral agencies and institutions.

Recommendations

In a further effort to acknowledge and publicise the contribution of South Asian businesses as well as other minority ethnic firms, certain steps must be taken to address firstly, issues; and secondly, to examine the gaps in researching minority (ethnic) entrepreneurs in Britain. By way of constructive action, we consider the following recommendations as urgent and necessary: -

- That further investigation is needed to determine the reason why most research on South Asian enterprise activities tend to be either London or Southeast-centric.
- That more focused work is required on the organisation and performance of minority firms to increase public understanding about entrepreneurs from various heritage ancestry in the UK.

- That additional empirical evidence is needed to identify the factors that are responsible for 'above average entrepreneurial achievements' by South Asians than other minorities.
- That further investigation is also needed to determine the difference in entrepreneurial success rates based on educational attainment, between male and female business owners (including young entrepreneurs).
- That greater analysis is needed to interpret Pakistanis' consistently high levels of self-employment vis-à-vis sharing Best Practice with other minorities with lower entrepreneurial rates.
- That additional field work is needed to establish intra-ethnic differences or commonalities on enterprise orientation between and among the six South Asian groups.
- That policy makers and other influential figures should formulate investment and business support policies that encourage growth and development of minority ethnic firms alongside mainstream entities.
- That top priority should be given to ethnic monitoring to reinforce the 'fairness doctrine' that Britain espouses as a fundamental principle.
- That business owners should allocate a percentage of their operating budget to improve market intelligence to sustain competitive advantage.
- That the enterprise activities of minority ethnic females and young business owners should be given prominence to measure the impact of the 'ethnic dividend' on the British economy.
- That [targeted] institutional funding should be allocated to research into the underperformance of minority ethnic firms with growth potential.
- That more ethnic firms should be encouraged to collaborate across industry sectors to increase competitive advantage in domestic and overseas markets.
- That Foreign Missions and Embassies should be encouraged to utilise 'Economic' or 'Trade Attaches' to promote South Asian and other ethnic firms' entry into regional and inter-regional (global) or mass markets.
- That South Asian business leaders should sponsor national and international apprenticeships/internships on commercial, industrial and social enterprises.
- That small business owners must be conduits in wealth creation campaigns –locally, nationally and internationally (http://www.isbe.org.uk/asianwealth).
- That business owners should develop consortia arrangements to orient young learners about money management and other complex investment models to assist in creating more prosperous communities thereby repairing

'structural damage' to disadvantaged or 'under-served' inner-city and suburban areas.

Several of the business owners felt that this book can be a forerunner to a more full-length publication on the economic contribution of minority ethnic communities in the whole of the UK. Some argued that not only will it add to the quality of literature on ethnic entrepreneurship, but it will help to reinforce the importance, relevance and value of migrants and their families as 'economic change agents' (www.casas.org.uk/papers/pdfpapers/southasianbritain.pdf). Further, the increasing presence of South Asian firms and other ethnic businesses, will undoubtedly, assist further to redefine diversity viz., the confluence of imaginative ideas, innovative products, tangible services and multiple capital for a 21st century corporate Britain.

Notes

Identify Quest

The citizenship factor is very important to South Asian and other minority groups. In terms of citizenship, 51% of Indians classed themselves as 'British' and 48% as 'Commonwealth'. Pakistanis 74% British and 25% Commonwealth and Bangladeshi 75% British and 23% Commonwealth (Rishi Sunak & Saratha Rajeswaran, A Portrait of Modern Britain, *Policy Exchange*, London 2014).

Philanthropy

A vital of area of ethnic entrepreneurship that is yet to be addressed in mainstream literature – either in Britain or North America. Private foundations or community trusts are legendary amongst members of the South Asian diasporic communities who donate millions in resources to various causes. Key features of this type of entrepreneurship are *'diversity in charitable motivation'*, application of *'business principles'*, focus on *'religious giving'* and *'giving abroad'* (Siridhar, Archana: An Opportunity to Lead: South Asian Philanthropy in Canada, *The Philanthropist*, 2011/Volume 24.1).

'Other Asian'

The 'Other Asian' category is reserved for other ethnic groups, Nepalese and Sri Lankans. For those born in the UK, 87% were both Sri Lankan and Nepalese accordingly (2001 Census, Office for National Statistics). One publication asserted that 'Asians' or 'Asian' immigrants referenced groups such as other minorities, other immigrants and native born which were consistently documented ('International Differences in Entrepreneurship', eds. Josh Lerner and Antoinette Schoar, *University of Chicago Press,* May 2010, USA).

Resilience
Our research showed that estimated lifespan of all British South Asian enterprises was 730 years plus. The average age for each South Asian business sector (overall) was 67 years.

South Asian
Except for Nepalese, Afghanis, Bangladeshis, Indians, Pakistanis and Sri Lankans, 'low skilled' migrants from these countries were properly identified as being part of 'South Asia' ('Migrants in low-skilled work', Migration Advisory Committee, *Full Report* July 2014 p37).

Super Diversity
A term that originated from 'different origins and circumstances' of 'established' and 'new immigrants' (Castles, S, Miller, MJ (2003) 'The Age of Migration: International Population Movements in the Modern World': New York: *The Guildford Press*). Vertovec, S. (2010) 'Towards post-multiculturalism? Changing communities, conditions and contexts of diversity', *International Social Science Journal* 61(1999): 83. These two authors referred to the emergence of a globalised market for high skills and their impact on countries of origin and recipient states.

Recognition
The University of Birmingham working paper, '*Super-diverse Britain and new migrant enterprises*' examined issues facing super-diverse migrants: recognition of migrants' input, industry sector composition, commercial motivations, access to financial capital, business performance and labour market discrimination etc. (Jones, T., Ram, M., Li, Y., Edwards, P. and Villares, M. (2015) 'Super-diverse Britain and new migrant enterprises', *IRiS Working Paper Series*, No. 8/2015. Birmingham: Institute for Research into Superdiversity)

Business Case
Business in the Community produced facts sheets to create a detailed picture of minority ethnic representation in England and Wales. This included a breakdown of data for population, religion, education, employment and leadership (Regional Fact Sheets – Ethnic Minorities in England and Wales: A Business Case for Inclusion, 2013).

Study
Scottish authorities conducted the first ever national study on minority ethnic enterprise in the country. The work examined the importance and the extent of these firms'- diversity. These ethnic business owners accounted for just over 3% of all self-employed in the country. It was estimated that there were over 4,400 minority ethnic businesses registered in Scotland. (www.gov.scot/Publications/2005/06/20132742/27457)

Sampled Firms

Our research of sampled firms showed that 4% of Afghani enterprises started in the 20th century (1980s) and 94% began in the 21st century. Approximately 21% of Bengali firms began in the 20th century (1960s) and 79% in the 21st century. Seventy eight (78%) of Indian companies were established in the 20th century 22% were founded in this century. An estimated 10% of Nepali firms were founded in the 20th century (1970s) and 90% in this century. About 14% of Pakistani firms were set up in the 20th century (1930s) and 86% in this century. Roughly 5% of Sri Lankan companies were incorporated in the 20th century and 95% this century.

Sector Dynamics

Dr Spinder Dhaliwal and Dr Andy Adcroft examined aspects of 'Asian' enterprise viz., traditional stereotypes, wealth creation and the sector contribution of Asian entrepreneurs. Nearly a dozen sectors were highlighted for the 1998-2004 period. Between them, 'the pharmaceutical, fashion and new economy sectors' generated wealth increases by more than £2.2 billion (Refereed Material *Volume I, Issue 2, 2005 Journal of Asia Entrepreneurship and Sustainability*, p13; www.asiaentrepreneurshipjournal.com)

Business Clusters

'Migrant infrastructure' on 'transaction economies is an evolving trend in modern ethnic entrepreneurship. It also reinforces the relevance of 'business clusters' in British inner-cities. A leading public research university studied the enterprise activities of over 360 migrant proprietors in the Midland Counties - Rookery Road (Birmingham) and Narborough Road (Leicester). The nationality of business owners included Bangladeshis, Indians, Pakistanis and Sri Lankans ('Migrant infrastructure: transaction economies in Birmingham and Leicester': *Urban Studies Journal Limited*, LSC Research Online February 2016).

Economic Value

The 'economic value' of Britain's South Asian creative industries sector is virtually unknown even though it has brought innovation, distinction, talent, technology and cultural tapestry to local neighbourhoods. The 40 years plus (since the 1970s) sector has business segments viz, dance, theatre, music, combined arts, literature and publishing, across London, the Home Counties, Scotland, Wales and Ireland (Singh, Jasjit (2014). 'The Cultural Value of South Asian Arts'. University of Leeds. *Arts & Humanities Research Council*, University of Leeds.

Ethnic Women

In Northern Island, Training for Women Network examined the contribution of minority ethnic women to self-employment activities. Among the 18,430 individuals sampled (from 23 nationalities), were Bangladeshis (450-500), Indians including Sikhs (1,750), Pakistanis (700), Africans and Afghanis (100-150). (www.twnonline.com/policy-research/research-reports/138-minority-ethnic-women-entrepreneurs-in-northern-ireland)

Uniqueness

Kumud Gandhi founder of the successful **Cooking Academy** and **The Saffron House** recognised the added value of 'Asian' foods, flavour and fusion. Her business specialises in authentic Indian/Asian foods and focuses on the presentation of the food by 'reengineering its manifestation'. The Saffron House is an integral part of 'our food value and ethos'. Gandhi's distinctive competence lies in teaching different cookery programmes including British, Japanese and Thai. "I want to share my passion for the knowledge of food whatever genre or ethnicity of food" ('Kumud Gandhi, The Saffron House', *Asian Lite*, June 2010).

Maximising Contribution

Gender equality amongst South Asian and other minorities is crucial. The benefits to enterprise are multiple; they are enabling women to understand the importance of enterprise as offering financial independence and workplace flexibility. Another advantage is 'increasing the availability of inspirational role models', by 'promoting support for women who want to start a business' ('*Maximising women's contribution to future economic growth'*, Women's Business Council, July 2015, London).

Youth Enterprises

Despite limited media coverage, trends in youth entrepreneurship are no longer a rarity. Thousands of under-35s in particular, are seeking self-employment as an alternative to chronic unemployment. Some leading young entrepreneurs emphasised key strategies for business growth. They consisted of increased transparency, collaboration, private investment, regulation, valuations of equity, innovation and demystifying complex settings ('A Few Minutes With Neha Manaktala, CEO/Founder, DealIndex', *AIMkts Editors*, September 23, 2015).

Generational Shifts

Send and third generation South Asian entrepreneurs have fused ancestral traditions with more modern approaches to business and industry. Hence some researchers asserted that factors such as 'the role of family members', 'co-ethnic', 'business expertise' and 'social connectedness'' are among the key drivers of enterprises success (Rafique 2014).

Education vs Enterprise

Apart from language dexterity and latent skills, educational attainment has been recognised as one of the factors contributing to 'entrepreneurial preferences and attitudes' among British South Asian-owned SMEs especially (Jones, T. Ram, M (2003)

South Asian businesses in retreat? The case of the UK. *Journal of ethnic and migration studies*, 29 (3), pp485-500.) Studies in both the UK and North America have shown that 'highly qualified entrepreneurs are likely to communicate more effectively and meaningfully with stakeholders than less qualified counterparts' (Hamilton, R., Dana, L.P. and Benfell, c. (2008) Changing cultures: an international study of migrant entrepreneurs. *Journal of Enterprising Culture*, 16 (01), pp89-105.

Standard Industrial Classification (SIC)

A system that is used to classify business establishments and other standard units by the type of economic activity in which they are engaged. The new version of these codes (SIC 2007) was adopted in the UK as from 1 January 2008. Approximately 7% of minority ethnic firms were engaged in industry sectors that represented categories or codes of the SIC ('Small Business Survey 2014: SME employers', *BIS Research Paper Number 214,* March 2015, Department for Business, Innovation & Skills UK).

Trading Characteristics

There are several factors that have motivated the business success of minorities in Britain. Some of these elements point to a '*culturalist viewpoint*' (Welbourne, T. M. and Pardo-del-Val, M. (2009) Relational capital: strategic advantage for small and medium-size enterprises (SMEs) through negotiation and collaboration. *Group Decision and Negotiation,* 18 (5), 483-497).

Structuralism

The '*structuralist viewpoint*' is founded on the belief that self-employment is the only alternative for disadvantaged minorities (Wang, C. L. and Altinay, L. (2012) Social embeddedness, entrepreneurial orientation and firm growth in ethnic minority small businesses in the UK. *International Small Business Journal,* 30 (1), 3-23.

Legendary

Historical success is built in the knowledge that South Asians came to the UK either as refugees or labourers. Thus their entrepreneurial success was a boost to their overall status (Basu, A. (1998) An exploration of entrepreneurial activity among Asian small businesses in Britain. *Small Business Economics,* 10 (4), pp313-326.

East End Foods plc

Over the past 40 years, this leading company has been contributing to the local and regional economies in the Midland Counties. It has a product range containing a 'massive 1250 lines' The Wouhra brothers have carved out a reputation of quality, market intelligence and customer care. Such outstanding achievements are also a reflection of the company's desire to sustain distinctive competence in the marketplace of products and services.

Missionary Zeal

Ram Gidoomal has combined faith, enterprise and a thirst for public service, to excel in business and industry. He remains a unique and formidable figure within the South Asian and minority ethnic community overall, capable of bringing together diverse communities. His leadership of numerous organisations is legendary, and one of his famous assertions was, "I wanted to make a difference, do something for the community" ('Ram Gidoomal's London mission', *BBC*, 23 March 2005).

Global Competition

The Global Competitiveness Report 2014–2015 was aimed at analysing the chain of economic, financial and social events as various issues loomed in the horizon to derail global recovery. The report is ideal for decision-makers, business and civic society leaders and other influential figures who are keen on employment-wealth creation

Web Links

http://www.theguardian.com/uk/2010/jul/13/uk-population-growth-ethnic-minorities Accessed on 23 September 2013.

www.casas.org.uk/papers/pdfpapers/southasianbritain.pdf.

www.gov.scot/Publications/2005/06/20132742/27457

www.asiaentrepreneurshipjournal.com

www.twnonline.com/policy-research/research-reports/138-minority-ethnic-women-entrepreneurs-in-northern-ireland

Selected References

How your businesses can harness performance "premium" from better ethnic diversity, *Institute of Directors, London Spring 2015*.

Sunak, Rishi and Rajeswaran, Saratha (2014): 'A Portrait of Modern Britain', *Policy Exchange*, London 2014.

Simpson, L., Gavalas, V. and Finney, N. (2008) Population dynamics in ethnically diverse towns: the long -term implications of immigration. *Urban Studies*, 45 (1), pp 163-183.

Khondker, Ayman: 'The Factors Affecting South Asian National Hierarchy', Undergraduate Class of 2015 Colgate University, Hamilton, NY.

'International Differences in Entrepreneurship', eds. Josh Lerner and Antoinette Schoar, *University of Chicago Press,* May 2010, USA.

Castles, S, Miller, MJ (2003) 'The Age of Migration: International Population Movements in the Modern World': New York: *The Guildford Press*.

Vertovec, S. (2010) 'Towards post-multiculturalism? Changing communities, conditions and contexts of diversity', *International Social Science Journal* 61(1999): 83.

Siridhar, Archana: An Opportunity to Lead: South Asian Philanthropy in Canada, *The Philanthropist*, 2011/Volume 24.1.

Office for National Statistics, England 2011.

" *Language and the BSA: Ethnicity & Race".* British Sociological Association. March 2005. Retrieved 27 April 2015.

Ethnic group statistics: A guide for the collection and classification of ethnicity data, Office for National Statistics, 2003.

Regional Fact Sheets –Ethnic Minorities in England and Wales: *A Business Case for Inclusion,* 2013.

Deakins, Professor David; Ishaq Dr Mohammed; Smallbone, David Professor; Whittam, Geoff and Wyper, Janette (2005): *Minority Ethnic Enterprise in Scotland*: A National Scoping Study, Paisley Enterprise Research Centre University of Paisley and Small Business Research Centre Kingston on behalf of the Scottish Executive 2005.

Refereed Material *Volume I, Issue 2, 2005 Journal of Asia Entrepreneurship and Sustainability*, p13.

Singh, Jasjit (2014). 'The Cultural Value of South Asian Arts'. University of Leeds. *Arts & Humanities Research Council*, University of Leeds.

Potter, Michael*: Minority Ethnic Women Entrepreneurs in Northern Ireland,* Training For Women Network 2008, pp 9-12.

'Kumud Gandhi, The Saffron House', *Asian Lite*, June 2010.

'*Maximising women's contribution to future economic growth'*, Women's Business Council, July 2015, London.

Alexander, C. and Kim, H., 2013. South Asian Youth Cultures. In *Handbook of the South Asian Diaspora*, ed. J. Chatterji & D. Washbrook, London: Routledge.

'A Few Minutes With Neha Manaktala, CEO/Founder, DealIndex', *AIMkts Editors*, September 23, 2015.

Jones, T. Ram, M (2003) South Asian businesses in retreat? The case of the UK. *Journal of ethnic and migration studies*, 29 (3), pp485-500.

Hamilton, R., Dana, L.P. and Benfell, c. (2008) Changing cultures: an international study of migrant entrepreneurs. *Journal of Enterprising Culture*, 16 (01), pp89-105.

'Small Business Survey 2014: SME employers', *BIS Research Paper Number 214,* March 2015, Department for Business, Innovation & Skills UK.

Welbourne, T. M. and Pardo-del-Val, M. (2009) Relational capital: strategic advantage for small and medium-size enterprises (SMEs) through negotiation and collaboration. *Group Decision and Negotiation,* 18 (5), 483-497).

Wang, C. L. and Altinay, L. (2012) Social embeddedness, entrepreneurial orientation and firm growth in ethnic minority small businesses in the UK. *International Small Business Journal,* 30 (1), 3-2.

Basu, A. (1998) An exploration of entrepreneurial activity among Asian small businesses in Britain. *Small Business Economics,* 10 (4), pp313-326.

The UK Competition Regime, House of Commons Library, 9 November 2015.

Centre for Entrepreneurs and DueDil, 2014 &Companies House UK,

Carter, Sara; Ram, Monder; Trehan, Kiran and Jones, Trevor: 'Diversity and SMEs', *ERC White Paper No.3 April 2013.*

Urban Studies Journal Limited, LSC Research Online February 2016.

ChamberLink, February 2013, Birmingham Chamber of Commerce Goup, England.

Gidoomal, Ram : *The British and How to Deal with Them: Doing Business with Britain's Ethnic Communities* 2001.

'Ram Gidoomal's London mission', *BBC*, 23 March 2005.

Author of Noon, *With a View: Courage and Integrity* (2008).

UNCTADStat, 2013.

Schwab, Klaus: *The Global Competitiveness Report* 2014-2015, World Economic Forum, 2014 pp4-8.

The World Factbook: South Asia, March 2015.

Haq, M. (2015). "South Asian ethnic minority small and medium enterprises in the UK: a review and research agenda". *International Journal of Entrepreneurship and Small Business*, 25(4), 494-516).

Epilogue

The new PM's Business Agenda is imperative
(By Dr Christopher A. Johnson, first published in *The Phoenix, August 2016* edition www.thephoenixnewspaper.com)

It is often said that 'a week in politics is a rather long time'. Fast forward, the former Home Secretary, Mrs Theresa Mary May, is the new Conservative Party Leader and **Britain's 76th Prime Minister** (the second woman to achieve such eminent status in the country). She pledged to govern the country, by emphasising; "A vision of a country that works not for the privileged few, but that works for every one of us because we're going to give people more control over their lives and that's how, together, we will build a better Britain" http://www.bbc.co.uk/news/uk-politics-36768148.

With her endurable stewardship at the Home Office and a brief stint as Minister responsible for Women and Equality, Mrs May will need to call on her dual public and private sector calculus, to place the minority ethnic dividend at the epicentre of UK macro-economic policy. Since changes to the equalities legislation in the first half of this century, ethnic monitoring has almost disappeared from the radar in terms of business and industry, except for a few areas in public life. And yet, the contribution of ethnic firms and women-owned businesses combined, exceeds over £30 billion, with the former input to the treasury estimated at £20 billion per annum (Diversity Magazine 9 June 2016).

Despite the incredible achievements of these 'captains of industry' for generations, the recent closure of Enterprise Development Agencies and the diminution of Business Links across the English Regions, have left thousands of existing and new minority entrepreneurs, without consistent and reliable technical assistance and enterprise support. The hundreds of 'arms-length' agencies set up to offer support to small and medium-enterprises (SMEs), is not 'seamlessly' working as was first mooted by state officials. The clamour by a leading business leader for a renewed 'SME Task Force' **(The Phoenix, July 2016**) is therefore opportune. With more women and young people of ethnic background setting up commercial firms and social enterprises, the necessity for additional support measures, is not altogether unreasonable.

Mrs May's depiction as a 'moral and ethical' politician, rather than a definitive 'ideologue', is an attribute that is needed to reinforce the 'fairness doctrine' Britain (so loudly) proclaims rather testily. With the post-EU Referendum uncertainty, the time is propitious for the review of a rationally inclusive SME Policy that gives credence to the contribution of ethnic firms to the national coffers. Certainly, this policy can be part of the new Premier's legacy of 'ethical integrity' which can be likened unto her renowned endowment of moral sensitivity.

Hundreds of ethnic businesses are located in diverse communities that experience incidences of economic deprivation and social exclusion. Much of these dislocations are due in part, to the velocity of public expenditure reduction especially, to essential services, over the past 6 years. In spite of this situation, business owners are contributing to jobs, wealth creation, social cohesion, scientific and technological advances and generally, helping to reduce material poverty (including the collapse of low-income economies), in the process.

Ethically, Madame Prime Minister May, will need to find a delicate balance between recognising the valuable input of 'Big Business' to large scale investments and the invaluable contribution of minority firms to the economy as a whole. The following actions by the May Administration will therefore go a far way to find a 'common ground' in the current 'ethical dilemma' on ethnic firms:-

- Undertake a comprehensive review of the organisation and performance of minority firms, as a first step towards recognising their contribution to the British economy.
- Re-integrate minority firms within wider macro-economic policy with a responsible 'Czar' leading on this.
- Offer greater prominence to women and young people's entrepreneurial flair and their influence on local economies.
- Encourage government departments and agencies to simply procurement and related tender procedures, to facilitate minority firms' access to commissioned work especially in their locale.
- Instruct the UK Trade and Investment (UKTI) to work with established minority entrepreneurs, to promote a culture of 'Ambassadorial Enterprise' in emerging [Commonwealth] democracies - Africa, the Caribbean, South Asia and the Pacific group of countries – particularly where material poverty tends to inhibit orderly development and growth spurts.

Undoubtedly, Mrs May's governance will seek to redefine Napoleon Bonaparte's famous assertion of Britain being 'a nation of shopkeepers'. The new PM's strategic trajectory will be perceived as more than an empty slogan, but one which bears the hallmark of modernising the 'ethnic business realm' across the British Isles.